Machine Learning with Spark™ and Python®

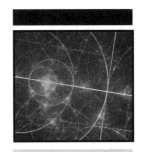

Machine Learning with Spark™ and Python®

Essential Techniques for Predictive Analytics

Second Edition

Michael Bowles

WILEY

Machine Learning with Spark™ and Python®: Essential Techniques for Predictive Analytics, Second Edition

Published by
John Wiley & Sons, Inc.
10475 Crosspoint Boulevard
Indianapolis, IN 46256
www.wiley.com

Copyright © 2020 by John Wiley & Sons, Inc., Indianapolis, Indiana
Published simultaneously in Canada

ISBN: 978-1-119-56193-4
ISBN: 978-1-119-56201-6 (ebk)
ISBN: 978-1-119-56195-8 (ebk)

Manufactured in the United States of America

For general information on our other products and services please contact our Customer Care Department within the United States at (877) 762-2974, outside the United States at (317) 572-3993 or fax (317) 572-4002.

Wiley publishes in a variety of print and electronic formats and by print-on-demand. Some material included with standard print versions of this book may not be included in e-books or in print-on-demand. If this book refers to media such as a CD or DVD that is not included in the version you purchased, you may download this material at http://booksupport.wiley.com. For more information about Wiley products, visit www.wiley.com.

Library of Congress Control Number: 2019940771

C10014390_100219

I dedicate this book to my expanding family of children and grandchildren, Scott, Seth, Cayley, Rees, and Lia. Being included in their lives is a constant source of joy for me. I hope it makes them smile to see their names in print. I also dedicate it to my close friend Dave, whose friendship remains steadfast in spite of my best efforts. I hope this makes him smile too.

Mike Bowles, Silicon Valley 2019

About the Author

Dr. Michael Bowles (Mike) holds bachelor's and master's degrees in mechanical engineering, an ScD in instrumentation, and an MBA. He has worked in academia, technology, and business. Mike currently works with companies where artificial intelligence or machine learning are integral to success. He serves variously as part of the management team, a consultant, or advisor. He also teaches machine learning courses at UC Berkeley and Hacker Dojo, a co-working space and startup incubator in Mountain View, CA.

Mike was born in Oklahoma and took his bachelor's and master's degrees there, then after a stint in Southeast Asia went to Cambridge for ScD and C. Stark Draper Chair at MIT after graduation. Mike left Boston to work on communications satellites at Hughes Aircraft Company in Southern California, and then after completing an MBA at UCLA moved to the San Francisco Bay Area to take roles as founder and CEO of two successful venture-backed startups.

Mike remains actively involved in technical and startup-related work. Recent projects include the use of machine learning in industrial inspection and automation, financial prediction, predicting biological outcomes on the basis of molecular graph structures, and financial risk estimation. He has participated in due diligence work on companies in the artificial intelligence and machine learning arenas. Mike can be reached through `mbowles.com`.

About the Technical Editor

James York-Winegar is an Infrastructure Principal with Accenture Enkitec Group. James helps companies of all sizes from startups to enterprises with their data lifecycle by helping them bridge the gap between systems management and data science. He started his career in physics, where he did large-scale quantum chemistry simulations on supercomputers, and went into technology. He holds a master's in Data Science from Berkeley.

Acknowledgments

I'd like to acknowledge the splendid support that people at Wiley have offered during the course of writing this book and making the revisions for this second edition. It began with Robert Elliot, the acquisitions editor who first contacted me about writing a book—very easy to work with. Tom Dinse has done a splendid job editing this second edition. He's been responsive, thorough, flexible, and completely professional, as I've come to expect from Wiley. I thank you.

I'd also like to acknowledge the enormous comfort that comes from having such a quick, capable computer scientist as James Winegar doing the technical editing on the book. James has brought a more consistent style and has made a number of improvements that will make the code that comes along with the book easier to use and understand. Thank you for that.

The example problems used in the book come from the University of California at Irvine's data repository. UCI does the machine learning community a great service by gathering these data sets, curating them, and making them freely available. The reference for this material is:

Bache, K. & Lichman, M. (2013). UCI Machine Learning Repository (`http://archive.ics.uci.edu/ml`). Irvine, CA: University of California, School of Information and Computer Science.

Contents at a Glance

Contents

Introduction

Extracting actionable information from data is changing the fabric of modern business in ways that directly affect programmers. One way is the demand for new programming skills. Market analysts predict demand for people with advanced statistics and machine learning skills will exceed supply by 140,000 to 190,000 by 2018. That means good salaries and a wide choice of interesting projects for those who have the requisite skills. Another development that affects programmers is progress in developing core tools for statistics and machine learning. This relieves programmers of the need to program intricate algorithms for themselves each time they want to try a new one. Among general-purpose programming languages, Python developers have been in the forefront, building state-of-the-art machine learning tools, but there is a gap between having the tools and being able to use them efficiently.

Programmers can gain general knowledge about machine learning in a number of ways: online courses, a number of well-written books, and so on. Many of these give excellent surveys of machine learning algorithms and examples of their use, but because of the availability of so many different algorithms, it's difficult to cover the details of their usage in a survey.

This leaves a gap for the practitioner. The number of algorithms available requires making choices that a programmer new to machine learning might not be equipped to make until trying several, and it leaves the programmer to fill in the details of the usage of these algorithms in the context of overall problem formulation and solution.

This book attempts to close that gap. The approach taken is to restrict the algorithms covered to two families of algorithms that have proven to give optimum performance for a wide variety of problems. This assertion is supported by their dominant usage in machine learning competitions, their early inclusion in newly developed packages of machine learning tools, and their performance in comparative studies (as discussed in Chapter 1, "The Two Essential Algorithms for Making Predictions"). Restricting attention to two algorithm families makes it possible to provide good coverage of the principles of operation and to run through the details of a number of examples showing how these algorithms apply to problems with different structures.

The book largely relies on code examples to illustrate the principles of operation for the algorithms discussed. I've discovered in the classes I have taught at University of California, Berkeley, Galvanize, University of New Haven, and Hacker Dojo, that programmers generally grasp principles more readily by seeing simple code illustrations than by looking at math.

This book focuses on Python because it offers a good blend of functionality and specialized packages containing machine learning algorithms. Python is an often-used language that is well known for producing compact, readable code. That fact has led a number of leading companies to adopt Python for prototyping and deployment. Python developers are supported by a large community of fellow developers, development tools, extensions, and so forth. Python is widely used in industrial applications and in scientific programming, as well. It has a number of packages that support computationally intensive applications like machine learning, and it is a good collection of the leading machine learning algorithms (so you don't have to code them yourself). Python is a better general-purpose programming language than specialized statistical languages such as R or SAS (Statistical Analysis System). Its collection of machine learning algorithms incorporates a number of top-flight algorithms and continues to expand.

Who This Book Is For

This book is intended for Python programmers who want to add machine learning to their repertoire, either for a specific project or as part of keeping their toolkit relevant. Perhaps a new problem has come up at work that requires machine learning. With machine learning being covered so much in the news these days, it's a useful skill to claim on a resume.

This book provides the following for Python programmers:

- A description of the basic problems that machine learning attacks
- Several state-of-the-art algorithms
- The principles of operation for these algorithms
- Process steps for specifying, designing, and qualifying a machine learning system

- Examples of the processes and algorithms
- Hackable code

To get through this book easily, your primary background requirements include an understanding of programming or computer science and the ability to read and write code. The code examples, libraries, and packages are all Python, so the book will prove most useful to Python programmers. In some cases, the book runs through code for the core of an algorithm to demonstrate the operating principles, but then uses a Python package incorporating the algorithm to apply the algorithm to problems. Seeing code often gives programmers an intuitive grasp of an algorithm in the way that seeing the math does for others. Once the understanding is in place, examples will use developed Python packages with the bells and whistles that are important for efficient use (error checking, handling input and output, developed data structures for the models, defined predictor methods incorporating the trained model, and so on).

In addition to having a programming background, some knowledge of math and statistics will help get you through the material easily. Math requirements include some undergraduate-level differential calculus (knowing how to take a derivative and a little bit of linear algebra), matrix notation, matrix multiplication, and matrix inverse. The main use of these will be to follow the derivations of some of the algorithms covered. Many times, that will be as simple as taking a derivative of a simple function or doing some basic matrix manipulations. Being able to follow the calculations at a conceptual level may aid your understanding of the algorithm. Understanding the steps in the derivation can help you to understand the strengths and weaknesses of an algorithm and can help you to decide which algorithm is likely to be the best choice for a particular problem.

This book also uses some general probability and statistics. The requirements for these include some familiarity with undergraduate-level probability and concepts such as the mean value of a list of real numbers, variance, and correlation. You can always look through the code if some of the concepts are rusty for you.

This book covers two broad classes of machine learning algorithms: penalized linear regression (for example, Ridge and Lasso) and ensemble methods (for example, Random Forest and Gradient Boosting). Each of these families contains variants that will solve regression and classification problems. (You learn the distinction between classification and regression early in the book.)

Readers who are already familiar with machine learning and are only interested in picking up one or the other of these can skip to the two chapters covering that family. Each method gets two chapters—one covering principles of operation and the other running through usage on different types of problems. Penalized linear regression is covered in Chapter 4, "Penalized Linear Regression," and Chapter 5, "Building Predictive Models Using Penalized Linear

Methods." Ensemble methods are covered in Chapter 6, "Ensemble Methods," and Chapter 7, "Building Ensemble Models with Python." To familiarize yourself with the problems addressed in the chapters on usage of the algorithms, you might find it helpful to skim Chapter 2, "Understand the Problem by Understanding the Data," which deals with data exploration. Readers who are just starting out with machine learning and want to go through from start to finish might want to save Chapter 2 until they start looking at the solutions to problems in later chapters.

What This Book Covers

As mentioned earlier, this book covers two algorithm families that are relatively recent developments and that are still being actively researched. They both depend on, and have somewhat eclipsed, earlier technologies.

Penalized linear regression represents a relatively recent development in ongoing research to improve on ordinary least squares regression. Penalized linear regression has several features that make it a top choice for predictive analytics. Penalized linear regression introduces a tunable parameter that makes it possible to balance the resulting model between overfitting and underfitting. It also yields information on the relative importance of the various inputs to the predictions it makes. Both of these features are vitally important to the process of developing predictive models. In addition, penalized linear regression yields the best prediction performance in some classes of problems, particularly underdetermined problems and problems with very many input parameters such as genetics and text mining. Furthermore, there's been a great deal of recent development of coordinate descent methods, making training penalized linear regression models extremely fast.

To help you understand penalized linear regression, this book recapitulates ordinary linear regression and other extensions to it, such as stepwise regression. The hope is that these will help cultivate intuition.

Ensemble methods are one of the most powerful predictive analytics tools available. They can model extremely complicated behavior, especially for problems that are vastly overdetermined, as is often the case for many web-based prediction problems (such as returning search results or predicting ad click-through rates). Many seasoned data scientists use ensemble methods as their first try because of their performance. They are relatively simple to use, and they also rank variables in terms of predictive performance.

Ensemble methods have followed a development path parallel to penalized linear regression. Whereas penalized linear regression evolved from overcoming the limitations of ordinary regression, ensemble methods evolved to overcome the limitations of binary decision trees. Correspondingly, this book's coverage of ensemble methods covers some background on binary decision trees because ensemble methods inherit some of their properties from binary decision trees. Understanding them helps cultivate intuition about ensemble methods.

What Has Changed Since the First Edition

In the three years since the first edition was published, Python has more firmly established itself as the primary language for data science. Developers of platforms like Spark for big data or TensorFlow and Torch for deep learning have adopted Python interfaces to reach the widest set of data scientists. The two classes of algorithms emphasized in the first edition continue to be heavy favorites and are now available as part of PySpark.

The beauty of this marriage is that the code required to build machine learning models on truly gargantuan data sets is no more complicated than what's required on smaller data sets.

PySpark illustrates several important developments, making it cleaner and easier to invoke very powerful machine learning tools through relatively simple easy to read and write Python code. When the first edition of this book was written, building machine learning models on very large data sets required spinning up hundreds of processors, which required vast knowledge of data center processes and programming. It was cumbersome and frankly not very effective. Spark architecture was developed to correct this difficulty.

Spark made it possible to easily rent and employ large numbers of processors for machine learning. PySpark added a Python interface. The result is that the code to run a machine learning algorithm in PySpark is not much more complicated than to run the plain Python versions of programs. The algorithms that were the focus of the first edition continue to be heavily used favorites and are available in Spark. So it seemed natural to add PySpark examples alongside the Python examples in order to familiarize readers with PySpark.

In this edition all the code examples are in Python 3, since Python 2 is due to fall out of support and, in addition to providing the code in text form, the code is also available in Jupyter notebooks for each chapter. The notebook code when executed will draw graphs and tables you see in the figures.

How This Book Is Structured

This book follows the basic order in which you would approach a new prediction problem. The beginning involves developing an understanding of the data and determining how to formulate the problem, and then proceeds to try an algorithm and measure the performance. In the midst of this sequence, the book outlines the methods and reasons for the steps as they come up. Chapter 1 gives a more thorough description of the types of problems that this book covers and the methods that are used. The book uses several data sets from the UC Irvine data repository as examples, and Chapter 2 exhibits some of the methods and tools that you can use for developing insight into a new data set. Chapter 3, "Predictive Model Building: Balancing Performance, Complexity, and Big Data," talks about the difficulties of predictive analytics and techniques for addressing them. It outlines the relationships between problem complexity, model complexity, data set size, and predictive performance. It discusses overfitting and how to reliably sense overfitting. It talks about performance metrics for different types of problems. Chapters 4 and 5, respectively, cover the background on penalized linear regression and its application to problems explored in Chapter 2. Chapters 6 and 7 cover background and application for ensemble methods.

What You Need to Use This Book

To run the code examples in the book, you need to have Python 3.x, SciPy, numpy, pandas, and scikit-learn and PySpark. These can be difficult to install due to cross-dependencies and version issues. To make the installation easy, I've used a free distribution of these packages that's available from Continuum Analytics (`http://continuum.io/`). Its Anaconda product is a free download and includes Python 3.x and all the packages you need to run the code in this book (and more). I've run the examples on Ubuntu 14.04 Linux but haven't tried them on other operating systems.

PySpark will need a Linux environment. If you're not running on Linux, then probably the easiest way to run the examples will be to use a virtual machine. Virtual Box is a free open source virtual machine—follow the directions to download Virtual Box and then install Ubuntu 18.05 and use Anaconda to install Python, PySpark, etc. You'll only need to employ a VM to run the PySpark examples. The non-Spark code will run anywhere you can open a Jupyter notebook.

Reader Support for This Book

Source code available in the book's repository can help you speed your learning. The chapters include installation instructions so that you can get coding along with reading the book.

Source Code

As you work through the examples in this book, you may choose either to type in all the code manually or to use the source code files that accompany the book.

All the source code used in this book is available for download from `http://www.wiley.com/go/pythonmachinelearning2e`. You will find the code snippets from the source code are accompanied by a download icon and note indicating the name of the program so that you know it's available for download and can easily locate it in the download file.

Besides providing the code in text form, it is also included in a Python notebook. If you know how to run a Jupyter notebook, you can run the code cell-by-cell. The output will appear in the notebook, the figures will get drawn, and printed output will appear below the code block.

After you download the code, just decompress it with your favorite compression tool.

How to Contact the Publisher

If you believe you've found a mistake in this book, please bring it to our attention. At John Wiley & Sons, we understand how important it is to provide our customers with accurate content, but even with our best efforts an error may occur.

In order to submit your possible errata, please email it to our Customer Service Team at `wileysupport@wiley.com` with the subject line "Possible Book Errata Submission".

The Two Essential Algorithms for Making Predictions

This book focuses on the machine learning process and so covers just a few of the most effective and widely used algorithms. It does not provide a survey of machine learning techniques. Too many of the algorithms that might be included in a survey are not actively used by practitioners.

This book deals with one class of machine learning problems, generally referred to as *function approximation*. Function approximation is a subset of problems that are called *supervised learning* problems. Linear regression and its classifier cousin, logistic regression, provide familiar examples of algorithms for function approximation problems. Function approximation problems include an enormous breadth of practical classification and regression problems in all sorts of arenas, including text classification, search responses, ad placements, spam filtering, predicting customer behavior, diagnostics, and so forth. The list is almost endless.

Broadly speaking, this book covers two classes of algorithms for solving function approximation problems: penalized linear regression methods and ensemble methods. This chapter introduces you to both of these algorithms, outlines some of their characteristics, and reviews the results of comparative studies of algorithm performance in order to demonstrate their consistent high performance.

This chapter then discusses the process of building predictive models. It describes the kinds of problems that you'll be able to address with the tools covered here and the flexibilities that you have in how you set up your problem and define the features that you'll use for making predictions. It describes process steps involved in building a predictive model and qualifying it for deployment.

Why Are These Two Algorithms So Useful?

Several factors make the penalized linear regression and ensemble methods a useful collection. Stated simply, they will provide optimum or near-optimum performance on the vast majority of predictive analytics (function approximation) problems encountered in practice, including big data sets, little data sets, wide data sets, tall skinny data sets, complicated problems, and simple problems. Evidence for this assertion can be found in two papers by Rich Caruana and his colleagues:

- "An Empirical Comparison of Supervised Learning Algorithms," by Rich Caruana and Alexandru Niculescu-Mizil[1]
- "An Empirical Evaluation of Supervised Learning in High Dimensions," by Rich Caruana, Nikos Karampatziakis, and Ainur Yessenalina[2]

In those two papers, the authors chose a variety of classification problems and applied a variety of different algorithms to build predictive models. The models were run on test data that were not included in training the models, and then the algorithms included in the studies were ranked on the basis of their performance on the problems. The first study compared 9 different basic algorithms on 11 different machine learning (binary classification) problems. The problems used in the study came from a wide variety of areas, including demographic data, text processing, pattern recognition, physics, and biology. Table 1.1 lists the data sets used in the study using the same names given by the study authors. The table shows how many attributes were available for predicting outcomes for each of the data sets, and it shows what percentage of the examples were positive.

Table 1.1: Sketch of Problems in Machine Learning Comparison Study

DATA SET NAME	NUMBER OF ATTRIBUTES	% OF EXAMPLES THAT ARE POSITIVE
Adult	14	25
Bact	11	69
Cod	15	50
Calhous	9	52
Cov_Type	54	36
HS	200	24

DATA SET NAME	NUMBER OF ATTRIBUTES	% OF EXAMPLES THAT ARE POSITIVE
Letter.p1	16	3
Letter.p2	16	53
Medis	63	11
Mg	124	17
Slac	59	50

The term *positive example* in a classification problem means an experiment (a line of data from the input data set) in which the outcome is positive. For example, if the classifier is being designed to determine whether a radar return signal indicates the presence of an airplane, then the positive example would be those returns where there was actually an airplane in the radar's field of view. The term *positive* comes from this sort of example where the two outcomes represent presence or absence. Other examples include presence or absence of disease in a medical test or presence or absence of cheating on a tax return.

Not all classification problems deal with presence or absence. For example, determining the gender of an author by machine-reading his or her text or machine-analyzing a handwriting sample has two classes—male and female— but there's no sense in which one is the absence of the other. In these cases, there's some arbitrariness in the assignment of the designations "positive" and "negative." The assignments of positive and negative can be arbitrary, but once chosen must be used consistently.

Some of the problems in the first study had many more examples of one class than the other. These are called *unbalanced*. For example, the two data sets Letter.p1 and Letter.p2 pose closely related problems in correctly classifying typed uppercase letters in a wide variety of fonts. The task with Letter.p1 is to correctly classify the letter *O* in a standard mix of letters. The task with Letter .p2 is to correctly classify *A–M* versus *N–Z*. The percentage of positives shown in Table 1.1 reflects this difference.

Table 1.1 also shows the number of "attributes" in each of the data sets. Attributes are the variables you have available to base a prediction on. For example, to predict whether or not an airplane will arrive at its destination on time, you might incorporate attributes such as the name of the airline company, the make and year of the airplane, the level of precipitation at the destination airport, the wind speed and direction along the flight path, and so on. Having a lot of attributes upon which to base a prediction can be a blessing and a curse. Attributes that relate directly to the outcomes being predicted are a blessing. Attributes that are unrelated to the outcomes are a curse. Telling the difference between blessed and cursed attributes requires data. Chapter 3, "Predictive Model Building: Balancing Performance, Complexity, and Big Data," goes into that in more detail.

Table 1.2 shows how the algorithms covered in this book fared relative to the other algorithms used in the study. Table 1.2 shows which algorithms showed the top five performance scores for each of the problems listed in Table 1.1. Algorithms covered in this book are spelled out (boosted decision trees, Random Forests, bagged decision trees, and logistic regression). The first three of these are ensemble methods. Penalized regression was not fully developed when the study was done and wasn't evaluated. Logistic regression is a close relative and is used to gauge the success of regression methods. Each of the 9 algorithms used in the study had 3 different data reduction techniques applied, for a total of 27 combinations. The top five positions represent roughly the top 20 percent of performance scores. The row next to the heading Covt indicates that the boosted decision trees algorithm was the first and second best relative to performance, the Random Forests algorithm was the fourth and fifth best, and the bagged decision trees algorithm was the third best. In the cases where algorithms not covered here were in the top five, an entry appears in the Other column. The algorithms that show up there are *k-nearest neighbors* (KNNs), *artificial neural nets* (ANNs), and *support vector machines* (SVMs).

Table 1.2: How the Algorithms Covered in This Book Compare on Different Problems

ALGORITHM	BOOSTED DECISION TREES	RANDOM FORESTS	BAGGED DECISION TREES	LOGISTIC REGRESSION	OTHER
Covt	1, 2	4, 5	3		
Adult	1, 4	2	3, 5		
LTR.P1	1				SVM, KNN
LTR.P2	1, 2	4, 5			SVM
MEDIS		1, 3		5	ANN
SLAC		1, 2, 3	4, 5		
HS	1, 3				ANN
MG		2, 4, 5	1, 3		
CALHOUS	1, 2	5	3, 4		
COD	1, 2		3, 4, 5		
BACT	2, 5		1, 3, 4		

Logistic regression captures top-five honors in only one case in Table 1.2. The reason for that is that these data sets have few attributes (at most 200) relative to examples (5,000 in each data set). There's plenty of data to resolve a model with so few attributes, and yet the training sets are small enough that the training time is not excessive.

As you'll see in Chapter 3 and in the examples covered in Chapter 5, "Building Predictive Models Using Penalized Linear Methods," and Chapter 7, "Building Ensemble Models with Python," the penalized regression methods perform best relative to other algorithms when there are numerous attributes and not enough examples or time to train a more complicated ensemble model.

Caruana et al. have run a newer study (2008) to address how these algorithms compare when the number of attributes increases. That is, how do these algorithms compare on big data? A number of fields have significantly more attributes than the data sets in the first study. For example, genomic problems have several tens of thousands of attributes (one attribute per gene), and text mining problems can have millions of attributes (one attribute per distinct word or per distinct pair of words). Table 1.3 shows how linear regression and ensemble methods fare as the number of attributes grows. The results in Table 1.3 show the ranking of the algorithms used in the second study. The table shows the performance on each of the problems individually and in the far right column shows the ranking of each algorithm's average score across all the problems. The algorithms used in the study are broken into two groups. The top group of algorithms are ones that will be covered in this book. The bottom group will not be covered.

The problems shown in Table 1.3 are arranged in order of their number of attributes, ranging from 761 to 685,569. Linear (logistic) regression is in the top three for 5 of the 11 test cases used in the study. Those superior scores were concentrated among the larger data sets. Notice that boosted decision tree (denoted by BSTDT in Table 1.3) and Random Forests (denoted by RF in Table 1.3) algorithms still perform near the top. They come in first and second for overall score on these problems.

The algorithms covered in this book have other advantages besides raw predictive performance. An important benefit of the penalized linear regression models that the book covers is the speed at which they train. On big problems, training speed can become an issue. In some problems, model training can take days or weeks. This time frame can be an intolerable delay, particularly early in development when iterations are required to home in on the best approach. Besides training very quickly, after being deployed a trained linear model can produce predictions very quickly—quickly enough for high-speed trading or Internet ad insertions. The study demonstrates that penalized linear regression can provide the best answers available in many cases and be near the top even in cases where they are not the best.

Table 1.3: How the Algorithms Covered in This Book Compare on Big Data Problems

DIM	761 STURN	761 CALAM	780 DIGITS	927 TIS	1344 CRYST	3448 KDD98	20958 R-S	105354 CITE	195203 DSE	405333 SPAM	685569 IMDB	MEAN
BSTDT	8	1	2	6	1	3	8	1	7	6	3	1
RF	9	4	3	3	2	1	6	5	3	1	3	2
BAGDT	5	2	6	4	3	1	9	1	6	7	3	4
BSTST	2	3	7	7	7	1	7	4	8	8	5	7
LR	4	8	9	1	4	1	2	2	2	4	4	6
SVM	3	5	5	2	5	2	1	1	5	5	3	3
ANN	6	7	4	5	8	1	4	2	1	3	3	5
KNN	1	6	1	9	6	2	10	1	7	9	6	8
PRC	7	9	8	8	7	1	3	3	4	2	2	9
NB	10	10	10	10	9	1	5	1	9	10	7	10

In addition, these algorithms are reasonably easy to use. They do not have very many tunable parameters. They have well-defined and well-structured input types. They solve several types of problems in regression and classification. It is not unusual to be able to arrange the input data and generate a first trained model and performance predictions within an hour or two of starting a new problem.

One of their most important features is that they indicate which of their input variables is most important for producing predictions. This turns out to be an invaluable feature in a machine learning algorithm. One of the most time-consuming steps in the development of a predictive model is what is sometimes called *feature selection* or *feature engineering*. This is the process whereby the data scientist chooses the variables that will be used to predict outcomes. By ranking features according to importance, the algorithms covered in this book aid in the feature-engineering process by taking some of the guesswork out of the development process and making the process more sure.

What Are Penalized Regression Methods?

Penalized linear regression is a derivative of *ordinary least squares* (OLS) regression—a method developed by Gauss and Legendre roughly 200 years ago. Penalized linear regression methods were designed to overcome some basic limitations of OLS regression. The basic problem with OLS is that sometimes it overfits the problem. Think of OLS as fitting a line through a group of points, as in Figure 1.1. This is a simple prediction problem: predicting y, the target value given a single attribute x. For example, the problem might be to predict men's salaries using only their heights. Height is slightly predictive of salaries for men (but not for women).

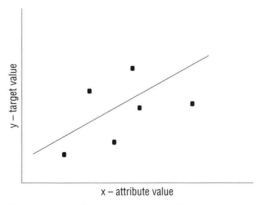

Figure 1.1: Ordinary least squares fit

The points represent men's salaries versus their heights. The line in Figure 1.1 represents the OLS solution to this prediction problem. In some sense, the line is the best predictive model for men's salaries given their heights. The data set has six points in it. Suppose that the data set had only two points in it. Imagine that there's a population of points, like the ones in Figure 1.1, but that you do not get to see all the points. Maybe they are too expensive to generate, like the genetic data mentioned earlier. There are enough humans available to isolate the gene that is the culprit; the problem is that you do not have gene sequences for many of them because of cost.

To simulate this in the simple example, imagine that instead of six points you're given only two of the six points. How would that change the nature of the line fit to those points? It would depend on which two points you happened to get. To see how much effect that would have, pick any two points from Figure 1.1 and imagine a line through them. Figure 1.2 shows some of the possible lines through pairs of points from Figure 1.1. Notice how much the lines vary depending on the choice of points.

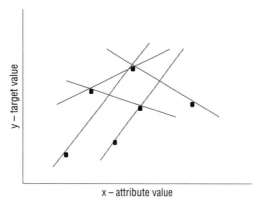

Figure 1.2: Fitting lines with only two points

The problem with having only two points to fit a line is that there is not enough data for the number of degrees of freedom. A line has two degrees of freedom. Having two degrees of freedom means that there are two independent parameters that uniquely determine a line. You can imagine grabbing hold of a line in the plane and sliding it up and down in the plane or twisting it to change its slope. So, vertical position and slope are independent. They can be changed separately, and together they completely specify a line. The degrees of freedom of a line can be expressed in several equivalent ways (where it intercepts the y-axis and its slope, two points that are on the line, and so on). All of these representations of a line require two parameters to specify.

When the number of degrees of freedom is equal to the number of points, the predictions are not very good. The lines hit the points used to draw them, but there is a lot of variation among lines drawn with different pairs of points. You cannot place much faith in a prediction that has as many degrees of freedom as the number of points in your data set. The plot in Figure 1.1 had six points and fit a line (two degrees of freedom) through them. That is six points and two degrees of freedom. The thought problem of determining the genes causing a heritable condition illustrated that having more genes to choose from makes it necessary to have more data in order to isolate a cause from among the 20,000 or so possible human genes. The 20,000 different genes represent 20,000 degrees of freedom. Data from even 20,000 different persons will not suffice to get a reliable answer, and in many cases, all that can be afforded within the scope of a reasonable study is a sample from 500 or so persons. That is where penalized linear regression may be the best algorithm choice.

Penalized linear regression provides a way to systematically reduce degrees of freedom to match the amount of data available and the complexity of the under-lying phenomena. These methods have become very popular for problems with very many degrees of freedom. They are a favorite for genetic problems where the number of degrees of freedom (that is, the number of genes) can be several tens of thousands and for problems like text classification where the number of degrees of freedom can be more than a million. Chapter 4, "Penalized Linear Regression," gives more detail on how these methods work, sample code that illustrates the mechanics of these algorithms, and examples of the process for implementing machine learning systems using available Python packages.

What Are Ensemble Methods?

The other family of algorithms covered in this book is ensemble methods. The basic idea with ensemble methods is to build a horde of different predictive models and then combine their outputs—by averaging the outputs or taking the majority answer (voting). The individual models are called *base learners*. Some results from computational learning theory show that if the base learners are just slightly better than random guessing, the performance of the ensemble can be very good if there is a sufficient number of independent models.

One of the problems spurring the development of ensemble methods has been the observation that some particular machine learning algorithms exhibit instability. For example, the addition of fresh data to the data set might result in a radical change in the resulting model or its performance. Binary decision trees and traditional neural nets exhibit this sort of instability. This instability causes high variance in the performance of models, and averaging many models can be viewed as a way to reduce the variance. The trick is how to generate large numbers of independent models, particularly if they are all using the same base learner. Chapter 6, "Ensemble Methods," will get into the details of how this is done. The techniques are ingenious, and it is relatively easy to understand their basic principles of operation. Here is a preview of what's in store.

The ensemble methods that enjoy the widest availability and usage incorporate binary decision trees as their base learners. Binary decision trees are often portrayed as shown in Figure 1.3. The tree in Figure 1.3 takes a real number, called x, as input at the top, and then uses a series of binary (two-valued) decisions to decide what value should be output in response to x. The first decision is whether x is less than 5. If the answer to that question is "no," the binary decision tree outputs the value 4 indicated in the circle below the No leg of the upper decision box. Every possible value for x leads to some output y from the tree. Figure 1.4 plots the output (y) as a function of the input to the tree (x).

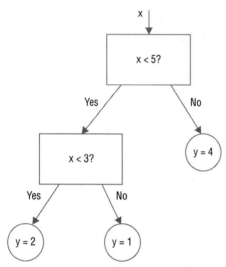

Figure 1.3: Binary decision tree example

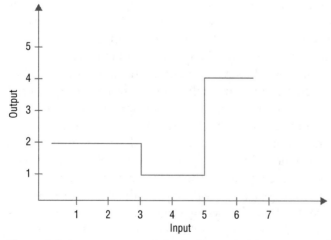

Figure 1.4: Input-output graph for the binary decision tree example

This description raises the question of where the comparisons (for example, $x < 5$?) come from and where the output values (in the circles at the bottom of the tree) come from. These values come from training the binary tree on the input data. The algorithm for doing that training is not difficult to understand and is covered in Chapter 6. The important thing to note at this point is that the values in the trained binary decision tree are fixed, given the data. The process for generating the tree is deterministic. One way to get differing models is to take random samples of the training data and train on these random subsets. That technique is called *Bagging* (short for *bootstrap aggregating*). It gives a way to generate a large number of slightly different binary decision trees. Those are then averaged (or voted for a classifier) to yield a final result. Chapter 6 describes in more detail this technique and other more powerful ones.

How to Decide Which Algorithm to Use

Table 1.4 gives a sketch comparison of these two families of algorithms. Penalized linear regression methods have the advantage that they train very quickly. Training times on large data sets can extend to hours, days, or even weeks. Training usually needs to be done several times before a deployable solution is arrived at. Long training times can stall development and deployment on large problems. The rapid training time for penalized linear methods makes them useful for the obvious reason that faster is better. Depending on the problem, these methods may suffer some performance disadvantages relative to ensemble methods. Chapter 3 gives more insight into the types of problems where penalized regression might be a better choice and those where ensemble methods might be a better choice. Penalized linear methods can sometimes be a useful first step in your development process even in the circumstance where they yield inferior performance to ensemble methods.

Table 1.4: High-Level Tradeoff between Penalized Linear Regression and Ensemble Algorithms

	TRAINING SPEED	PREDICTION SPEED	PROBLEM COMPLEXITY	DEALS WITH WIDE ATTRIBUTE
Penalized Linear Regression	+	+	–	+
Ensemble Methods	–	–	+	–

Early in development, a number of training iterations will be necessary for purposes of feature selection and feature engineering and for solidifying the mathematical problem statement. Deciding what you are going to use as input to your predictive model can take some time and thought. Sometimes that is obvious, but usually it requires some iteration. Throwing in everything you can find is not usually a good solution.

Trial and error is typically required to determine the best inputs for a model. For example, if you're trying to predict whether a visitor to your website will click a link for an ad, you might try using demographic data for the visitor. Maybe that does not give you the accuracy that you need, so you try incorporating data regarding the visitor's past behavior on the site—what ad the visitor clicked during past site visits or what products the visitor has bought. Maybe adding data about the site the visitor was on before coming to your site would help. These questions lead to a series of experiments where you incorporate the new data and see whether it hurts or helps. This iteration is generally time-consuming both for the data manipulations and for training your predictive model. Penalized linear regression will generally be faster than an ensemble method, and the time difference can be a material factor in the development process.

For example, if the training set is on the order of a gigabyte, training times may be on the order of 30 minutes for penalized linear regression and 5 or 6 hours for an ensemble method. If the feature engineering process requires 10 iterations to select the best feature set, the computation time alone comes to the difference between taking a day or taking a week to accomplish feature engineering. A useful process, therefore, is to train a penalized linear model in the early stages of development, feature engineering, and so on. That gives the data scientist a feel for which variables are going to be useful and important as well as a baseline performance for comparison with other algorithms later in development.

Besides enjoying a training time advantage, penalized linear methods generate predictions much faster than ensemble methods. Generating a prediction involves using the trained model. The trained model for penalized linear regression is simply a list of real numbers—one for each feature being used to make the predictions. The number of floating-point operations involved is the number of variables being used to make predictions. For highly time-sensitive predictions such as high-frequency trading or Internet ad insertions, computation time makes the difference between making money and losing money.

For some problems, linear methods may give equivalent or even better performance than ensemble methods. Some problems do not require complicated models. Chapter 3 goes into some detail about the nature of problem complexity and how the data scientist's task is to balance problem complexity, predictive model complexity, and data set size to achieve the best deployable model. The basic idea is that on problems that are not complex and problems for which sufficient data are not available, linear methods may achieve better overall performance than more complicated ensemble methods. Genetic data provide a good illustration of this type of problem.

The general perception is that there's an enormous amount of genetic data around. Genetic data sets are indeed large when measured in bytes, but in terms of generating accurate predictions, they aren't very large. To understand this distinction, consider the following thought experiment. Suppose that you have two people, one with a heritable condition and the other without. If you had genetic sequences for the two people, could you determine which gene was responsible for the condition? Obviously, that's not possible because many genes will differ between the two persons. So how many people would it take? At a minimum, it would take gene sequences for as many people as there are genes, and given any noise in the measurements, it would take even more. Humans have roughly 20,000 genes, depending on your count. And each datum costs roughly $1,000. So having just enough data to resolve the disease with perfect measurements would cost $20 million.

This situation is very similar to fitting a line to two points, as discussed earlier in this chapter. Models need to have fewer degrees of freedom than the number of data points. The data set typically needs to be a multiple of the degrees of freedom in the model. Because the data set size is fixed, the degrees of freedom in the model need to be adjustable. The chapters dealing with penalized linear regression will show you how the adjustability is built in to penalized linear regression and how to use it to achieve optimum performance.

NOTE The two broad categories of algorithms addressed in this book match those that Jeremy Howard and I presented at Strata Conference in 2012. Jeremy took ensemble methods, and I took penalized linear regression. We had fun arguing about the relative merits of the two groups. In reality, however, those two cover something like 80 percent of the model building that I do, and there are good reasons for that.

Chapter 3 goes into more detail about why one algorithm or another is a better choice for a given problem. It has to do with the complexity of the problem and the number of degrees of freedom inherent in the algorithms. The linear models tend to train rapidly and often give equivalent performance to nonlinear ensemble methods, especially if the data available are somewhat constrained. Because they're so rapid to train, it is often convenient to train linear models for early feature selection and to ballpark achievable performance for a specific problem. The linear models considered in this book can give information about variable importance to aid in the feature selection process. The ensemble methods often give better performance if there are adequate data and also give somewhat indirect measures of relative variable importance.

The Process Steps for Building a Predictive Model

Using machine learning requires several different skills. One is the required programming skill, which this book does not address. The other skills have to do with getting an appropriate model trained and deployed. These other skills are what the book does address. What do these other skills include?

Initially, problems are stated in somewhat vague language-based terms like "Show site visitors links that they're likely to click on." To turn this into a working system requires restating the problem in concrete mathematical terms, finding data to base the prediction on, and then training a predictive model that will predict the likelihood of site visitors clicking the links that are available for presentation. Stating the problem in mathematical terms makes assumptions about what features will be extracted from the available data sources and how they will be structured.

How do you get started with a new problem? First, you look through the available data to determine which of the data might be of use in prediction. "Looking through the data" means running various statistical tests on the data to get a feel for what they reveal and how they relate to what you're trying to predict. Intuition can guide you to some extent. You can also quantify the outcomes and test the degree to which potential prediction features correlate with these outcomes. Chapter 2, "Understand the Problem by Understanding the Data," goes through this process for the data sets that are used to characterize and compare the algorithms outlined in the rest of the book.

By some means, you develop a set of features and start training the machine learning algorithm that you have selected. That produces a trained model and estimates its performance. Next, you want to consider making changes to the features set, including adding new ones or removing some that proved unhelpful, or perhaps changing to a different type of training objective (also called a *target*) to see whether it improves performance. You'll iterate various design decisions to determine whether there's a possibility of improving performance. You may pull out the examples that show the worst performance and then attempt to determine if there's something that unites these examples. That may lead to another feature to add to the prediction process, or it might cause you to bifurcate the data and train different models on different populations.

The goal of this book is to make these processes familiar enough to you that you can march through these development steps confidently. That requires your familiarity with the input data structures required by different algorithms as you frame the problem and begin extracting the data to be used in training and testing algorithms. The process usually includes several of the following steps:

1. Extract and assemble features to be used for prediction.
2. Develop targets for the training.
3. Train a model.
4. Assess performance on test data.

NOTE   The first pass can usually be improved on by trying different sets of features, different types of targets, and so on.

Machine learning requires more than familiarization with a few packages. It requires understanding and having practiced the process involved in developing a deployable model. This book aims to give you that understanding. It assumes basic undergraduate math and some basic ideas from probability and statistics, but the book doesn't presuppose a background in machine learning. At the same time, it intends to arm readers with the very best algorithms for a wide class of problems, not necessarily to survey all machine learning algorithms or approaches. There are a number of algorithms that are interesting but that don't get used often, for a variety of reasons. For example, perhaps they don't scale well, maybe they don't give insight about what is going on inside, maybe they're difficult to use, and so on. It is well known, for example, that Gradient Boosting (one of the algorithms covered here) is the leading winner of online machine competitions by a wide margin. There are good reasons why some algorithms are more often used by practitioners, and this book will succeed to the extent that you understand these when you've finished reading.

Framing a Machine Learning Problem

Beginning work on a machine learning competition presents a simulation of a real machine learning problem. The competition presents a brief description (for example, announcing that an insurance company would like to better predict loss rates on their automobile policies). As a competitor, your first step is to open the data set, take a look at the data available, and identify what form a prediction needs to take to be useful. The inspection of the data will give an intuitive feel for what the data represent and how they relate to the prediction job at hand. The data can give insight regarding approaches. Figure 1.5 depicts the process of starting from a general language statement of objective and moving toward an arrangement of data that will serve as input for a machine learning algorithm.

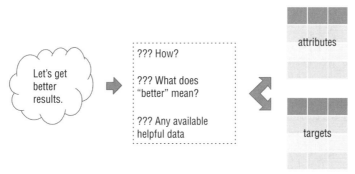

Figure 1.5: Framing a machine learning problem

The generalized statement caricatured as "Let's get better results" has first to be converted into specific goals that can be measured and optimized. For a website owner, specific performance might be improved click-through rates or more sales (or more contribution margin). The next step is to assemble data that might make it possible to predict how likely a given customer is to click various links or to purchase various products offered online. Figure 1.5 depicts these data as a matrix of attributes. For the website example, they might include other pages the visitor has viewed or items the visitor has purchased in the past. In addition to attributes that will be used to make predictions, the machine learning algorithms for this type of problem need to have correct answers to use for training. These are denoted as targets in Figure 1.5. The algorithms covered in this book learn by detecting patterns in past behaviors, but it is important that they not merely memorize past behavior; after all, a customer might not repeat a purchase of something he bought yesterday. Chapter 3 discusses in detail how this process of training without memorizing works.

Usually, several aspects of the problem formulation can be done in more than one way. This leads to some iteration between framing the problem, selecting and training a model, and producing performance estimates. Figure 1.6 depicts this process.

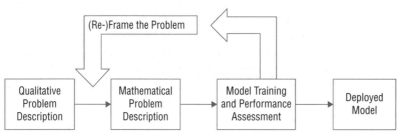

Figure 1.6: Iteration from formulation to performance

The problem may come with specific quantitative training objectives, or part of the job might be extracting these data (called *targets* or *labels*). Consider, for instance, the problem of building a system to automatically trade securities. To trade automatically, a first step might be to predict changes in the price of a security. The prices are easily available, so it is conceptually simple to use historical data to build training examples for which the future price changes are known. But even that involves choices and experimentation. Future price change could be computed in several different ways. The change could be the difference between the current price and the price 10 minutes in the future. It could also be the change between the current price and the price 10 days in the future. It could also be the difference between the current price and the maximum/minimum price over the next 10 minutes. The change in price could be characterized by a two-state variable taking values "higher" or "lower" depending on whether the price is higher or lower 10 minutes in the future. Each of these choices will lead to a predictive model, and the predictions will be used for deciding whether to buy or sell the security. Some experimentation will be required to determine the best choice.

Feature Extraction and Feature Engineering

Deciding which variables to use for making predictions can also involve experimentation. This process is known as *feature extraction* and *feature engineering*. Feature extraction is the process of taking data from a free-form arrangement, such as words in a document or on a web page, and arranging them into rows and columns of numbers. For example, a spam-filtering problem begins with text from emails and might extract things such as the number of capital letters in the document and the number of words in all caps, the number of times the word "buy" appears in the document and other numeric features selected to highlight the differences between spam and non-spam emails.

Feature engineering is the process of manipulating and combining features to arrive at more informative ones. Building a system for trading securities involves feature extraction and feature engineering. Feature extraction would be deciding what things will be used to predict prices. Past prices, prices of related securities, interest rates, and features extracted from news releases have all been incorporated into various trading systems that have been discussed publicly. In addition, securities prices have a number of engineered features with names like stochastic, MACD (*moving average convergence divergence*), and RSI (*relative strength index*) that are basically functions of past prices that their inventors believed to be useful in securities trading.

After a reasonable set of features is developed, you can train a predictive model like the ones described in this book, assess its performance, and make a decision about deploying the model. Generally, you'll want to make changes to the features used, if for no other reason than to confirm that your model's performance is adequate. One way to determine which features to use is to try all combinations, but that can take a lot of time. Inevitably, you'll face competing pressures to improve performance but also to get a trained model into use quickly. The algorithms discussed in this book have the beneficial property of providing metrics on the utility of each attribute in producing predictions. One training pass will generate rankings on the features to indicate their relative importance. This information helps speed the feature engineering process.

NOTE   Data preparation and feature engineering is estimated to take 80 to 90 percent of the time required to develop a machine learning model.

The model training process, which begins each time a baseline set of features is attempted, also involves a process. A modern machine learning algorithm, such as the ones described in this book, trains something like 100 to 5,000 different models that have to be winnowed down to a single model for deployment. The reason for generating so many models is to provide models of all different shades of complexity. This makes it possible to choose the model that is best suited to the problem and data set. You don't want a model that's too simple or you give up performance, but you don't want a model that's too complicated or you'll overfit the problem. Having models in all shades of complexity lets you pick one that is just right.

Determining Performance of a Trained Model

The fit of a model is determined by how well it performs on data that were not used to train the model. This is an important step and conceptually simple. Just set aside some data. Don't use it in training. After the training is finished, use the data you set aside to determine the performance of your algorithm. This book discusses several systematic ways to hold out data. Different methods have different advantages, depending mostly on the size of the training data. As easy as it sounds, people continually figure out complicated ways to let the test data "leak" into the training process. At the end of the process, you'll have an algorithm that will sift through incoming data and make accurate predictions for you. It might need monitoring as changing conditions alter the underlying statistics.

Chapter Contents and Dependencies

Different readers may want to take different paths through this book, depending on their backgrounds and whether they have time to understand the basic principles. Figure 1.7 shows how chapters in the book depend on one another.

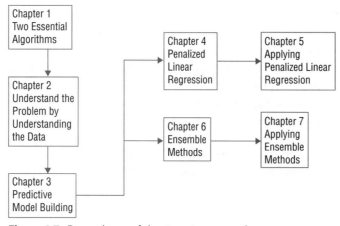

Figure 1.7: Dependence of chapters on one another

Chapter 2 goes through the various data sets that will be used for problem examples to illustrate the use of the algorithms that will be developed and to compare algorithms to each other based on performance and other features. The starting point with a new machine learning problem is digging into the data set to understand it better and to learn its problems and idiosyncrasies. Part of the point of Chapter 2 is to demonstrate some of the tools available in Python for data exploration. You might want to go through some but not all of the examples shown in Chapter 2 to become familiar with the process and then come back to Chapter 2 when diving into the solution examples later.

Chapter 3 explains the basic tradeoffs in a machine learning problem and introduces several key concepts that are used throughout the book. One key concept is the mathematical description of predictive problems. The basic distinctions between classification and regression problems are shown. Chapter 3 also introduces the concept of using out-of-sample data for determining the performance of a predictive model. Out-of-sample data are data that have not been included in the training of the model. Good machine learning practice demands that a developer produce solid estimates of how a predictive model will perform when it is deployed. This requires excluding some data from the training set and using it to simulate fresh data. The reasons for this requirement, the methods for accomplishing it, and the tradeoffs between different methods are described. Another key concept is that there are numerous measures of system performance. Chapter 3 outlines these methods and discusses tradeoffs between them. Readers who are already familiar with machine learning can browse this chapter and scan the code examples instead of reading it carefully and running the code.

Chapter 4 shows the core ideas of the algorithms for training penalized regression models. The chapter introduces the basic concepts and shows how the algorithms are derived. Some of the examples introduced in Chapter 3 are used to motivate the penalized linear regression methods and algorithms for their solution. The chapter runs through code for the core algorithms for solving penalized linear regression training. Chapter 4 also explains several extensions to linear regression methods. One of these extensions shows how to code factor variables as real numbers so that linear regression methods can be applied. Linear regression can be used only on problems where the predictors are real numbers; that is, the quantities being used to make predictions have to be numeric. Many practical and important problems have variables like "single, married, or divorced" that can be helpful in making predictions. To incorporate variables of this type (called *categorical variables*) in a linear regression model, means have been devised to convert categorical variables to real number variables. Chapter 4 covers those methods. In addition, Chapter 4 also shows methods (called *basis expansion*) for getting nonlinear functions out of nonlinear regression. Sometimes basis expansion can be used to squeeze a little more performance out of linear regression.

Chapter 5 applies the penalized regression algorithms developed in Chapter 4 to a number of the problems outlined in Chapter 2. The chapter outlines the Python packages that implement penalized regression methods and uses them to solve problems. The objective is to cover a wide enough variety of problems that practitioners can find a problem close to the one that they have in front of them to solve. Besides quantifying and comparing predictive performance, Chapter 5 looks at other properties of the trained algorithms. Variable selection and variable ranking are important to understand. This understanding will help speed development on new problems.

Chapter 6 develops ensemble methods. Because ensemble methods are most frequently based on binary decision trees, the first step is to understand the principles of training and using binary decision trees. Many of the properties of ensemble methods are ones that they inherit directly from binary decision trees. With that understanding in place, the chapter explains the three principal ensemble methods covered in the book. The common names for these are Bagging, Boosting, and Random Forest. For each of these, the principles of operation are outlined and the code for the core algorithm is developed so that you can understand the principles of operation.

Chapter 7 uses ensemble methods to solve problems from Chapter 2 and then compares the various algorithms that have been developed. The comparison involves a number of elements. Predictive performance is one element of comparison. The time required for training and performance is another element. All the algorithms covered give variable importance ranking, and this information is compared on a given problem across several different algorithms.

In my experience, teaching machine learning to programmers and computer scientists, I've learned that code examples work better than mathematics for some people. The approach taken here is to provide some mathematics, algorithm sketches, and code examples to illustrate the important points. Nearly all the methods that are discussed will be found in the code included in the book and on the website. The intent is to provide hackable code to help you get up and running on your own problems as quickly as possible.

Summary

This chapter has given a specification for the kinds of problems that you'll be able to solve and a description of the process steps for building predictive models. The book concentrates on two algorithm families. Limiting the number of algorithms covered allows for a more thorough explanation of the background for these algorithms and of the mechanics of using them. This chapter showed some comparative performance results to motivate the choice of these two particular families. The chapter discussed the different strengths and characteristics of these two families and gave some description of the types of problems that would favor one or the other of the two.

The chapter also laid out the steps in the process of developing a predictive model and elaborated on the tradeoffs and outcomes for each step. The use of data not included in model training was suggested for generating performance estimates for predictive models.

This book's goal is to bring programmers with little or no machine learning experience to the point where they feel competent and comfortable incorporating machine learning into projects. The book does not survey a wide number of algorithms. Instead, it covers several best-in-class algorithms that can offer you performance, flexibility, and clarity. Once you understand a little about how these work and have some experience using them, you'll find them easy and quick to use. They will enable you to solve a wide variety of problems without having to do a lot of fussing to get them trained, and they'll give you insight into the sources of their performance.

References

1. Caruana, Rich, and Alexandru Niculescu-Mizil. "An Empirical Comparison of Supervised Learning Algorithms." *Proceedings of the 23rd International Conference on Machine Learning.* ACM, 2006.

2. Caruana, Rich, Nikos Karampatziakis, and Ainur Yessenalina. "An Empirical Evaluation of Supervised Learning in High Dimensions." *Proceedings of the 25th International Conference on Machine Learning.* ACM, 2008.

## CHAPTER 2

Understand the Problem by Understanding the Data

A new data set (problem) is a wrapped gift. It's full of promise and anticipation at the miracles you can perform once you've solved it. But it remains a mystery until you've opened it. This chapter is about opening up your new data set so you can see what's inside, get an appreciation for what you'll be able to do with the data, and start thinking about how you'll approach model building with it.

This chapter has two purposes. One is to familiarize you with data sets that will be used later as examples of different types of problems to be solved using the algorithms you'll learn in Chapter 4, "Penalized Linear Regression," and Chapter 6, "Ensemble Methods." The other purpose is to demonstrate some of the tools available in Python for data exploration.

The chapter uses a simple example to review some basic problem structure, nomenclature, and characteristics of a machine learning data set. The language introduced in this section will be used throughout the rest of the book. After establishing some common language, the chapter goes one by one through several different types of function approximation problems. These problems illustrate common variations of machine learning problems so that you'll know how to recognize the variants when you see them and will know how to handle them (and will have code examples for them).

The Anatomy of a New Problem

The algorithms covered in this book start with a matrix (or table) full of numbers and perhaps some character variables. The example in Table 2.1 establishes some nomenclature and represents a small machine learning data set in a two-dimensional table. The table will give you a mental image of a data set so that references to "columns corresponding to attributes" or "rows corresponding to individual examples" will be familiar. In this example, the predictive analytics problem is to predict how much money individuals will spend buying books online over the next year.

Table 2.1: Data for a Machine Learning Problem

USERID	ATTRIBUTE 1	ATTRIBUTE 2	ATTRIBUTE 3	LABELS
001	6.5	Male	12	$120
004	4.2	Female	17	$270
007	5.7	Male	3	$75
008	5.8	Female	8	$600

The data are arranged into rows and columns. Each row represents an individual case (also called an *instance, example,* or *observation*). The columns in Table 2.1 are given designations that indicate the roles they will play in the machine learning problem. The columns designated as attributes will be used to make predictions of the dollars spent on books. In the column designated as labels, you'll see how much each customer spent last year on books.

> **NOTE**   Machine learning data sets are most commonly arranged with columns corresponding to a single attribute and rows corresponding to a single observation, but not always. For example, some text mining literature arranges the matrix the other way around—with columns corresponding to an observation and rows corresponding to an attribute.

In Table 2.1, a row represents an individual customer, and the data in the row all pertain to that individual. The first column is called UserID and contains an identifier that is unique for each row (case). A unique identifier may or may not be present in your problem. For instance, websites typically tag site visitors with a user ID that is associated with them for the duration of their visit. If a user does not register with the site, the same user gets a different ID with each visit. The ID is usually assigned to each observation, which will be the subject of the prediction you're going to build. Columns 2, 3, and 4 are called Attributes instead of being given more specific names like Height or Gender. The point is to highlight their role in the prediction process. Attributes are data available about the case that will be used to make predictions.

Labels are the things you want to predict. In this example, UserID is a simple number, Attribute 1 is height, Attribute 2 is gender, and Attribute 3 is how many books the person read last year. The column under Labels contains how much money the individual spent on books online last year. What are the roles that these different categories of data will play? What use does a machine learning algorithm make of user ID, attributes, and labels? The short answer is this: You ignore the user ID. You use the attributes to predict the labels.

The unique ID is for bookkeeping purposes and allows you to refer back to the other data available for the specific case. Generally, the unique ID does not get used directly in a machine learning algorithm. Attributes are the things that you've chosen to use for making predictions. Labels are observed outcomes that the machine learning algorithm will use to build a predictive model.

User ID doesn't usually get used for making predictions because it is too specific. It pertains to only a single example. The trick with machine learning is to build a model that generalizes to new cases (not merely memorizing past cases). To achieve that, the algorithm must be derived so that it is forced to pay attention to more than one row of data. One possible exception to excluding user ID is when the user ID is numeric and assigned in the order that users are signed up. Basically, it's indicating signup date in that case and can be useful because users with close IDs signed up at similar times and can be considered as a group on that basis.

The process of building a predictive model is called *training*. The way the process proceeds depends on the algorithm, and later chapters cover the details, but it is often iterative. The algorithm postulates a predictive relationship between the attributes and the labels, observes the mistakes that it makes, makes some correction, and then iterates on that process until a sound model is achieved. A number of technicalities are addressed later, but that's the basic idea.

WHAT'S IN A NAME?

Attributes and labels go by a variety of names, and new machine learners can get tripped up by the name switching from one author to another or even one paragraph to another from a single author.

Attributes (the variables being used to make predictions) are also known as the following:

- Predictors
- Features
- Independent variables
- Inputs

Labels are also known as the following:

- ▪ Outcomes
- ▪ Targets
- ▪ Dependent variables
- ▪ Responses

Different Types of Attributes and Labels Drive Modeling Choices

The attributes shown in Table 2.1 come in two different types: numeric variables and categorical (or factor) variables. Attribute 1 (height) is a numeric variable and is the most usual type of attribute. Attribute 2 is gender and is indicated by the entry Male or Female. This type of attribute is called a *categorical* or *factor* variable. Categorical variables have the property that there's no order relation between the various values. There's no sense to Male < Female (despite centuries of squabbling). Categorical variables can be two-valued, like Male Female, or multivalued, like states (AL, AK, AR . . . WY). Other distinctions can be drawn regarding attributes (integer versus float, for example), but they do not have the same impact on machine learning algorithms. The reason for this is that many machine learning algorithms take numeric attributes only; they cannot handle categorical or factor variables. Penalized regression algorithms deal only with numeric attributes. The same is true for support vector machines, kernel methods, and k-nearest neighbors. Chapter 4 will cover methods for converting categorical variables to numeric variables. The nature of the variables will shape your algorithm choices and the direction you take in developing a predictive model, so it's one of the things you need to pay attention to when you face a new problem.

A similar dichotomy arises for the labels. The labels shown in Table 2.1 are numeric: the amount of money that the individual spent on books online last year. In other problems, though, the labels may also be categorical. For example, if the job with Table 2.1 were to predict which individuals would spend more than $200 next year the problem would change, and the problem approach would change. The new problem of predicting which customers would spend more than $200 would have new labels. The new labels would take one of two values. Table 2.2 shows the relationship between the labels given in Table 2.1 and new labels based on the logical proposition Spending > $200. The new labels shown in Table 2.2 take one of two values—True or False.

Table 2.2: Numeric Targets versus Categorical Targets

TABLE 1 LABELS	>$200 ?
$120	False
$270	True
$75	False
$600	True

When the labels are numeric, the problem is called a *regression problem*. When the labels are categorical, the problem is called a *classification problem*. If the categorical target takes only two values, the problem is called a *binary classification problem*. If it takes more than two values, the problem is called a *multiclass classification problem*.

In many cases, the choice of problem type is up to the designer. You've just seen that this example problem can be converted from a regression problem to a binary classification problem by the simple transformation of the labels. These are tradeoffs that you might make as part of your attack on a problem. For example, classification targets might better support a decision between two courses of action.

The classification problem might also be simpler than the regression problem. Consider, for instance, the difference in complexity between a topographic map with a single contour line (say, the 100-foot contour line) and a topographic map with contour lines every 10 feet. The single contour divides the map into the areas that are higher than 100 feet and those that are lower and contains considerably less information than the more detailed contour map. A classifier is trying to compute a single dividing contour without regard for behavior distant from the decision boundary, whereas regression is trying to draw the whole map.

Things to Notice about Your New Data Set

You'll want to ascertain a number of other features of the data set as part of your initial inspection of the data. The following is a checklist and a sequence of things to learn about your data set to familiarize yourself with the data and to formulate the predictive model development steps that you want to follow. These are simple things to check and directly impact your next steps. In addition, the process gets you moving around the data and learning its properties.

Here are the Items to Check

- Number of rows and columns
- Number of categorical variables and number of unique values for each
- Missing values
- Summary statistics for attributes and labels

One of the first things to check is the size and shape of the data. Read the data into a list of lists; then the dimension of the outer list is the number of rows, and the dimension of one of the inner lists is the number of columns. The next section shows the concrete application of this to one of the data sets that you'll see used later to illustrate the properties of an algorithm that will be developed.

The next step in the process is to determine how many missing values there are in each row. The reason for doing it on a row-by-row basis is that the simplest way to deal with missing values is to throw away instances that aren't complete (examples with at least one missing value). In many situations, this can bias the results, but just a few incomplete examples will not make a material difference. By counting the rows with missing data (in addition to the total number of missing entries), you'll know how much of the data set you have to discard if you use the easy method.

If you have a large number of rows, as you might if you're collecting web data, the number you'll lose may be small compared to the number of rows of data you have available. If you're working on biological problems where the data are expensive and you have many attributes, you might not be able to afford to throw data out. In that case, you'll have to figure out some ways to fill in the missing values or use an algorithm that can deal with them. Filling them in is called *imputation*. The easiest way to impute the missing data is to fill in the missing entries using average values of the entries in each row. A more sophisticated method is to use one of the predictive methods covered in Chapters 4 and 6. To use a predictive method, you treat a column of attributes with missing values as though it were labels. Be sure to remove the original problem labels before undertaking this process.

The next several sections are going to go through the process outlined here and will introduce some methods for characterizing your data set to help you decide how to attack the modeling process.

Classification Problems: Detecting Unexploded Mines Using Sonar

This section steps through several checks that you might make on a classification problem as you begin digging into it. It starts with simple measurements of size and shape, reporting data types, counting missing values, and so forth. Then it moves on to statistical properties of the data and interrelationships between attributes and between attributes and the labels. The data set comes from the UC Irvine Data Repository [Ref 1988]. The data result from some experiments to determine if sonar can be used to detect unexploded mines left in harbors subsequent to military actions. The sonar signal is what's called a *chirped signal*. That means that the signal rises (or falls) in frequency over the duration of the sound pulse. The measurements in the data set represent the power measurements collected in the sonar receiver at different points in the returned signal. For roughly half of the examples, the sonar is illuminating a rock, and for the other half a metal cylinder having the shape of a mine. The data set goes by the name of "Rocks versus Mines."

Physical Characteristics of the Rocks Versus Mines Data Set

The first thing to do with a new data set is to determine its size and shape. Listing 2-1 shows code for determining the size and shape of the "Rocks versus Mines" data set from the UC Irvine Data Repository: the rocks versus mines data. Later in this chapter, you'll learn more about this data set, and the book will use it for example purposes as the algorithms are introduced. The process for determining the number of rows and columns is pretty simple in this case. The file is comma delimited, with the data for one experiment occupying one line of text. This makes it a simple matter to read a line, split it on the comma delimiters, and stack the resulting lists into an outer list containing the whole data set.

Listing 2-1: Sizing Up a New Data Set — rockVmineSummaries.py

```
__author__ = 'mike_bowles'

#read data from uci data repository
xList = list_read_rvm()

print('Number of Rows of Data = ' + str(len(xList)))
print('Number of Columns of Data = ' + str(len(xList[1])))

Printed Output:
Number of Rows of Data = 208
Number of Columns of Data = 61
```

As you can see in the sample output, this data set has 208 rows (lines) and 61 columns (fields per line). What difference does this make? The number of rows and columns has several impacts on how you proceed. First, the overall size gives you a rough idea of how long your training times are going to be. For a small data set like the rocks versus mines data, training time will be less than a minute, which will facilitate iterating through the process of training and tweaking. If the data set grows to 1,000 x 1,000, the training times will grow to a fraction of a minute for penalized linear regression and a few minutes for an ensemble method. As the data set gets to several tens of thousands of rows and columns, the training times will expand to 3 or 4 hours for penalized linear regression and 12 to 24 hours for an ensemble method. The larger training times will have an impact on your development time because you'll iterate a number of times.

The second important observation regarding row and column counts is that if the data set has many more columns than rows, you may be more likely to get the best prediction with penalized linear regression and vice versa. Chapter 3, "Predictive Model Building: Balancing Performance, Complexity, and Big Data," and the examples you'll run later will give you a better understanding of why that's true.

The next step in the checklist is to determine how many of the columns of data are numeric versus categorical. Listing 2-2 shows code to accomplish this for the rocks versus mines data set. The code runs down each column and adds up the number of entries that are numeric (int or float), the number of entries that are nonempty strings, and the number that are empty. The result is that the first 60 columns contain all numeric values and the last column contains all strings. The string values are the labels. Generally, categorical variables are presented as strings, as in this example. In some cases, binary-valued categorical variables are presented as a 0,1 numeric variable.

Listing 2-2: Determining the Nature of Attributes — rockVmineContents.py

```
__author__ = 'mike_bowles'

#read rvm data from uci url
xList = list_read_rvm()

nrow = len(xList)
ncol = len(xList[1])

type = [0]*3
colCounts = []

for col in range(ncol):
    for row in xList:
        try:
            a = float(row[col])
            if isinstance(a, float):
                type[0] += 1
        except ValueError:
            if len(row[col]) > 0:
                type[1] += 1
            else:
                type[2] += 1

    colCounts.append(type)
    type = [0]*3

print('Col#' + '\t\t' + 'Number' + '\t\t' +
                'Strings' + '\t\t ' + 'Other\n')
iCol = 0
for types in colCounts:
    print(str(iCol) + '\t\t' + str(types[0]) + '\t\t' +
```

```
                         str(types[1]) + '\t\t' + str(types[2]))
     iCol += 1
```

Printed Output:

Col#	Number	Strings	Other
0	208	0	0
1	208	0	0
2	208	0	0
3	208	0	0
4	208	0	0
5	208	0	0
6	208	0	0
7	208	0	0
8	208	0	0
9	208	0	0
10	208	0	0
11	208	0	0
12	208	0	0
13	208	0	0
14	208	0	0
15	208	0	0
16	208	0	0
17	208	0	0
18	208	0	0
19	208	0	0
20	208	0	0
.	.	.	.
.	.	.	.
.	.	.	.
40	208	0	0
41	208	0	0
42	208	0	0
43	208	0	0
44	208	0	0
45	208	0	0
46	208	0	0
47	208	0	0
48	208	0	0
49	208	0	0
50	208	0	0
51	208	0	0
52	208	0	0
53	208	0	0
54	208	0	0
55	208	0	0
56	208	0	0
57	208	0	0
58	208	0	0
59	208	0	0
60	0	208	0

Statistical Summaries of the Rocks Versus Mines Data Set

After determining which attributes are categorical and which are numeric, you'll want some descriptive statistics for the numeric variables and a count of the unique categories in each categorical attribute. Listing 2-3 gives some examples of these two procedures.

Listing 2-3: Summary Statistics for Numeric and Categorical Attributes — rVMSummaryStats.py

```
__author__ = 'mike_bowles'
import numpy as np

#read data from uci data repository
xList = list_read_rvm()

nrow = len(xList)
ncol = len(xList[1])

type = [0]*3
colCounts = []

#generate summary statistics for column 3 (e.g.)
col = 3
colData = []
for row in xList:
    colData.append(float(row[col]))

colArray = np.array(colData)
colMean = np.mean(colArray)
colsd = np.std(colArray)
print("Mean = " + '\t' + str(colMean) + '\t\t' +
            "Standard Deviation = " + '\t ' + str(colsd))


#calculate quantile boundaries
ntiles = 4

percentBdry = []

for i in range(ntiles+1):
    percentBdry.append(np.percentile(colArray, i*(100)/ntiles))

print("\nBoundaries for 4 Equal Percentiles")
print(percentBdry)
print(" \n")

Printed Output:
 Mean =        0.053892307692307684
Standard Deviation =        0.04641598322260027
```

```
Boundaries for 4 Equal Percentiles
[0.0058, 0.024375, 0.04405, 0.0645, 0.4264]


Boundaries for 10 Equal Percentiles

[0.0058, 0.0141, 0.022740000000000003, 0.027869999999999995, 0.03622,
0.04405, 0.050719999999999, 0.0599599999999999, 0.07794000000000001,
0.10836, 0.4264]


Unique Label Values
{'M', 'R'}

Counts for Each Value of Categorical Label
['M', 'R']
[111, 97]
```

The first section of the code picks up one column of numeric data, and then generates some statistics for it. The first step is to calculate the mean and standard deviation for the chosen attribute. Knowing these will undergird your intuition as you're developing models.

The next section of code looks for outliers. Here's how that works. Suppose that you're trying to determine whether you've got an outlier in the following list of numbers: [0.1, 0.15, 0.2, 0.25, 0.3, 0.35, 0.4, 4]. This example is constructed to have an outlier. The last number (4) is clearly out of scale with the rest of the numbers.

One way to reveal this sort of mismatch is to divide a set of numbers into percentiles. For example, the 25th percentile contains the smallest 25 percent of the data. The 50th percentile contains the smallest 50 percent of the data. The easiest way to visualize forming these groupings is to imagine that the data are sorted into numeric order. The numbers in the preceding list are arranged in numeric order. That makes it easy to see where the percentile boundaries go. Some often-used percentiles are given special names. The percentiles defined by dividing the set into equal quarters, fifths, and tenths are called respectively *quartiles*, *quintiles*, and *deciles*.

With the preceding list, it's easy to define the quartiles because the list is ordered and there are eight elements in the list. The first quartile contains 0.1 and 0.15 and so on. Notice how wide these quartiles are. The first quartile has a range of 0.5 (0.15–0.1). The second quartile is roughly the same. However, the last quartile has a range of 4.6, which is 100 times larger than the range of the other quartiles.

You can see similar behavior in the quartile boundaries that are calculated in Listing 2-3. First the program calculates the quartiles. That shows that the upper quartile is much wider than the others. To be more certain, the decile boundaries are also calculated and similarly demonstrate that the upper decile is unusually wide. Some widening is normal because distributions often thin out in the tails.

Visualization of Outliers Using a Quantile-Quantile Plot

One way to study outliers in more detail is to plot the distribution of the data in question relative to some reasonable distributions to see whether the relative numbers match up. Listing 2-4 shows how to use the Python function `probplot` to help determine whether or not the data set has outliers. The resulting plot shows how the boundaries associated with empirical percentiles in the data compare to the boundaries for the same percentiles of a Gaussian distribution. If the data being analyzed comes from a Gaussian distribution, the point being plotted will lie on a straight line. Figure 2.1 shows that a couple of points from column 4 of the rocks versus mines data are very far from the line. That means that the tails of the rocks versus mines data contain more examples than the tails of a Gaussian density.

Listing 2-4: Quantile-Quantile Plot for 4th Rocks Versus Mines Attribute — qqplotAttribute.py

```python
__author__ = 'mike_bowles'
import numpy as np

import scipy.stats as stats

#read rocks v mines data
xList = list_read_rvm()
nrow = len(xList)
ncol = len(xList[1])

type = [0]*3
colCounts = []

#generate summary statistics for column 3 (e.g.)
col = 3
colData = []
for row in xList:
    colData.append(float(row[col]))


stats.probplot(colData, dist="norm", plot=plt)
plt.show()
```

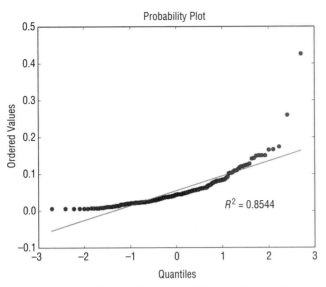

Figure 2.1: Quantile-quantile plot of attribute 4 from rocks versus mines data

What do you do with this information? Outliers may cause trouble either for model building or prediction. After you've trained a model on this data set, you can look at the errors your model makes and see whether the errors are correlated with these outliers. If they are, you can then take steps to correct them. For example, you can replicate the poor-performing examples to force them to be more heavily represented. You can segregate them out and train on them as a separate class. You can also edit them out of the data if they represent an abnormality that won't be present in the data your model will see when deployed. A reasonable process for this might be to generate quartile boundaries during the exploration phase and note potential outliers to get a feel for how much of a problem you might (or might not) have with it. Then when you're evaluating performance data, use quantile-quantile (Q-Q) plots to determine which points to call outliers for use in your error analysis.

Statistical Characterization of Categorical Attributes

The process just described applies to numeric attributes. But what about categorical attributes? You want to check to see how many categories they have and how many examples there are from each category. You want to learn these things for a couple of reasons. The gender attribute has two possible values (Male and Female), but if the attribute had been the state of the United States, there would have been 50 possible categories. As the number of attributes grows, the complexity of dealing with them mounts. Most binary tree algorithms, which are the basis for ensemble methods, have a cutoff on how many categories they can handle. The popular Random Forests package written by Breiman and Cutler (the inventors of the algorithm) has a cutoff of 32 categories. If an attribute has more than 32 categories, you'll need to aggregate them.

You'll see later that training involves taking a random subset of the data and training a series of models on it. Suppose, for instance, that the category is the state of the United States and that Idaho has only two examples. A random draw of training examples might not get any from Idaho. You need to see those kinds of problems before they occur so that you can address them. In the case of the two Idaho examples, you might merge them with Montana or Wyoming, you might duplicate them, or you might manage the random draw so that you ensure getting Idaho examples (a procedure called *stratified sampling*).

How to Use Python Pandas to Summarize the Rocks Versus Mines Data Set

The Python package pandas can help automate the process of data inspection and handling. It proves particularly useful for the early stages of data inspection and preprocessing. The pandas package makes it possible to read data into a specialized data structure called a *data frame*. The data frame is modeled after the CRAN-R data structure of the same name.

NOTE   The pandas package can be difficult to install because it has a number of dependencies that need to be correctly versioned and each of those has to be correctly matched to one another (and so on). An easy way around this hurdle is to use the Anaconda Python distribution available for free download from Continuum Analytics (`http://continuum.io`). The installation procedures are easy to follow and result in compatible installations of a wide variety of packages for data analysis and machine learning.

You can think of a data frame as a table or matrix-like structure as in Table 2.1. The data frame is oriented with a row representing a single case (experiment, example, measurement) and columns representing particular attributes. The structure is matrix-like, but not a matrix because the elements in various columns may be of different types. Formally, a matrix is defined over a field (like the real numbers, binary numbers, complex numbers), and all the entries in a matrix are elements from that field. For statistical problems, the matrix is too confining because statistical samples typically have a mix of different types.

The simple example in Table 2.1 has real values in the Attribute 1 column, categorical variables in the Attribute 2 column, and integer variables in the Attribute 3 column. Within a column, the entries are all the same type, but they differ from one column to the next. The data frame structure enables access to individual elements through an index roughly similar to addressing an entry in a Python numpy array or a list of lists. Similarly, index slicing can be used to address an entire row or column from the array. In addition, the pandas data frame enables addressing rows and columns by means of their names. This turns out to be very handy, particularly for a small to medium number of columns. (A search on "pandas introduction" will give you a number of links that can guide you through the basics of using pandas.)

Listing 2-5 shows how simple it is to read in the rocks versus mines CSV file from the UC Irvine Data Repository website. The output shown as part of the listing is truncated from the actual output. You can get the full version by running the code for yourself.

Listing 2-5: Using Python pandas to Read and Summarize Data — pandasReadSummarize.py

```
__author__ = 'mike_bowles'

#read rocks versus mines data into pandas data frame
rocksVMines = pd_read_rvm()

#print head and tail of data frame
print(rocksVMines.head())
print(rocksVMines.tail())

#print summary of data frame
summary = rocksVMines.describe()
print(summary)

Printed Output:
        V0      V1      V2      V3      V4      V5      V6      V7
1   0.0453  0.0523  0.0843  0.0689  0.1183  0.2583  0.2156  0.3481  . . .
2   0.0262  0.0582  0.1099  0.1083  0.0974  0.2280  0.2431  0.3771  . . .
3   0.0100  0.0171  0.0623  0.0205  0.0205  0.0368  0.1098  0.1276  . . .
4   0.0762  0.0666  0.0481  0.0394  0.0590  0.0649  0.1209  0.2467  . . .


        V58     V59     V60
0   0.0090  0.0032    R
1   0.0052  0.0044    R
2   0.0095  0.0078    R
3   0.0040  0.0117    R
4   0.0107  0.0094    R

[5 rows x 61 columns]
          V0      V1      V2      V3      V4      V5      V6      V7
203   0.0187  0.0346  0.0168  0.0177  0.0393  0.1630  0.2028  0.1694  . . .
```

```
204   0.0323   0.0101   0.0298   0.0564   0.0760   0.0958   0.0990   0.1018  . . .
205   0.0522   0.0437   0.0180   0.0292   0.0351   0.1171   0.1257   0.1178  . . .
206   0.0303   0.0353   0.0490   0.0608   0.0167   0.1354   0.1465   0.1123  . . .
207   0.0260   0.0363   0.0136   0.0272   0.0214   0.0338   0.0655   0.1400  . . .


      V8       V58      V59  V60
203   0.0193   0.0157    M
204   0.0062   0.0067    M
205   0.0077   0.0031    M
206   0.0036   0.0048    M
207   0.0061   0.0115    M


[5 rows x 61 columns]
              V0           V1           V2           V3           V4
count  208.000000   208.000000   208.000000   208.000000   208.000000
mean     0.029164     0.038437     0.043832     0.053892     0.075202
std      0.022991     0.032960     0.038428     0.046528     0.055552
min      0.001500     0.000600     0.001500     0.005800     0.006700
25%      0.013350     0.016450     0.018950     0.024375     0.038050
50%      0.022800     0.030800     0.034300     0.044050     0.062500
75%      0.035550     0.047950     0.057950     0.064500     0.100275
max      0.137100     0.233900     0.305900     0.426400     0.401000


              V57          V58          V59
count  208.000000   208.000000   208.000000
mean     0.007949     0.007941     0.006507
std      0.006470     0.006181     0.005031
min      0.000300     0.000100     0.000600
25%      0.003600     0.003675     0.003100
50%      0.005800     0.006400     0.005300
75%      0.010350     0.010325     0.008525
max      0.044000     0.036400     0.043900


[8 rows x 60 columns]

Output truncated.  To see the full output run the code or python
notebook found in the book's code repo.
```

After reading in the file, the first section of the program prints out the head and the tail of the data set. Notice that all the head examples have R labels, and the tail examples have M labels. With this data set, the Rs all come first and the Ms second. Note things like that during your inspection of the data. You'll see in later sections that determining the quality of your models requires sampling the data. Structure in the way the data are stored might need to be factored into your approach for doing subsequent sampling. The last bit of the code snippet prints out summaries of the real-valued columns in the data set.

Pandas makes it possible to automate the steps of calculating mean, variance, and quantiles. Notice that the summary produced by the `describe` function is itself a data frame so that you can automate the process of screening for attributes that have outliers. To do that, you can compare the differences between the various quantiles and raise a flag if any of the differences for an attribute are out of scale with the other differences for the same attributes. The attributes that are shown in the output indicate that several of them have outliers. It would be worth looking to determine how many rows are involved in the outliers. They might all come from a handful of examples. This can point out data that needs to be inspected more closely.

Visualizing Properties of the Rocks Versus Mines Data Set

Visualizations can sometimes give you insights into your data that would be difficult to see in tables of numbers. This section introduces several that you may find useful. Some of the visualizations take slightly different forms for classification problems than for regression problems. You'll see the regression variants of the methods in the sections covering the abalone data set and the wine quality data set.

Visualizing with Parallel Coordinates Plots

One visualization that is useful for problems with more than a few attributes is called a *parallel coordinates plot*. Figure 2.2 depicts the construction of a parallel coordinates plot. The vector of numbers on the right-hand side of the figure represents a row of attribute data from a machine learning data set. The parallel coordinates plot of that vector of numbers is shown in the line plot in Figure 2.2. The line plots the value of each attribute versus its index. The parallel coordinates plot for the whole data set has a line for each row of attributes in the data set. Color-coding based on the labels can help you see some types of systematic relationships between the attribute values and the labels. Plot the real-valued attributes from a row versus the index of the attribute. (Search "parallel coordinates" and check out the Wikipedia page for some more examples.)

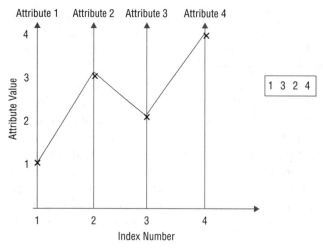

Figure 2.2: Constructing a parallel coordinates plot

Listing 2-6 shows how this process works for the rocks versus mines data set. Figure 2.3 shows the resulting plotted line graphs. The lines are color-coded according to their labels: blue for R (rock), and red for M (mine). Sometimes a plot of this type will show clear areas of separation between the classes. The famous "Iris data" show very clear separation that machine learning algorithms will exploit for classification purposes. For the rocks versus mines data set, no extremely clear separation is evident in the line plot, but there are some areas where the blues and reds are separated. Along the bottom of the plot, the blues stand out a bit, and in the range of attribute indices from 30 to 40, the blues are somewhat higher than the reds. These kinds of insights can help in interpreting and confirming predictions made by your trained model.

Listing 2-6: Parallel Coordinates Graph for Real Attribute Visualization — linePlots.py

```
__author__ = 'mike_bowles'

#read rocks versus mines data into pandas data frame
rocksVMines = pd_read_rvm()

for i in range(208):
    #assign color based on color based on "M" or "R" labels
    if rocksVMines.iat[i,60] == "M":
        pcolor = "red"
    else:
        pcolor = "blue"

    #plot rows of data as if they were series data
    dataRow = rocksVMines.iloc[i,0:60]
    dataRow.plot(color=pcolor, alpha=0.5)
```

```
plt.xlabel("Attribute Index")
plt.ylabel(("Attribute Values"))
plt.show()
```

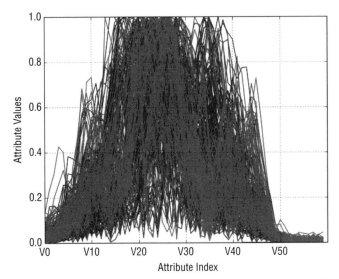

Figure 2.3: Parallel coordinates graph of rocks versus mines attributes

Visualizing Interrelationships between Attributes and Labels

Another question you might ask of the data is how the various attributes relate to one another. One quick way to get an idea of pair-wise relationships is to cross-plot the attributes with the labels. Listing 2-7 shows what's required to generate cross-plots for a couple of representative pairs of attributes. These cross-plots (also called scatter plots) show you how closely related the pairs of variables are.

Listing 2-7: Cross-Plotting Pairs of Attributes — corrPlot.py

```
_author__ = 'mike_bowles'

#read rocks versus mines data into pandas data frame
rocksVMines = pd_read_rvm()

#calculate correlations between real-valued attributes
dataRow2 = rocksVMines.iloc[1,0:60]
dataRow3 = rocksVMines.iloc[2,0:60]

plt.scatter(dataRow2, dataRow3)


plt.xlabel("2nd Attribute")
plt.ylabel(("3rd Attribute"))
plt.show()
```

```
dataRow21 = rocksVMines.iloc[20,0:60]

plt.scatter(dataRow2, dataRow21)


plt.xlabel("2nd Attribute")
plt.ylabel(("21st Attribute"))
plt.show()
```

Figures 2.4 and 2.5 show the scatter plots for two pairs of attributes from the rocks versus mines data set. The rocks versus mines attributes are samples from sonar returns. The sonar signal is called a *chirped* waveform because it's a pulse that starts at low frequency and rises higher over the duration of the pulse. The attributes in the rocks versus mines data set are time samples of the sound waves that bounce off the rock or mine. These returned acoustic signals bear the same relationship between time and frequency as the outgoing transmission. The 60 attributes in the rocks versus mines data are samples of the return taken at 60 different times (and therefore 60 different frequencies). You'd expect that adjacent attributes would be more correlated than attributes separated in time from one another because there's not much difference in frequency between adjacent time samples.

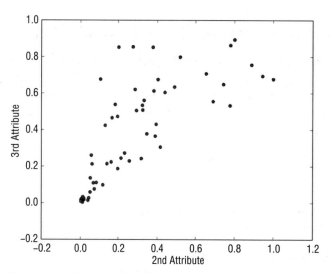

Figure 2.4: Cross-plot of rocks versus mines attributes 2 and 3

This intuition is borne out in Figures 2.4 and 2.5. The points in the scatter plot in Figure 2.4 are more closely grouped around a straight line than those in Figure 2.5. If you want to develop your intuition about the relation between numeric correlation and the shape of the scatter plot, just search "correlation" and have a look at the Wikipedia page that comes up. That shows some scatter plots and the associated numeric correlation. Basically, if the points in the scatter plot lie along a thin straight line, the two variables are highly correlated; if they form a ball of points, they're uncorrelated.

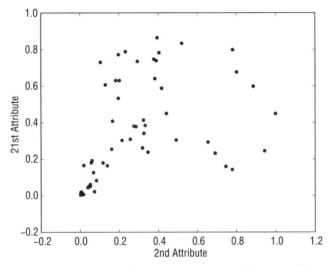

Figure 2.5: Cross-plot of rocks versus mines attributes 2 and 21

You can apply the same principle to plotting the correlation between each of the attributes and the target. For a problem where the targets are real numbers (a regression problem), the plots look much the same as Figures 2.4 and 2.5. The rocks versus mines data set is a classification problem. The targets are two-valued. You can follow the same general procedure.

Listing 2-8 shows the code for plotting a scatter plot between the targets and attribute 35. The idea of using attribute 35 for the example showing correlation with the target came from the parallel coordinates graph in Figure 2.3. That graph shows some separation between the rocks and mines (red lines and blue lines) around index value 35. The correlation between the target and one of the attributes around that index value should also show some separation. Figures 2.6 and 2.7 plot the results.

Listing 2-8: Correlation between Classification Target and Real Attributes — targetCorr.py

```
__author__ = 'mike_bowles'
from random import uniform

#read rocks versus mines data into pandas data frame
rocksVMines = pd_read_rvm()
```

```
#change the targets to numeric values
target = []
for i in range(208):
    #assign 0 or 1 target value based on "M" or "R" labels
    if rocksVMines.iat[i,60] == "M":
        target.append(1.0)
    else:
        target.append(0.0)

    #plot rows of data as if they were series data
dataRow = rocksVMines.iloc[0:208,35]
plt.scatter(dataRow, target)

plt.xlabel("Attribute Value")
plt.ylabel("Target Value")
plt.show()

#
#To improve the visualization, this version dithers the points a little
# and makes them somewhat transparent
target = []
for i in range(208):
    #assign 0 or 1 target value based on "M" or "R" labels
    # and add some dither
    if rocksVMines.iat[i,60] == "M":
        target.append(1.0 + uniform(-0.1, 0.1))
    else:
        target.append(0.0 + uniform(-0.1, 0.1))

    #plot rows of data as if they were series data
dataRow = rocksVMines.iloc[0:208,35]
plt.scatter(dataRow, target, alpha=0.5, s=120)

plt.xlabel("Attribute Value")
plt.ylabel("Target Value")
plt.show()
```

The plots show what happens if you make a list corresponding to the list of R or M targets but with the substitution of 1 for M and 0 for R. Then you can plot a scatter plot as shown in Figure 2.6. Figure 2.6 highlights a common problem with cross-plots. When one of the variables being plotted takes on a small number of values, the points get plotted on top of one another. If there are a lot of them, you just get a thick dark line, and you don't get a feel for how the points are distributed along the line.

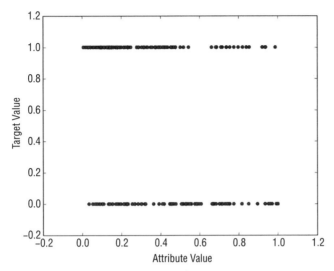

Figure 2.6: Target-attribute cross-plot

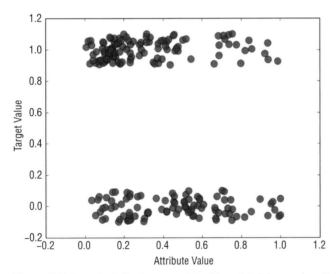

Figure 2.7: Target-attribute cross-plot with point dither and partial opacity

The code in Listing 2-8 generates a second plot with two small changes to overcome this problem. A small random number is added to each of the points and takes a small number of discrete values (the targets in this case). The target values are either 0 or 1 by construction. In the code, you'll see that the added random number is uniformly distributed between –0.1 and 0.1. That spreads the points apart, but not so far as to confuse the two lines. Second, the points are plotted with alpha=0.5 in order that the points are only partially opaque. Then any overplotting shows up as a darkened region in the scatter plot. You may have to adjust these numbers a little to make the plot show you what you need to know.

Figure 2.7 shows the effect of these two alterations. Notice the somewhat higher concentration of attribute 35 on the left end of the upper band of points, whereas the points are more uniformly spread from right to left in the lower band. The upper band of points corresponds to mines. The lower band corresponds to rocks. You could build a classifier for this problem by testing whether attribute 35 is greater than or less than 0.5. If it is greater than 0.5 call it a rock, and if it is less than 0.5, call it a mine. The examples where attribute 35 is less than 0.5 contain a higher concentration of mines than rock, and the examples where attribute 35 is less than 0.5 contain a lower density, so you'd get better performance than you would with random guessing.

> **NOTE**   You'll see much more systematic approaches to building classifiers in Chapter 5, "Building Predictive Models Using Penalized Linear Methods," and Chapter 7, "Building Ensemble Models with Python." They'll use all the attributes instead of just one or two. However, when you look at what they're using to make their decisions, you can refer back to these types of studies to help you gain confidence that what they're doing is sensible.

The degree of correlation between two attributes (or an attribute and a target) can be quantified using Pearson's correlation coefficient. Pearson's correlation coefficient is defined for two equal length vectors u and v, as follows (see Equations 2.1 and 2.2). First subtract the mean value of u from all the elements of u (see Equation 2.3) and do the same for v.

$$u = \begin{matrix} u_1 \\ u_2 \\ \vdots \\ u_n \end{matrix}$$

Equation 2.1: Elements of a vector u

$$\bar{u} = avg(u)$$

Equation 2.2: Average values of the entries in u

$$\Delta u = \begin{matrix} u_1 - \bar{u} \\ u_2 - \bar{u} \\ \vdots \\ u_n - \bar{u} \end{matrix}$$

Equation 2.3: Subtract the average from each element in u

For the second vector v, define a vector Δv in the same way as Δu was defined corresponding to the vector u.

Then Pearson's correlation between u and v is shown in Equation 2.4.

$$corr(u,v) = \frac{\Delta u^T * \Delta v}{\sqrt{(\Delta u^T * \Delta u) * (\Delta v^T * \Delta v)}}$$

Equation 2.4: Definition of Pearson's correlation coefficient

Listing 2-9 shows a Python implementation of this function to calculate correlation for the pairs of attributes plotted in Figures 2.3 and 2.5. The correlation numbers agree with plotted data. The attributes that have close index numbers have relatively higher correlations than those that are separated further.

Listing 2-9: Pearson's Correlation Calculation for Attributes 2 Versus 3 and 2 Versus 21 — corrCalc.py

```
__author__ = 'mike_bowles'
from math import sqrt
from Read_Fcns import pd_read_rvm
from scipy.stats.stats import pearsonr

rocksVMines = pd_read_rvm()

#calculate correlations between real-valued attributes
dataRow2 = np.array(rocksVMines.iloc[1,0:60])
dataRow3 = np.array(rocksVMines.iloc[2,0:60])
dataRow21 = np.array(rocksVMines.iloc[20,0:60])

mean2 = 0.0; mean3 = 0.0; mean21 = 0.0
numElt = len(dataRow2)
for i in range(numElt):
    mean2 += dataRow2[i]/numElt
    mean3 += dataRow3[i]/numElt
    mean21 += dataRow21[i]/numElt

var2 = 0.0; var3 = 0.0; var21 = 0.0
for i in range(numElt):
```

```
            var2 += (dataRow2[i] - mean2) * (dataRow2[i] - mean2)/numElt
            var3 += (dataRow3[i] - mean3) * (dataRow3[i] - mean3)/numElt
            var21 += (dataRow21[i] - mean21) * (dataRow21[i] - mean21)/numElt

    corr23 = 0.0; corr221 = 0.0
    for i in range(numElt):
        corr23 += (dataRow2[i] - mean2) * \
                  (dataRow3[i] - mean3) / (sqrt(var2*var3) * numElt)
        corr221 += (dataRow2[i] - mean2) * \
                   (dataRow21[i] - mean21) / (sqrt(var2*var21) * numElt)

    print('Correlation between attribute 2 and 3')
    print(corr23, '\n')


    print('Correlation between attribute 2 and 21')
    print(corr221, '\n')

    print('Now that you see how the calculation is done, using the python \
    pearsonr function will save you time')
    print(pearsonr(dataRow2, dataRow3))

    Printed Output:
    Correlation between attribute 2 and 3
    0.7709381211911223

    Correlation between attribute 2 and 21
    0.46654808078868865

    Now that you see how the calculation is done, using the python pearsonr
    function will save you time
    (0.7709381211911221, 5.79499196668097e-13)
```

Visualizing Attribute and Label Correlations Using a Heat Map

Calculating the correlations and printing them or drawing cross-plots works fine for a few correlations, but it is difficult to get a grasp of a large table of numbers, and it is difficult to squeeze all the cross-plots onto a page if the problem has 100 attributes.

One way to check correlations with a large number of attributes is to calculate the Pearson's correlation coefficient for pairs of attributes, arrange those correlations into a matrix where the i, j-th entry is the correlation between the ith attribute and the jth attribute, and then plot them in a heat map. Listing 2-10 gives the code to make this plot. Figure 2.8 shows the plot. The light areas along the diagonal confirm that attributes close to one another in index have relatively high correlations. As mentioned earlier, this is due to the way in which the data are generated. Close indices are sampled at short time intervals from one another and consequently have similar frequencies. Similar frequencies reflect off the targets similarly (and so on).

Listing 2-10: Presenting Attribute Correlations Visually — sampleCorrHeatMap.py

```
__author__ = 'mike_bowles'

#read rocks versus mines data into pandas data frame
rocksVMines = pd_read_rvm()

#calculate correlations between real-valued attributes

corMat = DataFrame(rocksVMines.corr())

#visualize correlations using heatmap
plt.pcolor(corMat)
plt.show()
```

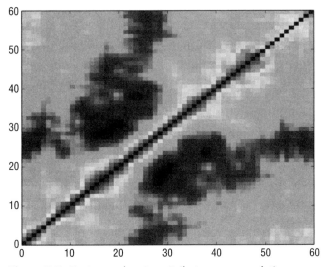

Figure 2.8: Heat map showing attribute cross-correlations

Perfect correlation (correlation = 1) between attributes means that you may have made a mistake and included the same thing twice. Very high correlation between a set of attributes (pairwise correlations > 0.7) is known as *multicollinearity* and can lead to unstable estimates. Correlation with the targets is a different matter. Having an attribute that's correlated with the target generally indicates a predictive relation.

Summarizing the Process for Understanding the Rocks Versus Mines Data Set

In the process of understanding the rocks versus mines data set, this section has introduced a number of tools for you to use to gain understanding and intuition about your data sets. The section has gone into some detail to make their derivation and use clear. The next sections will use several of these same tools to inspect the other data sets that the book will use to develop machine learning algorithms. Since you're now familiar with the tools for doing data inspection, the next sections will comment on the tools only to the extent that they need to be modified because of the different nature of a problem.

Real-Valued Predictions with Factor Variables: How Old Is Your Abalone?

Most of the tools you've seen used for understanding the problem of detecting unexploded mines can be applied to regression problems. Predicting the age of an abalone, given physical measurements, provides an example of such a problem. The abalone attributes also include an attribute that is a factor variable, which will illustrate the differences involved with factor variables.

The abalone data set poses the problem of predicting the age of an abalone by taking several measurements. It is possible to get a precise reading on the age of an abalone by slicing the shell and counting growth rings, much like gauging the age of a tree by counting rings. The problem for scientists studying abalone populations is that it is expensive and time-consuming to slice the shells and count the rings under a microscope. It would be more convenient and economical to be able to make simple physical measurements like length, width, weight, and so forth and then to use a predictive model to process the measurements and make an accurate determination of the age of the abalone. There are myriad scientific applications for predictive analytics, and one of the benefits of studying machine learning is being able to contribute to an interesting array of different problems.

The data for this problem are available through the UC Irvine Data Repository. The URL for this data set is `http://archive.ics.uci.edu/ml/machine-learning-databases/abalone/abalone.data`. This data set is in the form of a comma-delimited file with no column headers. The names of the columns are in a separate file. Listing 2-11 reads the abalone data set into a pandas data frame and runs through some of the same analyses that you saw in "Classification Problems: Detecting Unexploded Mines Using Sonar." For the rocks versus mines data set, the column names were somewhat generic because of the nature of the data. For the abalone data set, the different columns of data have meanings that can be critical to cultivating an intuitive understanding of your progress toward an acceptable model. For this reason, you'll see in the code that the column names have been copy-pasted into the code and attached to the data set to help you make sense of what subsequent machine learning algorithms are doing to make predictions. The columns of data available for building a predictive model are Sex, Length, Diameter, Height, Whole Weight, Shucked Weight, Viscera Weight, Shell Weight, and Rings. The last column, Rings, is measured by the laborious process of sawing the shell and counting under a microscope. This is the usual arrangement for a supervised learning problem. You've got a special data set for which the answer is known so as to build a model that will generate predictions when the answer is not known.

In addition to showing the code for producing the summaries, Listing 2-11 shows the printed output from the summarization. The first section prints the head and tail of the data set. Only the head is shown in the output to save space. When you run the code for yourself, you'll see both. Most of the data frame is filled with floating-point numbers. The first column, which contains the gender of the animal, contains the letters M (male), F (female), and I (indeterminate). The gender of an abalone is not determined at birth, but after it has matured a little. Therefore, the gender is indeterminate for younger abalones. The gender of the abalone is a three-valued categorical variable. Categorical attributes require special attention. Some algorithms only deal with real-valued attributes (for example, support vector machines, k-nearest neighbors, and penalized linear regression, which is introduced in Chapter 4). Chapter 4 discusses techniques for translating categorical variables into real-valued variables so that you can employ these algorithms. Listing 2-11 also shows the column-by-column statistical summaries for the real-valued attributes.

Listing 2-11: Read and Summarize the Abalone Data Set — abaloneSummary.py

```
__author__ = 'mike_bowles'

from Read_Fcns import pd_read_abalone
#read abalone data
abalone = pd_read_abalone()

print(abalone.head())
print(abalone.tail())


#print summary of data frame
summary = abalone.describe()
print(summary)


#box plot the real-valued attributes
#convert to array for plot routine
array = abalone.iloc[:,1:9].values
plt.boxplot(array)
```

```
plt.xlabel("Attribute Index")
plt.ylabel(("Quartile Ranges"))
plt.show()

#the last column (rings) is out of scale with the rest
# - remove and replot
array2 = abalone.iloc[:,1:8].values
plt.boxplot(array2)
plt.xlabel("Attribute Index")
plt.ylabel(("Quartile Ranges"))
plt.show()

#removing is okay but renormalizing the variables generalizes better.
#renormalize columns to zero mean and unit standard deviation
#this is a common normalization and desirable for other operations
# (like k-means clustering or k-nearest neighbors
abaloneNormalized = abalone.iloc[:,1:9]


for i in range(8):
    mean = summary.iloc[1, i]
    sd = summary.iloc[2, i]
    abaloneNormalized.iloc[:,i:(i + 1)] = (
                    abaloneNormalized.iloc[:,i:(i + 1)] - mean) / sd

array3 = abaloneNormalized.values
plt.boxplot(array3)
plt.xlabel("Attribute Index")
plt.ylabel(("Quartile Ranges - Normalized "))
plt.show()
```

Printed Output:

	Sex	Length	Diameter	Height	Whole wt	Shucked wt	Viscera weight
0	M	0.455	0.365	0.095	0.5140	0.2245	0.1010
1	M	0.350	0.265	0.090	0.2255	0.0995	0.0485
2	F	0.530	0.420	0.135	0.6770	0.2565	0.1415
3	M	0.440	0.365	0.125	0.5160	0.2155	0.1140
4	I	0.330	0.255	0.080	0.2050	0.0895	0.0395

	Shell weight	Rings
0	0.150	15
1	0.070	7
2	0.210	9
3	0.155	10
4	0.055	7

	Sex	Length	Diameter	Height	Whole weight	Shucked weight	\
4172	F	0.565	0.450	0.165	0.8870	0.3700	
4173	M	0.590	0.440	0.135	0.9660	0.4390	
4174	M	0.600	0.475	0.205	1.1760	0.5255	
4175	F	0.625	0.485	0.150	1.0945	0.5310	
4176	M	0.710	0.555	0.195	1.9485	0.9455	

	Viscera weight	Shell weight	Rings
4172	0.2390	0.2490	11
4173	0.2145	0.2605	10
4174	0.2875	0.3080	9
4175	0.2610	0.2960	10
4176	0.3765	0.4950	12

	Length	Diameter	Height	Whole wt	Shucked wt
count	4177.000000	4177.000000	4177.000000	4177.000000	4177.0000
mean	0.523992	0.407881	0.139516	0.828742	0.359367
std	0.120093	0.099240	0.041827	0.490389	0.221963
min	0.075000	0.055000	0.000000	0.002000	0.001000
25%	0.450000	0.350000	0.115000	0.441500	0.186000
50%	0.545000	0.425000	0.140000	0.799500	0.336000
75%	0.615000	0.480000	0.165000	1.153000	0.502000
max	0.815000	0.650000	1.130000	2.825500	1.488000

	Viscera weight	Shell weight	Rings
count	4177.000000	4177.000000	4177.000000
mean	0.180594	0.238831	9.933684
std	0.109614	0.139203	3.224169
min	0.000500	0.001500	1.000000
25%	0.093500	0.130000	8.000000
50%	0.171000	0.234000	9.000000
75%	0.253000	0.329000	11.000000
max	0.760000	1.005000	29.000000

As an alternative to the listing of the statistical summaries, Listing 2-11 generates box plots for each of the real-valued columns of data. The first of these is shown in Figure 2.9. In Figure 2.9, the statistical summaries are represented by box plots, which are also called *box and whisker* plots. These plots show a small rectangle with a red line through it. The red line marks the median value (or 50th percentile) for the column of data. The top and bottom of the rectangle mark the 25th percentile and the 75th percentile, respectively. You can compare the numbers in the printed summary to the levels in the box plot to confirm this. Above and below the box, you'll see small horizontal ticks, the so-called whiskers. These are drawn in at levels that are 1.4 times the interquartile spacing above and below the box. Interquartile spacing is the difference between the 75th percentile and the 25th percentile. In other words, the space between the top of the box and the upper whisker is 1.4 times the height of the box. The 1.4x spacing for the whisker is adjustable; see the box plot documentation. You'll notice that in some cases the whiskers are closer than the 1.4x spacing. For these cases the data values do not extend all the way to the calculated whisker locations. In these cases, the whisker is placed at the most extreme data point. In other cases, the data extend for a considerable distance beyond the calculated whisker locations. These points can be considered outliers.

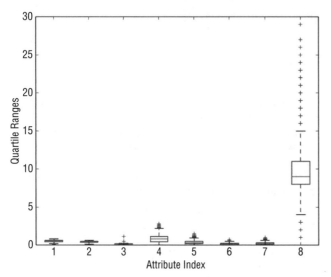

Figure 2.9: Box plot of real-valued attributes from the abalone data set

The box plot in Figure 2.9 is a faster, more visual way to identify outliers than the printed data, but the scale on the rings attributes (the rightmost box plot) causes the other attributes to be compressed (making them hard to see). One way to deal with this is to simply eliminate the larger-scale attributes. The result of that is shown in Figure 2.10. But that approach is unsatisfying because it doesn't automate or scale very well.

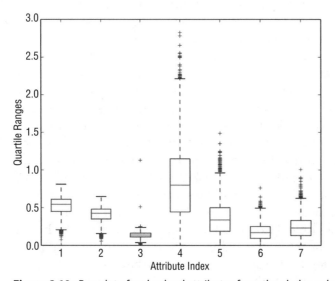

Figure 2.10: Box plot of real-valued attributes from the abalone data set

The last section of the code in Listing 2-11 normalizes all the data columns before box plotting. *Normalization* in this case means centering and scaling each column so that a unit of attribute number 1 means the same thing as a unit of attribute number 2. A number of algorithms and operations in data science require this type of normalization. For example, K-means clustering builds clusters based on vector distance between rows of data. Distance is measured by subtracting one point from another and squaring. If the units are different, the numeric distances are different. The distance to the grocery store can be 1 if measured in miles or 5,280 if measured in feet. The normalization indicated in Listing 2-11 adjusts the variables so that they all have 0 mean and a standard deviation of 1. This is a very common normalization. The calculations for the normalization make use of the numbers generated by the summary()function. The results are plotted in Figure 2.11.

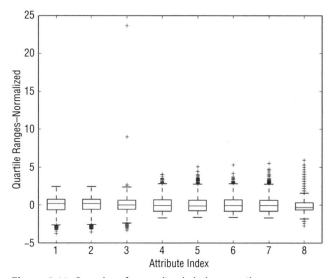

Figure 2.11: Box plot of normalized abalone attributes

Notice that normalizing to standard deviation of 1.0 does not mean that the data all fit between –1.0 and +1.0. It more or less places the lower and upper edges of the boxes at –1.0 and +1.0, but much of the data are outside these boundaries.

Parallel Coordinates for Regression Problems—Visualize Variable Relationships for the Abalone Problem

The next step is to get some ideas about the relationship among the attributes and between attributes and labels. For the rocks versus mines data, the color-coded parallel coordinates plot portrayed these relationships graphically. That approach needs some modification to work for the abalone problem. Rocks versus mines was a classifier problem. The parallel coordinates plot for that problem color-coded the lines representing rows of data according to their true classification. That helps to visualize the relationship between prediction and predictors. The abalone problem is a regression problem, so the color-coding in this example needs to be shades of color corresponding to higher or lower target values. To assign shades of color to real values, the real values need to be compressed into the interval [0.0, 1.0]. Listing 2-12 uses the min and max values generated by the summary() function from pandas to accomplish this. Figure 2.12 shows the results.

Listing 2-12: Parallel Coordinate Plot for Abalone Data — abaloneParallelPlot.py

```
__author__ = 'mike_bowles'

from math import exp
from Read_Fcns import pd_read_abalone

abalone = pd_read_abalone()

#get summary to use for scaling
summary = abalone.describe()
min_rings = summary.iloc[3,7]
max_rings = summary.iloc[7,7]
nrows = len(abalone.index)

for i in range(nrows):
    #plot rows of data as if they were series data
    data_row = abalone.iloc[i,1:8]
    label_color = (abalone.iloc[i,8] - min_rings) / (max_rings - \
        min_rings)
    data_row.plot(color=plt.cm.RdYlBu(label_color), alpha=0.5)

plt.xlabel("Attribute Index")
plt.ylabel(("Attribute Values"))
plt.show()

#renormalize using mean and standard variation, then compress
# with logit function

mean_rings = summary.iloc[1,7]
sd_rings = summary.iloc[2,7]

for i in range(nrows):
    #plot rows of data as if they were series data
    data_row = abalone.iloc[i,1:8]
    norm_target = (abalone.iloc[i,8] - mean_rings)/sd_rings
    label_color = 1.0/(1.0 + exp(-norm_target))
    data_row.plot(color=plt.cm.RdYlBu(label_color), alpha=0.5)
```

```
plt.xlabel("Attribute Index")
plt.ylabel(("Attribute Values"))
plt.show()
```

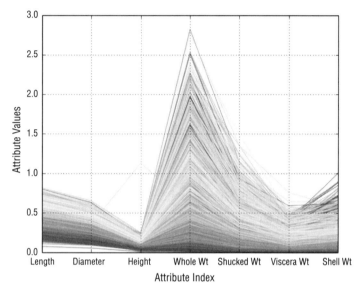

Figure 2.12: Color-coded parallel coordinate plot for abalone

The parallel coordinates plot in Figure 2.12 illustrates a direct relationship between abalone age (number of shell rings) and the attributes available for predicting age. The color scale used to produce this plot ranges from very dark reddish brown through lighter shades, yellow, light blue, and very dark blue. The box plot in Figure 2.11 shows that the maximum and minimum values are widely separated from the bulk of the data. This has the effect of compressing the scale so that most of the data are mid-range on the color scale. Nonetheless, Figure 2.12 indicates significant correlation between each of the attributes and the number of rings measured for each of the examples. Similar shades of color are grouped together at similar values of several of the attributes. This correlation suggests that you'll be able to build an accurate predictive model. Contrary to the generally favorable correlation between attributes and target, some faint blue lines are mixed among the darker orange areas of the graph, indicating that there are some examples that will be difficult to correctly predict.

Changing the color mapping can help you visualize relationships at different levels of target values. The last section of the code in Listing 2-11 uses the normalization that you saw used in the box plot graphs. That normalization doesn't make all the values fit between 0 and 1. For one thing, the resulting values take as many negative values as positive ones. The program in

Listing 2-11 employs the logit transform to get values in (0, 1). The logit transform is given by the expression shown in Equation 2.5. The plot for this function is given in Figure 2.13.

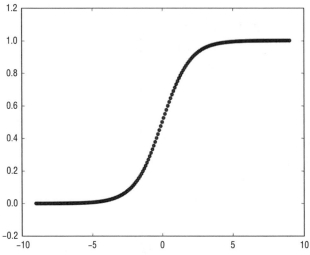

Figure 2.13: Graph of the logit function (logitCurve.png)

$$logittransform(x) = \frac{1}{\left(1 + e^{-x}\right)}$$

Equation 2.5: Using logit transform for soft range compression

The plot for this function is given in Figure 2.13. As you can see, the logit transform maps large negative values to 0 (almost) and large positive numbers to 1 (almost); it maps 0 to 0.5. You'll see the logit function again in Chapter 4, where it plays a critical role relating a linear function to a probability.

Figure 2.14 shows the results of these steps. These transformations have resulted in better usage of the full range of colors available. Notice that there are several darker blue lines (corresponding to specimens with large numbers of rings) mixed in among lighter blue examples, and even yellow and light red specimens for the graphs in the area of Whole Weight and Shucked Weight. That suggests that those attributes might not be enough to correctly predict the ages (number of rings) in the older specimens. Fortunately, some of the other attributes (Diameter and Shell Weight) do a better job of correctly ordering the dark blue lines. Those observations will prove helpful when you're analyzing the prediction errors later.

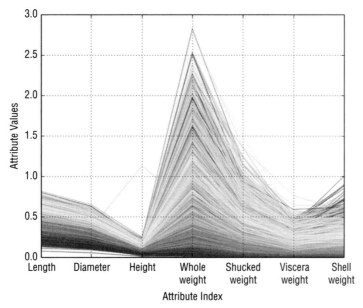

Figure 2.14: Parallel coordinate plot for the abalone data

How to Use a Correlation Heat Map for Regression—Visualize Pair-Wise Correlations for the Abalone Problem

The last step is to have a look at the correlations between the various attributes and between the attributes and the targets. Listing 2-13 shows the code for generating a correlation heat map and a correlation matrix for the abalone data. These calculations follow the same method outlined for the rocks versus mines data, but with one important difference: Because the abalone problem calls for making real number predictions, the correlation calculations can include the targets in the correlation matrix.

Listing 2-13: Correlation Calculations for the Abalone Data — abaloneCorrHeat.py

```
__author__ = 'mike_bowles'

abalone = pd_read_abalone()

#calculate correlation matrix
corr_mat = DataFrame(abalone.iloc[:,1:9].corr())
#print correlation matrix
print(corr_mat)
```

```
#visualize correlations using heatmap
plt.pcolor(corr_mat)
plt.show()
Printed Output:
```

	Length	Diameter	Height	Whole weight	Shucked wt
Length	1.000000	0.986812	0.827554	0.925261	0.897914
Diameter	0.986812	1.000000	0.833684	0.925452	0.893162
Height	0.827554	0.833684	1.000000	0.819221	0.774972
Whole weight	0.925261	0.925452	0.819221	1.000000	0.969405
Shucked weight	0.897914	0.893162	0.774972	0.969405	1.000000
Viscera weight	0.903018	0.899724	0.798319	0.966375	0.931961
Shell weight	0.897706	0.905330	0.817338	0.955355	0.882617
Rings	0.556720	0.574660	0.557467	0.540390	0.420884

	Viscera weight	Shell weight	Rings
Length	0.903018	0.897706	0.556720
Diameter	0.899724	0.905330	0.574660
Height	0.798319	0.817338	0.557467
Whole weight	0.966375	0.955355	0.540390
Shucked weight	0.931961	0.882617	0.420884
Viscera weight	1.000000	0.907656	0.503819
Shell weight	0.907656	1.000000	0.627574
Rings	0.503819	0.627574	1.000000

Figure 2.15 shows the correlation heat map. In this map, red indicates high correlation, and blue represents weak correlation. The targets (the number of rings in the shell) are the last item, which is the top row of the heat map and the rightmost column. The blue values in those positions mean that the attributes are weakly correlated with the targets. The light blue corresponds to the correlation between the target and the shell weight. That confirms what you saw in the parallel coordinates plot. The reddish values in the other off-diagonal cell in Figure 2.15 indicate that the attributes are highly correlated with one another. This somewhat contradicts the picture given by the parallel coordinates map where visually the correspondence between the target and the attributes seemed fairly tight. Listing 2-13 shows the numeric values for correlation.

In this section you've seen how to modify the tools described for a classification problem (rocks versus mines) to a regression problem (abalone). The modifications all stemmed from the basic difference between the two problem types—labels that are real numbers for a regression problem versus labels that are two-valued for a binary classification problem. The next section will conduct the same set of studies on a regression problem having all numeric attributes. Because it's a regression problem, the same tools used in this section for the abalone problem can be used. Because it has all numeric attributes, all of the attributes can be included in the studies, like correlation and plotting along the real number line.

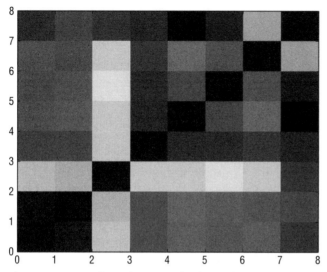

Figure 2.15: Correlation heat map for the abalone data

Real-Valued Predictions Using Real-Valued Attributes: Calculate How Your Wine Tastes

The wine taste data set contains data for approximately 1,500 red wines. For each wine there are a number of measurements of chemical composition, including things like alcohol content, volatile acidity, and sulphites. Each wine also has a taste score determined by averaging the scores given by three professional wine tasters. The problem is to build a model that will incorporate the chemical measurements and predict taste scores to match those given by the human tasters.

Listing 2-14 shows the code for producing summaries of the wine data set. The code prints out a numeric summary of the data, which is included at the bottom of the listing. The code also generates a box plot of the normalized variables so that you can visualize the outliers in the data. Figure 2.16 shows the box plots. The numeric summaries and the box plots indicate numerous outlying values. This is something to keep in mind during training on this data set. When analyzing the performance of the trained models, these outlying examples will be one place to look to understand the source of errors in your models.

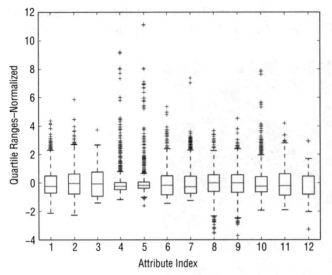

Figure 2.16: Attribute and target box plots of normalized wine data

Listing 2-14: Wine Data Summary — wineSummary.py

```
__author__ = 'mike_bowles'

#read wine data into pandas data frame
wine = pd_read_wine()

print(wine.head())

#generate statistical summaries
summary = wine.describe()
print(summary)

wineNormalized = wine
ncols = len(wineNormalized.columns)

for i in range(ncols):
    mean = summary.iloc[1, i]
    sd = summary.iloc[2, i]
    wineNormalized.iloc[:,i:(i + 1)] = \
        (wineNormalized.iloc[:,i:(i + 1)] - mean) / sd

array = wineNormalized.values
plt.boxplot(array)
plt.xlabel("Attribute Index")
plt.ylabel(("Quartile Ranges - Normalized "))
plt.show()

Printed Output:

   fixed acidity  volatile acidity  citric acid  resid sugar  chlorides
0            7.4              0.70         0.00          1.9      0.076
```

1	7.8	0.88	0.00	2.6	0.098
2	7.8	0.76	0.04	2.3	0.092
3	11.2	0.28	0.56	1.9	0.075
4	7.4	0.70	0.00	1.9	0.076

	free sulfur dioxide	total sulfur dioxide	density	pH	sulphates
0	11.0	34.0	0.9978	3.51	0.56
1	25.0	67.0	0.9968	3.20	0.68
2	15.0	54.0	0.9970	3.26	0.65
3	17.0	60.0	0.9980	3.16	0.58
4	11.0	34.0	0.9978	3.51	0.56

	alcohol	quality
0	9.4	5
1	9.8	5
2	9.8	5
3	9.8	6
4	9.4	5

	fixed acidity	volatile acidity	citric acid	residual sugar
count	1599.000000	1599.000000	1599.000000	1599.000000
mean	8.319637	0.527821	0.270976	2.538806
std	1.741096	0.179060	0.194801	1.409928
min	4.600000	0.120000	0.000000	0.900000
25%	7.100000	0.390000	0.090000	1.900000
50%	7.900000	0.520000	0.260000	2.200000
75%	9.200000	0.640000	0.420000	2.600000
max	15.900000	1.580000	1.000000	15.500000

	chlorides	free sulfur dioxide	tot sulfur dioxide	density
count	1599.000000	1599.000000	1599.000000	1599.00000
mean	0.087467	15.874922	46.467792	0.996747
std	0.047065	10.460157	32.895324	0.001887
min	0.012000	1.000000	6.000000	0.990070
25%	0.070000	7.000000	22.000000	0.995600
50%	0.079000	14.000000	38.000000	0.996750
75%	0.090000	21.000000	62.000000	0.997835
max	0.611000	72.000000	289.000000	1.003690

	pH	sulphates	alcohol	quality
count	1599.000000	1599.000000	1599.000000	1599.000000
mean	3.311113	0.658149	10.422983	5.636023
std	0.154386	0.169507	1.065668	0.807569
min	2.740000	0.330000	8.400000	3.000000
25%	3.210000	0.550000	9.500000	5.000000
50%	3.310000	0.620000	10.200000	6.000000
75%	3.400000	0.730000	11.100000	6.000000
max	4.010000	2.000000	14.900000	8.000000

A color-coded parallel coordinates plot for the wine data will give some idea of how well correlated the attributes are with the targets. Listing 2-15 shows the code for producing that plot. Figure 2.17 shows the resulting parallel coordinates plot. The plot in Figure 2.17 suffers from compressing the graph along the variable directions that have smaller scale values.

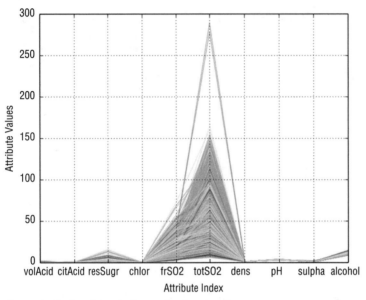

Figure 2.17: Parallel coordinate plot for wine data

Listing 2-15: Producing a Parallel Coordinate Plot for Wine Data — wineParallelPlot.py

```
__author__ = 'mike_bowles'

from math import exp

wine = pd_read_wine()

#print column names in order to have the full versions
print(wine.columns)

#change column names to shorter ones to fit graph
wine.columns = ['fixAcid', 'volAcid', 'citAcid',
    'resSugr', 'chlor', 'frSO2', 'totSO2',
    'dens', 'pH', 'sulpha', 'alcohol', 'quality']

#generate statistical summaries
summary = wine.describe()
nrows = len(wine.index)
tasteCol = len(summary.columns)
meanTaste = summary.iloc[1,tasteCol - 1]
sdTaste = summary.iloc[2,tasteCol - 1]
nDataCol = len(wine.columns) -1
```

```
for i in range(nrows):
    #plot rows of data as if they were series data
    dataRow = wine.iloc[i,1:nDataCol]
    normTarget = (wine.iloc[i,nDataCol] - meanTaste)/sdTaste
    labelColor = 1.0/(1.0 + exp(-normTarget))
    dataRow.plot(color=plt.cm.RdYlBu(labelColor), alpha=0.5)

plt.xlabel("Attribute Index")
plt.ylabel(("Attribute Values"))
plt.show()


wineNormalized = wine
ncols = len(wineNormalized.columns)

for i in range(ncols):
    mean = summary.iloc[1, i]
    sd = summary.iloc[2, i]
    wineNormalized.iloc[:,i:(i + 1)] = \
        (wineNormalized.iloc[:,i:(i + 1)] - mean) / sd

#Try again with normalized values
for i in range(nrows):
    #plot rows of data as if they were series data
    dataRow = wineNormalized.iloc[i,1:nDataCol]
    normTarget = wineNormalized.iloc[i,nDataCol]
    labelColor = 1.0/(1.0 + exp(-normTarget))
    dataRow.plot(color=plt.cm.RdYlBu(labelColor), alpha=0.5)

plt.xlabel("Attribute Index")
plt.ylabel(("Attribute Values"))
plt.show()


Printed Output:

Index(['fixed acidity', 'volatile acidity', 'citric acid',
   'residual sugar', 'chlorides', 'free sulfur dioxide',
   'total sulfur dioxide', 'density', 'pH', 'sulphates',
   'alcohol', 'quality'], dtype='object')
```

To overcome this limitation, Listing 2-15 normalizes the wine data and re-plots it. Figure 2.18 shows the resulting parallel coordinates plot.

The plot of the normalized wine data gives a better simultaneous view of the correlation with the targets along all the coordinate directions. Figure 2.18 shows a clear correlation between several of the attributes. On the far right of the plot, dark blue lines (high taste scores) aggregate at high values of alcohol. On the far left, the dark red lines (low taste scores) aggregate at high values of volatile acidity. Those are the most obviously correlated attributes. The predictive models that you'll see in Chapters 5 and 7 will rank attributes on the basis of their importance in generating predictions. You'll see how these visual observations are supported by the predictive models.

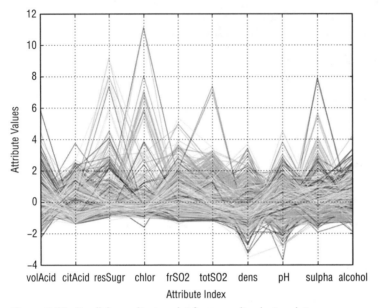

Figure 2.18: Parallel coordinates plot for normalized wine data

Figure 2.19 shows the heat map of the correlations between attributes and other attributes and between the attributes and the target. In the heat map, hot colors correspond to high levels (the opposite of the color scale used in the

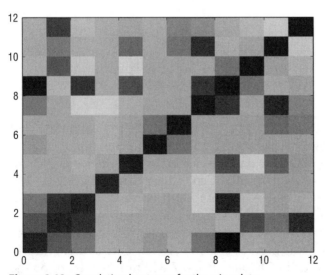

Figure 2.19: Correlation heat map for the wine data

parallel coordinates plots). The heat map for the wine data shows relatively high correlation between taste (the last column) and alcohol (the next-to-last column), and very low levels (high correlation but with negative sign) for several of the other attributes, including the first one (volatile acidity).

Exploration of the wine data set was accomplished with tools that have already been explained and used. The wine data set shows off what these tools can reveal. Both the parallel coordinates plot and the correlation heat map show that high levels of alcohol go with high taste scores, while high levels of volatile acidity go with low taste scores. You'll see in Chapters 5 and 7 that the variable importance studies that come as part of predictive modeling will echo these findings. The wine data gives a good example of how far data exploration can take you toward building and qualifying a predictive model. The next section will explore data for a multiclass classification problem.

Multiclass Classification Problem: What Type of Glass Is That?

Multiclass classifications are similar to binary classifications, with the difference that there are several possible discrete outcomes instead of just two. Recall that the problem of detecting unexploded mines involved two possible outcomes: that the object being illuminated by the sonar was a rock or that it was a mine. The problem of determining wine taste from measurements of chemical composition had several possible outcomes (taste scores from 3 to 8). But with the wine problem, an order relationship existed among the scores. A wine that had a score of 5 was better than one with a score of 3, but worse than one with a score of 8. With a multiclass problem, no sense of order exists among the outcomes. The glass problem described in this section provides an example of a multiclass problem.

In this section, the glass problem presents chemical compositions of various types of glass. The objective of the problem is to determine the use for the glass. The possible types of glass include glass from building windows, glass from vehicle windows, glass containers, and so on. The motivation for determining the type of glass is forensics. At the scene of an accident or a crime, there are fragments of glass, and determining their origin can help determine who is at fault or who committed the crime. Listing 2-16 shows the code for generating summaries of the glass data set. Figure 2.20 shows the box plot on the normalized data. The box plot shows a fair number of extreme values.

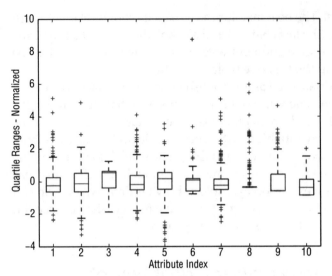

Figure 2.20: Box plot of the glass data

Listing 2-16: Summary of the Glass Data Set — glassSummary.py

```
__author__ = 'mike_bowles'

glass = pd_read_glass()

print(glass.head())

#generate statistical summaries
summary = glass.describe()
print(summary)
ncol1 = len(glass.columns)

glassNormalized = glass.iloc[:, 1:ncol1]
ncol2 = len(glassNormalized.columns)
summary2 = glassNormalized.describe()

for i in range(ncol2):
    mean = summary2.iloc[1, i]
    sd = summary2.iloc[2, i]
    glassNormalized.iloc[:,i:(i + 1)] = \
        (glassNormalized.iloc[:,i:(i + 1)] - mean) / sd

array = glassNormalized.values
plt.boxplot(array)
plt.xlabel("Attribute Index")
plt.ylabel(("Quartile Ranges - Normalized "))
plt.show()
```

```
Printed Output:
     Id       RI     Na    Mg    Al     Si     K     Ca   Ba   Fe  Type
0     1  1.52101  13.64  4.49  1.10  71.78  0.06  8.75  0.0  0.0     1
1     2  1.51761  13.89  3.60  1.36  72.73  0.48  7.83  0.0  0.0     1
```

2	3	1.51618	13.53	3.55	1.54	72.99	0.39	7.78	0.0 0.0	1
3	4	1.51766	13.21	3.69	1.29	72.61	0.57	8.22	0.0 0.0	1
4	5	1.51742	13.27	3.62	1.24	73.08	0.55	8.07	0.0 0.0	1

	Id	RI	Na	Mg	Al	Si
count	214.00000	214.00000	214.00000	214.00000	214.00000	214.00000
mean	107.50000	1.51836	13.40785	2.68453	1.44490	72.65093
std	61.92064	0.00303	0.81660	1.44240	0.49927	0.77454
min	1.00000	1.51115	10.73000	0.00000	0.29000	69.81000
25%	54.25000	1.51652	12.90750	2.11500	1.19000	72.28000
50%	107.50000	1.51768	13.30000	3.48000	1.36000	72.79000
75%	160.75000	1.51915	13.82500	3.60000	1.63000	73.08750
max	214.00000	1.53393	17.38000	4.49000	3.50000	75.41000

	K	Ca	Ba	Fe	Type
count	214.000000	214.000000	214.000000	214.000000	214.000000
mean	0.497056	8.956963	0.175047	0.057009	2.780374
std	0.652192	1.423153	0.497219	0.097439	2.103739
min	0.000000	5.430000	0.000000	0.000000	1.000000
25%	0.122500	8.240000	0.000000	0.000000	1.000000
50%	0.555000	8.600000	0.000000	0.000000	2.000000
75%	0.610000	9.172500	0.000000	0.100000	3.000000
max	6.210000	16.190000	3.150000	0.510000	7.000000

The box plot of the glass data attributes shows a remarkable number of outliers—remarkable at least by comparison to some of the other example problems. The glass data have a couple of elements that may drive the outlier behavior. One is that the problem is a classification problem. There's not necessarily any continuity in relationship between attribute values and class membership—no reason to expect proximity of attribute values across classes. Another unique feature of the glass data is that it is somewhat unbalanced. The number of examples of each class runs from 76 for the most populous class to 9 for the least populous. The average statistics can be dominated by the values for the most populous classes and there's no reason to expect members of other classes to have similar attribute values. The radical behavior can be a good thing for distinguishing classes from one another, but it also means that a method for making predictions has to be able to trace a fairly complicated boundary between the different classes. You'll learn in Chapter 3 that ensemble methods are producing more complicated decision boundaries than penalized linear regression if they are given enough data, and you'll see in Chapters 5 and 7 which family performs better on this data set.

The parallel coordinates plot might shed some more light on the behavior of these data. Figure 2.21 shows the parallel coordinates plot. The data is plotted using discrete colors for each possible output classification. Some of the variables in the plot show fairly distinct paths of color. For example, the dark blue lines group together fairly well and are well separated from the other classes along a number of the attributes. The dark blue lines are at the edges of the data for several attributes—in other words, outliers along those attributes. The light blue lines are less numerous than the dark blue ones and are at the edges for some of the same attributes as dark blue, but not for all of the same attributes. The middle brown lines also group together but toward the mid-range in value. Listing 2-17 shows the code to produce a parallel coordinates plot of the glass data. With the rocks versus mines problem, the lines in the parallel coordinates plot were two-colored to account for the two different label values. In the regression problems (wine taste and abalone age), the labels could take any real value, and the lines in the plots were drawn in a spectrum of different colors. In this multiclass problem, each class gets its own color. There are six discrete colors. The labels run from 1 to 7; there are no 4s. The calculation of the color is similar to the calculation done in the regression problem—divide the numeric label by its maximum value. The resulting lines in the plots take six discrete colors.

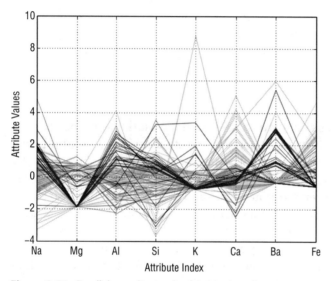

Figure 2.21: Parallel coordinate plot for the glass data

Listing 2-17: Parallel Coordinate Plot for the Glass Data — glassParallelPlot.py

```
__author__ = 'mike_bowles'

glass = pd_read_glass()

glassNormalized = glass
ncols = len(glassNormalized.columns)
nrows = len(glassNormalized.index)
summary = glassNormalized.describe()
nDataCol = ncols - 1

#normalize except for labels
for i in range(ncols - 1):
    mean = summary.iloc[1, i]
```

```
        sd = summary.iloc[2, i]
        glassNormalized.iloc[:,i:(i + 1)] = \
            (glassNormalized.iloc[:,i:(i + 1)] - mean) / sd

#Plot Parallel Coordinate Graph with normalized values
for i in range(nrows):
    #plot rows of data as if they were series data
    dataRow = glassNormalized.iloc[i,1:nDataCol]
    labelColor = glassNormalized.iloc[i,nDataCol]/7.0
    dataRow.plot(color=plt.cm.RdYlBu(labelColor), alpha=0.5)

plt.xlabel("Attribute Index")
plt.ylabel(("Attribute Values"))
plt.show()
```

Figure 2.22 shows the correlation heat map for the glass data. The plot shows mostly low correlation between attributes. That means the attributes are mostly independent of one another, which is a good thing. The targets are not included in the correlation map because the problem has targets that take on one of several discrete values. This robs the correlation heat map of some explanatory power.

Exploratory studies for the glass data have revealed a very interesting problem. In particular, the box plots, coupled with the parallel coordinates plot, suggest that a good choice of algorithm might be an ensemble method if there's enough data to fit it. The sets of attributes corresponding to one class or another apparently have a complicated boundary between them. What algorithm will give the best predictive performance remains to be seen. The exploratory methods you have learned have done their job. They have given a good understanding of the tradeoffs for this problem, leading to some guesses about what algorithm will give the best performance.

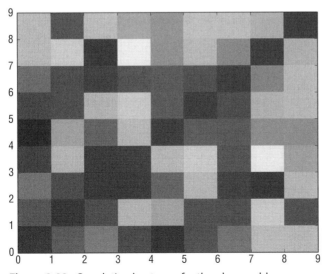

Figure 2.22: Correlation heat map for the glass problem

Using PySpark to Understand Large Data Sets

The only difference between understanding large data sets and small data sets is that large data set are larger. Why is that a problem? For one thing they can be so large that they don't fit into your RAM or maybe not even on your hard drive. Then inspecting the data becomes difficult. This is where PySpark comes in.

PySpark basically allows you to apply the techniques that you've seen in this chapter to really large data sets. And the code required is strikingly simple. There's a lot of furious activity in the background to make this work, but from the data scientist's standpoint, it's fairly straightforward.

Getting a large data set onto a computing cluster can cause some headaches. There are several approaches to getting this done. Cloud computing vendors such as Amazon, Google, Microsoft, and DataBricks offer services to make it easier to get data uploaded to the cloud and running on Spark. The process for doing that will vary from one vendor to another and they change as technology moves forward. Generally, the processes are getting easier and easier to use. Describing how to get the data uploaded currently is beyond the scope of this book for two reasons: There are a number of different vendor-dependent approaches and they are changing.

In the examples that follow, you'll see how to do machine learning on the data sets once they're up and running on the cloud. The approach will be to take the data sets that you're running in Python, convert them to PySpark data sets, and then use PySpark machine learning tools.

The code in Listing 2-18 shows how to generate the same statistical summaries using PySpark that you saw generated with Listings 2-11, 2-14, and 2-16. These calculations are done over the entire data set, even if the data set is spread over several computers.

Listing 2-18: Using PySpark to Summarize a Data Set—SparkDataFrameProperties.py

```
__author__ = 'mike_bowles'

from Read_Fcns import pd_read_abalone
from pyspark.sql import SparkSession
spark = SparkSession.builder.appName("explore").getOrCreate()

import pandas as pd
from pandas import DataFrame

abalone_df = pd_read_abalone()
abalone_sp_df = spark.createDataFrame(abalone_df)
```

```
#look at some of the properties of the spark data frame you've just
#created
print('Number of rows = ', abalone_sp_df.count())
print('Number of columns = ', len(abalone_sp_df.columns))
print('Column Names', abalone_sp_df.columns, '\n\n')

#generate sample rows from spark dataframe
abalone_sp_df.show()
```

Printed Output:

Number of rows = 4177
Number of columns = 9

Column Names ['Sex', 'Length', 'Diameter', 'Height', 'Whole weight',
'Shucked weight', 'Viscera weight', 'Shell weight', 'Rings']

Printed Output:

```
+---+------+--------+------+------------+------------------+
|Sex|Length|Diameter|Height|Whole weight|    Shucked weight|
+---+------+--------+------+------------+------------------+
|  M| 0.455|   0.365| 0.095|       0.514|            0.2245|
|  M|  0.35|   0.265|  0.09|      0.2255|            0.0995|
|  F|  0.53|    0.42| 0.135|       0.677|            0.2565|
|  M|  0.44|   0.365| 0.125|       0.516|            0.2155|
|  I|  0.33|   0.255|  0.08|       0.205|            0.0895|
|  I| 0.425|     0.3| 0.095|      0.3515|             0.141|
|  F|  0.53|   0.415|  0.15|      0.7775|             0.237|
|  F| 0.545|   0.425| 0.125|       0.768|             0.294|
|  M| 0.475|    0.37| 0.125|      0.5095|            0.2165|
|  F|  0.55|    0.44|  0.15|      0.8945|            0.3145|
|  F| 0.525|    0.38|  0.14|      0.6065|0.19399999999999998|
|  M|  0.43|    0.35|  0.11|       0.406|            0.1675|
|  M|  0.49|    0.38| 0.135|      0.5415|            0.2175|
|  F| 0.535|   0.405| 0.145|      0.6845|            0.2725|
|  F|  0.47|   0.355|   0.1|      0.4755|            0.1675|
|  M|   0.5|     0.4|  0.13|      0.6645|             0.258|
|  I| 0.355|    0.28| 0.085|      0.2905|             0.095|
|  F|  0.44|    0.34|   0.1|       0.451|             0.188|
|  M| 0.365|   0.295|  0.08|      0.2555|0.09699999999999999|
|  M|  0.45|    0.32|   0.1|       0.381|            0.1705|
+---+------+--------+------+------------+------------------+
```
only showing top 20 rows and first 6 columns to see the full output
run the jupyter notebook for this chapter.

```
+-------+----+-------------------+-------------------+
|summary| Sex|             Length|           Diameter|
+-------+----+-------------------+-------------------+
|  count|4177|               4177|               4177|
|   mean|null| 0.5239920995930093| 0.4078812544888676|
| stddev|null|0.12009291256479956|0.09923986613365948|
|    min|   F|              0.075|              0.055|
|    max|   M|              0.815|               0.65|
+-------+----+-------------------+-------------------+
```

```
+-------------------+-------------------+-------------------+----------+
|      Shucked weight|     Viscera weight|       Shell weight|     Rings|
+-------------------+-------------------+-------------------+----------+
|               4177|               4177|               4177|      4177|
|0.35936748862820195|0.18059360785252573|0.23883085946851815|9.93368446|
| 0.2219629490332201|0.10961425025968448|0.13920266952238614|3.22416903|
|              0.001|             5.0E-4|             0.0015|          |
| 1.4880000000000002|               0.76|              1.005|        29|
+-------------------+-------------------+-------------------+----------+
```

The calculations in Listing 2-18 can be done efficiently over a big data set. Some of the exploratory tools you've seen cannot. For example, doing a parallel plot of millions of variables might be too time-consuming. Something that will always work is to sample the data set and take a small enough sample that the result can be handled on a single processor.

Listing 2-19: Using PySpark to Sample Data—SamplingSparkDataFrame.py

```python
__author__ = 'mike_bowles'

from Read_Fcns import pd_read_abalone
from pyspark.sql import SparkSession
spark = SparkSession.builder.appName("explore").getOrCreate()

import pandas as pd
from pandas import DataFrame

abalone_df = pd_read_abalone()
abalone_sp_df = spark.createDataFrame(abalone_df)

print('Number of rows before sampling  = ', abalone_sp_df.count())
abalone_smaller = abalone_sp_df.sample(0.5)
print('Number of rows after sampling   = ', abalone_smaller.count())

Printed Output:
Number of rows before sampling  =   4177
Number of rows after sampling   =   2058
```

Any data set can be sampled and the sample inspected, plotted, heat mapped, etc. The natural question is whether the samples are representative. By taking several samples, you can get a handle on that.

Summary

This chapter introduced you to several tools for delving into new data sets and coming away with an understanding of how to proceed to building predictive models. The tools began with simply learning the size and shape of the data set and determining the types of attributes and labels. These facts about your data set will help you set your course through preprocessing the data and training predictive models. The chapter also covered several different statistical studies that can help you understand your data set. These included simple descriptive statistics (mean, variance, and quantiles) and second order statistics like correlations between attributes and correlations between attributes and labels. The correlation of attributes and binary labels required some techniques different from real numbers (regression labels). The chapter also introduced several visualization techniques. One was a Q-Q plot for visualizing outlier behavior in your data. Another was the parallel coordinates plot for visualizing the relationship between attributes and labels. All of these were applied to the problems that will be used in the rest of the book for demonstrating the algorithms covered and for comparing them.

Reference

1. Gorman, R. P., and Sejnowski, T. J. (1988). UCI Machine Learning Repository. `https://archive.ics.uci.edu/ml/datasets/Connectionist+Bench+%28Sonar,+Mines+vs.+Rocks%29`. Irvine, CA: University of California, School of Information and Computer Science.

Predictive Model Building: Balancing Performance, Complexity, and Big Data

This chapter discusses the factors affecting the performance of machine learning models. The chapter provides technical definitions of *performance* for different types of machine learning problems. In an ecommerce application, for example, good performance might mean returning correct search results or presenting ads that site visitors frequently click. In a genetic problem, it might mean isolating a few genes responsible for a heritable condition. The chapter describes relevant performance measures for these different problems.

The goal of selecting and fitting a predictive algorithm is to achieve the best possible performance. Achieving performance goals involves three factors: complexity of the problem, complexity of the predictive model employed, and the amount and richness of the data available.

In this chapter you will learn that achieving high performance on a complicated problem requires a complicated model, but that a complicated model requires a large, rich data set for adequate training. When your problem is less complicated or not much data is available, then a less complicated model will be the best choice. This process involves two things. First, you need models whose complexity is easily adjustable and second, you need a way to measure their performance. This chapter will discuss both of those things for some particular examples, with a particular focus on performance measurements. Subsequent chapters will go into more detail on particular predictive models.

NOTE   You'll also see the tradeoff between complex and simple models referred to as the "bias variance tradeoff." Simple models have high bias errors and complex models have high variance.

The chapter includes some visual examples that demonstrate the relationship between problem and model complexity and then provides technical guidelines for use in design and development.

The Basic Problem: Understanding Function Approximation

The algorithms covered in this book address a specific class of predictive problem. The problem statement for these problems has two types of variables:

- The variable that you are attempting to predict (for example, whether a visitor to a website will click an ad)
- Other variables (for example, the visitor's demographics or past behavior on the site) that you can use to make the prediction

Problems of this type are referred to as *function approximation problems* because the goal is to construct a model generating predictions of the first of these as a function of the second.

In a function approximation problem, the designer starts with a collection of historical examples for which the correct answer is known. For example, historical web log files will indicate whether a visitor clicked an ad when shown the ad. The data scientist next has to find other data that can be used to build a predictive model. For example, to predict whether a site visitor will click an ad, the data scientist might try using other pages that the visitor viewed before seeing the ad. If the user is registered with the site, data on past purchases or pages viewed might be available for making a prediction.

The variable being predicted is referred to by a number of different names, such as *target*, *label*, and *outcome*. The variables being used to make the predictions are variously called *predictors*, *regressors*, *features*, and *attributes*. These terms are used interchangeably in this text, as they are in general practice. Determining what attributes to use for making predictions is called *feature engineering*. Data cleaning and feature engineering take 80 percent to 90 percent of a data scientist's time.

Feature engineering usually requires a manual, iterative process for selecting features, determining optimal potential, and experimenting with different combinations of features. The algorithms covered in this book assign numeric importance values to each attribute. These values indicate the relative importance of attributes in making predictions. That information helps speed up the feature engineering process.

Working with Training Data

The data scientist starts algorithm development with a training set. The training set consists of outcome examples and the assemblage of features chosen by the data scientist. The training set comprises two types of data:

- The outcomes you want to predict
- The features available for making the prediction

Table 3.1 provides an example of a training set. The leftmost column contains outcomes (whether a site visitor clicked a link) and features to be used to make predictions about whether visitors will click the link in the future.

Table 3.1: Example Training Set

OUTCOMES: CLICKED ON LINK	FEATURE1: GENDER	FEATURE2: MONEY SPENT ON SITE	FEATURE3: GENDER
Yes	M	0	25
No	F	250	32
Yes	F	12	17

The predictor values (a.k.a., features, attributes, and so on) can be arranged in the form of a matrix (see Equation 3.1). The notational convention used in this book is as follows. The table of predictors will be called X, and it has the following form:

$$X = \begin{matrix} x_{11} & x_{12} & \cdots & x_{1n} \\ x_{21} & x_{22} & \cdots & x_{2n} \\ \vdots & \vdots & & \ddots \\ x_{m1} & x_{m2} & \cdots & x_{mn} \end{matrix}$$

Equation 3.1: Notation for set of predictors

Referring to the data set in Table 3.1, x_{11} would be M (gender), x_{12} would be 0.00 (money spent on site), x_{21} would be F (gender), and so on.

Sometimes it will be convenient to refer to all the attribute values for a particular example. For that purpose, x_i (with a single index) will refer to the ith row of X. For the data set in Table 3.1, x_2 would be a row vector containing the values F, 250, 32.

Strictly speaking, the X is not a matrix because the predictors may not all be the same type of variable. A proper matrix contains variables that are all the same type. Predictors, however, come in different types. Using the example of predicting ad clicks, the predictors might include demographic data about the site visitor. Those data could include marital status and yearly income, among other things. Yearly income is a real number, and marital status is a categorical variable. That means that marital status does not admit arithmetic operations such as adding or multiplication and that no order relation exists between *single*, *married*, and *divorced*. The entries in a column from X all have the same type, but the type may vary from one column to the next.

Attributes such as marital status, gender, or the state of residence go by several different designations. They may be called *factor* or *categorical*. Attributes like age or income that are represented by numbers are called *numeric* or *real-valued*. The distinction between these two types of attributes is important because some algorithms may not handle one type or the other. For example, linear methods, including the ones covered in this book, require numeric attributes. The PySpark algorithms that you'll see all require all the features to be numeric. Chapter 4, "Penalized Linear Regression," which covers linear methods, shows methods for converting (or coding) categorical variables to numeric in order to apply linear methods to problems with categorical variables. You'll also learn to use the PySpark functions for coding categorical variables as numeric.

The targets corresponding to each row in X are arranged in a column vector Y (see Equation 3.2), as follows:

$$Y = \begin{matrix} y_1 \\ y_2 \\ \vdots \\ y_m \end{matrix}$$

Equation 3.2: Notation for vector of targets

The target y_i corresponds to x_i—the predictors in the ith row of X. Referring to the data in Table 3.1, y_1 is Yes, and y_2 is No.

Targets may be of several different forms. For example, they may be real numbers, like if the objective were to predict how much a customer will spend. When the targets are real numbers, the problem is called a *regression problem*. Linear regression implies using a linear method to solve a regression problem. (This book covers both linear and nonlinear regression methods.)

If the targets are two-valued, as in Table 3.1, the problem is called a *binary classification problem*. Predicting whether a customer will click an advertisement is a binary classification problem. If the targets contain several discrete values, the problem is a *multiclass classification problem*. Predicting which of several ads a customer will click would be a multiclass classification problem.

The basic problem is to find a prediction function, `pred()`, that uses the attributes to predict outcomes (see Equation 3.3):

$$y_t \sim pred(x_t)$$

Equation 3.3: Basic equation for making predictions

The function `pred()` uses the attribute x_i to predict y_i. This book describes some of the very best current methods for producing the function `pred()`. These algorithms are available across a wide variety of platforms. In this book you'll see how to use them in Python and PySpark. If you're ever required to implement them in another language, the understanding you gain will carry over.

Assessing Performance of Predictive Models

Good performance means using the attributes x_i to generate a prediction that is close to y_i, but *close* has different meanings for different problems. For a regression problem where y_i is a real number, performance is measured in terms like the mean squared error (MSE) or the mean absolute error (MAE) (see Equation 3.4):

$$Mean\,squared\,error = \left(\frac{1}{m}\right)\sum_{i=1}^{m}(y_i - pred(x_i))^2$$

Equation 3.4: Performance measure for a regression problem

In a regression problem, the target $(y_i x_i)$, are both real numbers, so it makes sense to describe the error as being the numeric difference between them. Equation 3.4 for MSE squares the errors and averages over the data set to produce a measure of the overall level of errors. MAE averages the absolute values of the errors (see Equation 3.5) instead of averaging the squares of the errors.

$$Mean\,absolute\,error = \left(\frac{1}{m}\right)\sum_{i=1}^{m}|y_i - pred(x_i)|$$

Equation 3.5: Another performance measure for regression

If the problem is a classification problem, you must use some other measure of performance. One of the most used is the misclassification error—that is, the fraction of examples that the function `pred()` predicts incorrectly. The section "Performance Measures for Different Types of Problems" shows how to calculate misclassification.

For our function `pred()` to be useful for making predictions, there must be some way to predict what level of errors it will generate on new examples as they arrive. What is the performance on new data—data that were not involved in developing the function `pred()`? This chapter covers the best methods for estimating performance on new data.

This section introduced the basic type of prediction problem that will be addressed in this book and described how constructing these prediction models amounts to constructing a function that maps attributes (or features) into predicted outcomes. It also gave an overview of how the errors in these predictions can be assessed. Performing these steps leads to several complications. The remaining sections of this chapter describe these complications, how to deal with them, and how to arrive at the best possible model given the constraints of the problem and the data available.

Factors Driving Algorithm Choices and Performance—Complexity and Data

Several factors affect the overall performance of a predictive algorithm. Among these factors are the complexity of the problem, the complexity of the model used, and the amount of training data available. The following sections describe how these factors interrelate to determine performance.

Contrast between a Simple Problem and a Complex Problem

The preceding section of this chapter described several ways to quantify performance and highlighted the importance of performance on new data. The goal of designing a predictive model is to make accurate predictions on new examples (such as new visitors to your site). As a practicing data scientist, you will want an estimate of an algorithm's performance so that you can set expectations with your customer and compare algorithms with one another. Best practice in predictive modeling requires that you hold out some data from the training set. These held-out examples have labels associated with them and can be compared to predictions produced by models training on the remaining data. Statisticians refer to this technique as *out-of-sample error* because it is an error on data not used in training. (The section "Measuring the Performance of Predictive Models" later in this chapter goes into more detail about the mechanics of this process.) The important thing is that the only performance that counts is the performance of the model when it is run against new examples.

One of the factors affecting performance is the complexity of the problem being solved. Figure 3.1 shows a relatively simple classification problem in two dimensions. There are two groups of points: dark and light points. The dark points are randomly drawn from a 2D Gaussian distribution centered at (1,0) with unit variance in both dimensions. The light points are also drawn from a Gaussian distribution having the same variance but centered at (0,1). The attributes for the problem are the two axes in the plot: x_1 and x_2. The classification task is to draw some boundaries in the x_1, x_2 plane to separate the light points from the dark points. About the best that can be done in this circumstance is to draw a 45-degree line in the plot—that is the line where x_1 equals x_2. In a precise probabilistic sense, that is the best possible classifier for this problem. Because a straight line separates the lights and darks as well as possible, a linear classifier will do as well as nonlinear classifier. The linear methods covered in this book will do a splendid job on this problem.

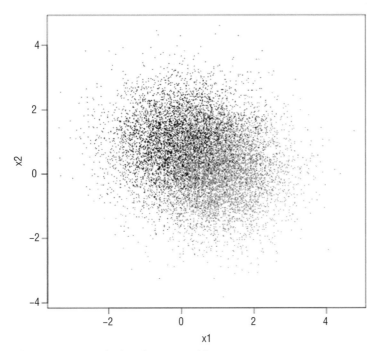

Figure 3.1: A simple classification problem

Figure 3.2 depicts a more complicated problem. The points shown in Figure 3.2 are generated by drawing points at random. The main difference from the random draw that generated Figure 3.1 is that the points in Figure 3.2 are drawn from several distributions for the light points and several different ones for dark. This is called a *mixture model*. The general goal is basically the same: draw boundaries in the x_1, x_2 plane to separate the light points from the dark points. In Figure 3.2, however, it is clear that a linear boundary will not separate the points as well as a curve. The ensemble methods covered in Chapter 6, "Ensemble Methods," will work well on this problem.

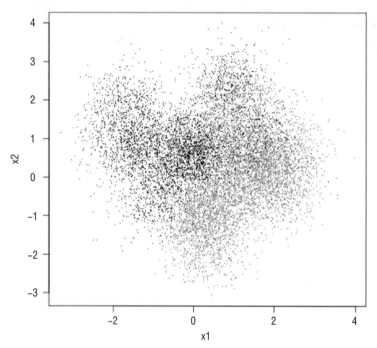

Figure 3.2: A complicated classification problem

However, complexity of the decision boundaries is not the only factor influencing whether linear or nonlinear methods will deliver better performance. Another important factor is the size of the data set. Figure 3.3 illustrates this element of performance. The points plotted in Figure 3.3 are a 1 percent subsample of data plotted in Figure 3.2.

In Figure 3.2, there was enough data to visualize the curved boundaries delineating the sets of light and dark points. Without as much data, the sets are not so easily discerned visually, and in this circumstance, a linear model may give equal or better performance than a nonlinear model. With less data, the boundaries are harder to visualize, and they are more difficult to compute. This gives a graphic demonstration of the value of having a large volume of data. If

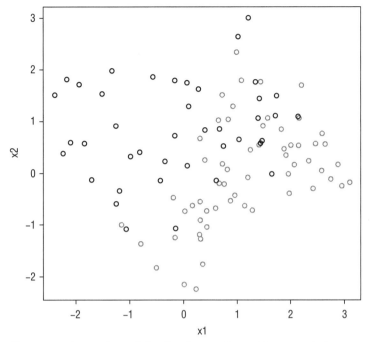

Figure 3.3: A complicated classification problem without much data

the underlying problem is complicated (for example, personalizing responses for individual shoppers), a complicated model with a lot of data can produce accurate results. However, if the model is not complicated, as in Figure 3.1, or there is not sufficient data, as in Figure 3.3, a linear model may produce the best answer.

Contrast between a Simple Model and a Complex Model

The previous section showed visual comparisons between simple and complex problems. This section describes how the various models available to solve these problems differ from one another. Intuitively, it seems that a complex model should be fit to a complex problem, but the visual example from the previous section demonstrates that data set size may dictate that a simple model fits a complex problem better than a complex model.

Another important concept is that modern machine learning algorithms generate families of models, not just single models. The algorithms covered in this book each generate hundreds or even thousands of different models. Generally, the ensemble methods covered in Chapter 6 yield more complex models than linear methods covered in Chapter 4, but both of these methods generate multiple models of varying complexity. (This will become clearer in Chapters 4 and 6, which cover linear and ensemble techniques in detail.)

Figure 3.4 shows a linear model fit to the simple problem introduced in the previous section. The linear model shown in Figure 3.4 was generated using the glmnet algorithm (covered in Chapter 4). The linear model fit to these data divides the data roughly in half. The line in the figure is given by Equation 3.6.

$$x_2 = -0.01 + 0.99x_1$$

Equation 3.6: Linear model fit to simple problem

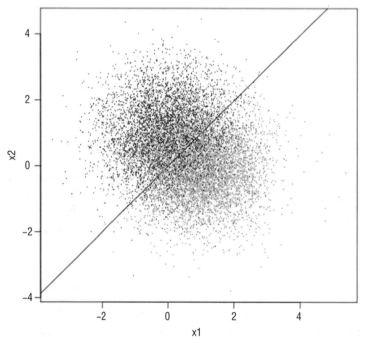

Figure 3.4: Linear model fit to simple data

This is very close to the line where x_2 equals x_1, which is the best possible boundary in a probabilistic sense. The boundary appears sensible from a visual intuitive standpoint. Fitting a more complicated model to this simple problem is not going to improve performance.

A more complicated problem with more complicated decision boundaries gives a complicated model an opportunity to outperform a simple linear model. Figure 3.5 shows a linear model fit to data indicating a nonlinear decision boundary. In this circumstance, the linear model misclassifies regions as dark when they should be light and vice versa.

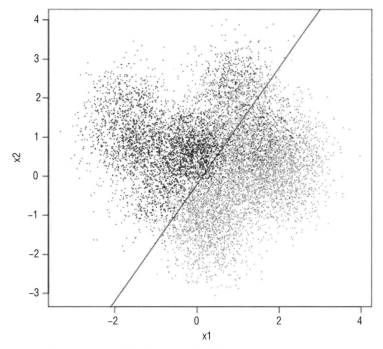

Figure 3.5: Linear model fit to complex data

Figure 3.6 shows how much better a complicated model can do with complicated data. The model used to generate this decision boundary is an ensemble (collection) of 1,000 binary decision trees constructed using the gradient boosting algorithm. (Gradient boosted decision trees are covered in detail in Chapter 6.) The nonlinear decision boundary curves are used to better delineate regions where the dark points are denser and regions where the light points are denser.

It is tempting to draw the conclusion that the best approach is to use complicated models for complicated problems and simple models for simple problems. But, you must consider one more dimension to the problem. As mentioned in the previous section, you must consider data set size. Figures 3.7 and 3.8 show 1 percent of the data from a complicated problem. Figure 3.7 shows a linear model fit to the data, and Figure 3.8 shows an ensemble model fit to the data. Count the number of points that are misclassified. There are 100 points in the data set. The linear model in Figure 3.7 misclassifies 11 points, for a misclassification error rate of 11 percent. The complex model misclassifies 8, for an 8 percent error rate. Their performance is roughly equal.

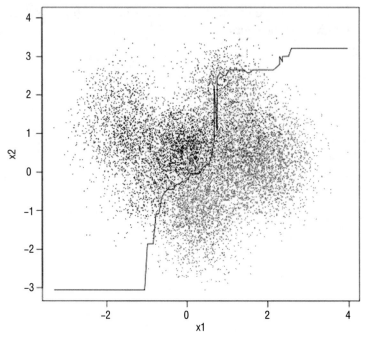

Figure 3.6: Ensemble model fit to complex data

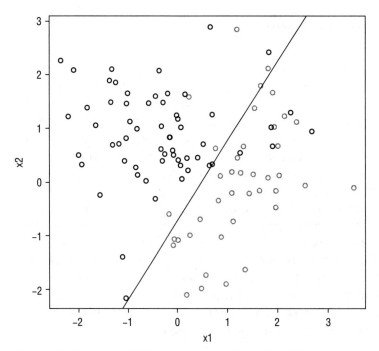

Figure 3.7: Linear model fit to small sample of complex data

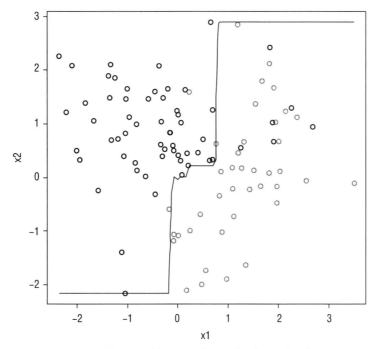

Figure 3.8: Ensemble model fit to small sample of complex data

Factors Driving Predictive Algorithm Performance

These results explain the excitement over large volumes of data. Accurate predictions for complicated problems require large volumes of data. But the size isn't quite a precise enough measure. The shape of the data also matters.

Equation 3.1 portrayed predictor data as a matrix having a number of rows (height) and a number of columns (width). The number of entries in the matrix is the product of the number of rows and the number of columns. An important difference exists between the number of rows and the number of columns when the data are being used for predictive modeling. Adding a column means adding a new attribute. Adding a new row means getting an additional historical example of the existing attributes. To understand how the effects of a new row differ from the effects of a new column, consider a linear model relating the attributes from Equation 3.1 to the labels of Equation 3.2.

Assume a model of the following form (see Equation 3.7):

$$y_i \sim x_i * \beta$$
$$= x_{i1} * \beta 1 + x_{i2} * \beta 2 + \ldots + x_i m * \beta m$$

Equation 3.7: Linear relation between attributes and outcomes

Here, x_i is a row of attributes, and is a column vector of coefficients to be determined. Adding a column to the matrix of attributes adds another coefficient that needs to be determined. This added coefficient is also called *degree of freedom*. Adding another degree of freedom is making the model more complicated. The preceding examples demonstrated that making the model more complicated required more data. For this reason, it is common to think in terms of the ratio of rows to columns—the aspect ratio. Biological data sets and natural language processing data sets are examples that are quite large because they have a lot of columns, but they are sometimes not large enough to get good performance out of a complex modeling approach. In biology, genomic data sets can easily contain 10,000 to 50,000 attributes. Even with tens of thousands of individual experiments (rows of data), a genomic data set may not be enough to train a complex ensemble model. A linear model may give equivalent or better performance. Genomic data are expensive. One of the experiments (rows) can cost upward of $5,000, making the full data set cost upward of $50 million. Text can be relatively inexpensive to collect and store, but can also be even wider than genomic data. In some natural language processing problems, the attributes are words, and rows are documents. Entries in the matrix of attributes are the number of times a word appears in a document. The number of columns is the vocabulary size for a document collection. Depending on preprocessing (for example, removing common words like *a*, *and*, and *of*), the vocabulary can be from a few thousand to a few tens of thousands. The attribute matrix for text becomes very wide when n-grams are counted alongside words. N-grams are groups of two, three, or four words that appear next to one another (or close enough to be a phrase). When groups of two, three, or four words are also counted, the attribute space for natural language processing can grow to more than a million attributes. Once again, a linear model may give equivalent or better performance than a more complicated ensemble model.

Choosing an Algorithm: Linear or Nonlinear?

The visual examples you have just seen give some idea of the performance tradeoffs between linear and nonlinear predictive models. Linear models are preferable when the data set has more columns than rows or when the underlying problem is simple. Nonlinear models are preferable for complex problems with many more rows than columns of data. An additional factor is training time. Fast linear techniques train much faster than nonlinear techniques. (You will have more of a basis for making this decision after we've covered the techniques described in Chapter 4 and Chapter 6 and have worked through some examples.)

Choosing a nonlinear model (say, an ensemble method) entails training a number of different models of differing complexity. For example, the ensemble model that generated the decision boundary in Figure 3.6 was one of roughly a thousand different models generated during the training process. These models had a variety of different complexities. Some of them would have given a much cruder approximation to the boundaries that are visually apparent in Figure 3.6. The model that generated the decision boundary in Figure 3.6 was chosen because it performed the best on out-of-sample data. This process holds for many modern machine learning algorithms. Examples will be covered in covered in the section "Choosing a Model to Balance Problem Complexity, Model Complexity, and Data Set Size."

This section has used data sets and classifier solutions that can be visualized in order to give you an intuitive grasp of the factors affecting the performance of the predictive models you build. Generally, you'll use numeric measures of performance instead of relying on pictures. The next section describes the methods and considerations for producing numeric performance measures for predictive models and how to use these to estimate the performance your models will achieve when deployed.

Measuring the Performance of Predictive Models

This section covers two broad areas relating to performance measures for predictive models. The first one is the different metrics that you can use for different types of problems (for example, using MSE for a regression problem and misclassification error for a classification problem). In the literature (and in machine learning competitions), you will also see measures like receiver operating curves (ROC curves) and area under the curve (AUC). Besides that, these ideas are useful for optimizing performance.

The second broad area consists of techniques for gathering out-of-sample error estimates. Recall that out-of-sample errors are meant to simulate errors on new data. It's an important part of design practice to use these techniques to compare different algorithms and to select the best model complexity for a given problem complexity and data set size. That process is discussed in detail later in this chapter and is then used in examples throughout the rest of the book.

Performance Measures for Different Types of Problems

Performance measures for regression problems are relatively straightforward. In a regression problem, both the target and the prediction are real numbers. Error is naturally defined as the difference between the target and the prediction. It is useful to generate statistical summaries of the errors for comparisons and for diagnostics. The most frequently used summaries are the mean squared error (MSE) and the mean absolute error (MAE). Listing 3.1 compares the calculation of the MSE, MAE, and root MSE (RMSE, which is the square root of MSE).

Listing 3.1: Comparison of MSE, MAE, and RMSE—regressionErrorMeasures.py

```python
__author__ = 'mike_bowles'
from math import sqrt

#here are some made-up numbers to start with
target = [1.5, 2.1, 3.3, -4.7, -2.3, 0.75]
prediction = [0.5, 1.5, 2.1, -2.2, 0.1, -0.5]

error = []
for i in range(len(target)):
    error.append(target[i] - prediction[i])

#print the errors
print("Errors ",)
print(error, '\n')

#calculate the squared errors and absolute value of errors
squaredError = []
absError = []
for val in error:
    squaredError.append(val*val)
    absError.append(abs(val))


#print squared errors and absolute value of errors
print("Squared Error")
print(squaredError, '\n')

print("Absolute Value of Error")
print(absError, '\n')

#calculate and print mean squared error MSE
print("MSE = ", sum(squaredError)/len(squaredError))

#calculate and print square root of MSE (RMSE)
print("RMSE = ", sqrt(sum(squaredError)/len(squaredError)))

#calculate and print mean absolute error MAE
print("MAE = ", sum(absError)/len(absError))

#compare MSE to target variance
targetDeviation = []
targetMean = sum(target)/len(target)
for val in target:
    targetDeviation.append((val - targetMean)*(val - targetMean))

#print the target variance
print("Target Variance = ", sum(targetDeviation)/len(targetDeviation))

#print the target standard deviation (square root of variance)
```

```
print("Target Standard Deviation = ", sqrt(sum(targetDeviation)/
                                      len(targetDeviation)))


Printed Output:
Errors
[1.0, 0.6000000000000001, 1.1999999999999997, -2.5, -2.4, 1.25]


Squared Error
[1.0, 0.3600000000000001, 1.4399999999999993, 6.25, 5.76, 1.5625]


Absolute Value of Error
[1.0, 0.6000000000000001, 1.1999999999999997, 2.5, 2.4, 1.25]


MSE =  2.72875
RMSE =  1.651892853668179
MAE =  1.4916666666666665
Target Variance =  7.570347222222222
Target Standard Deviation =  2.7514263977475797
```

The example starts with some made-up numbers for the targets and the predictions. First, it calculates the errors by simple subtraction; then it shows the calculation of MSE, MAE, and RMSE. Notice that MSE comes out markedly different in magnitude than MAE and RMSE. That's because MSE is in squared units. For that reason, the RMSE is usually a more usable number to calculate. At the bottom of the listing is a calculation of the variance (mean squared deviation from the mean) and the standard deviation (square root of variance) of the targets. These quantities are useful to compare (respectively) to the MSE and RMSE of the prediction errors. For example, if the MSE of the prediction error is roughly the same as the target variance (or the RMSE is roughly the same as target standard deviation), the prediction algorithm is not performing well. You could replace the prediction algorithm with a simple calculation of the mean of the targets and perform as well. The errors in Listing 3.1 have RMSE that's about half the standard deviation of the targets. That is fairly good performance.

Besides calculating summary statistics for the error, it may sometimes be useful for analyzing sources and magnitudes of error to look at things like histogram of the error or tail behavior (quantile or decile boundaries), degree of normality, and so forth. Sometimes those investigations will yield insights into error sources and potential performance improvements.

Classification problems require different treatment. The approaches to classification problems generally revolve around misclassification error rates—the fraction of examples that are incorrectly classified. Suppose, for instance, that the classification problem is to predict click or not-click on a link being considered for presentation to a site visitor. Generally, algorithms for doing classification can present predictions in the form of a probability instead of a hard click versus not-click decision. The algorithms considered in this book all output probabilities.

Here's why that's useful. If the prediction of click or not-click is given as a probability—say 80 percent chance of click (and correspondingly 20 percent chance of not-click)—the data scientist has the option to use 50 percent as a threshold for presenting the link or not presenting the link. In some cases, however, a higher or lower threshold value will give a better end result.

Suppose, for example, that the problem is fraud detection (for credit cards, automatic clearinghouses [checking], insurance claims, and so on). The actions that proceed from making a fraud-or-not decision are to have a call center representative intervene in the transaction or to let it go. There are costs involved with either decision. If the call is made, there's the call center cost and the cost of the customer's reaction. If the call isn't made, there's the cost of the potential fraud. If the costs of taking the action are very low relative to the costs of not taking the action, the minimum total comes at a relatively low threshold. More transactions get flagged for intervention.

But where do you draw the line for interrupting your customer's checkout and requiring the customer to call card services to proceed? Do you interrupt the transactions where your predictive algorithm indicates a 20 percent, 50 percent, or 80 percent probability that the transaction is fraudulent? If you place the threshold for interruption at 20 percent, you'll be intervening more frequently—preventing more fraudulent transactions—but also irritating more customers and keeping many call center reps busy. Maybe it is better to place the threshold higher (say 80 percent) and to accept more fraud.

A useful way to think about this is to arrange the possible outcomes into what is called a *confusion matrix* or *contingency table* (http://en.wikipedia.org/wiki/Confusion _ matrix). Figure 3.9 shows a toy example of a contingency matrix. The numbers in the contingency table represent the performance based on a choice for the threshold value discussed in the last paragraph. The contingency matrix in Figure 3.9 summarizes the results of making predictions for 135 test examples for a particular choice of the threshold probability. The matrix has two columns representing the possible predictions. It also has two rows representing the truth (label) for each example. So, each example in the test set can be assigned to one of the four cells in the table. The two classifications portrayed in Figure 3.9 are "click" and "not click," appropriate for selecting an ad. These could also correspond to "fraud" and "not fraud"—or other pairs—depending on the specific problem being addressed.

The upper-left cell contains examples that are predicted as click and where that matches the label (truth). These are called *true positive* and are generally abbreviated as TP. The entries in the lower-left box correspond to examples where the prediction was positive (click) but the truth was negative (not-click). These are called *false positive* and abbreviated as FP. The right column of the matrix contains the examples that were predicted not-click. The examples in the upper right were click in truth and are called *false negatives* or FN. The lower-right examples were predicted not-click and agree with the real outcome. They are called *false negative* or FN.

	Predicted Class		
Actual Class		Positive (Click)	Negative (Not-Click)
	Positive (Click)	True Positive 10	False Negative 7
	Negative (Not-Click)	False Positive 22	True Negative 96

Figure 3.9: Confusion matrix example

What happens when the probability threshold is changed? Consider the extreme values. If the probability threshold is set to 0.0, no matter what probability your model predicts, it will get designated as a click. All the examples wind up in the left column. There are only 0s in the right column. The number of TPs would go up to 17. The number of FPs would go up to 118. If there were no cost for an FP and no reward for a true negative (TN), that might be a good choice, but no predictive algorithm is required to assume click for every input example. Similarly, if there is no cost for an FN and no benefit for a TP, the threshold can be set at 1.0 so that all examples are classified as not-click. These extremes aid understanding, but they're not useful in a deployed system. The following example shows how the process would work to build a classifier for the rocks-versus-mines data set.

The rocks-versus-mines data set presents the problem of building a classifier that uses sonar data to determine whether seabed objects are rocks or mines. (For a more thorough discussion and exploration of the data set, see Chapter 2, "Understand the Problem by Understanding the Data.") Listing 3.2 shows the Python code for training a simple classifier on the rocks-versus-mines data set and then predicts performance for the classifier.

Listing 3.2: Measuring Performance for Classifier Trained on Rocks-Versus-Mines— classifierPerformance_RocksVMines.py

```
__author__ = 'mike_bowles'

from Read_Fcns import list_read_rvm
import numpy as np
import random
from sklearn import datasets, linear_model
```

```python
from sklearn.metrics import roc_curve, auc
import matplotlib.pyplot as plt


def confusionMatrix(predicted, actual, threshold):
    if len(predicted) != len(actual): return -1
    tp = 0.0
    fp = 0.0
    tn = 0.0
    fn = 0.0
    for i in range(len(actual)):
        if actual[i] > 0.5: #labels that are 1.0  (positive examples)
            if predicted[i] > threshold:
                tp += 1.0 #correctly predicted positive
            else:
                fn += 1.0 #incorrectly predicted negative
        else:              #labels that are 0.0 (negative examples)
            if predicted[i] < threshold:
                tn += 1.0 #correctly predicted negative
            else:
                fp += 1.0 #incorrectly predicted positive
    rtn = [tp, fn, fp, tn]
    return rtn

#use scikit learn package to perform linear regression
#read in the rocks versus mines data set from uci.edu data repository
xList, labels = list_read_rvm()

#divide attribute and labels into training and test sets (2/3 and 1/3)
indices = range(len(xList))
xListTest = [xList[i] for i in indices if i%3 == 0 ]
xListTrain = [xList[i] for i in indices if i%3 != 0 ]
labelsTest = [labels[i] for i in indices if i%3 == 0]
labelsTrain = [labels[i] for i in indices if i%3 != 0]

#form train and test data arrays
xTrain = np.array(xListTrain); yTrain = np.array(labelsTrain)
xTest = np.array(xListTest); yTest = np.array(labelsTest)

#check shapes to see what they look like
print("Shape of xTrain array", xTrain.shape)
print("Shape of yTrain array", yTrain.shape)
print("Shape of xTest array", xTest.shape)
print("Shape of yTest array", yTest.shape)

#train linear regression model
rocksVMinesModel = linear_model.LinearRegression()
rocksVMinesModel.fit(xTrain,yTrain)

#generate predictions on in-sample error
```

```
trainingPredictions = rocksVMinesModel.predict(xTrain)
print("\nSome values predicted by model", trainingPredictions[0:5], \
      trainingPredictions[-6:-1])

#generate confusion matrix for predictions on training set (in-sample
confusionMatTrain = confusionMatrix(trainingPredictions, yTrain, 0.5)
#pick threshold value and generate confusion matrix entries
tp = confusionMatTrain[0]; fn = confusionMatTrain[1]
fp = confusionMatTrain[2]; tn = confusionMatTrain[3]

print("\ntp = " + str(tp) + "\tfn = " + str(fn) + "\n" + "fp = " + \
      str(fp) + "\ttn = " + str(tn) + '\n')

#generate predictions on out-of-sample data
testPredictions = rocksVMinesModel.predict(xTest)

#generate confusion matrix from predictions on out-of-sample data
conMatTest = confusionMatrix(testPredictions, yTest, 0.5)

#pick threshold value and generate confusion matrix entries
tp = conMatTest[0]; fn = conMatTest[1]
fp = conMatTest[2]; tn = conMatTest[3]
print("tp = " + str(tp) + "\tfn = " + str(fn) + "\n" + "fp = " + \
      str(fp) + "\ttn = " + str(tn) + '\n')

#generate ROC curve for in-sample

fpr, tpr, thresholds = roc_curve(yTrain,trainingPredictions)
roc_auc = auc(fpr, tpr)
print( 'AUC for in-sample ROC curve: %f' % roc_auc)

# Plot ROC curve
plt.clf()
plt.plot(fpr, tpr, label='ROC curve (area = %0.2f)' % roc_auc)
plt.plot([0, 1], [0, 1], 'k--')
plt.xlim([0.0, 1.0])
plt.ylim([0.0, 1.0])
plt.xlabel('False Positive Rate')
plt.ylabel('True Positive Rate')
plt.title('In sample ROC rocks versus mines')
plt.legend(loc="lower right")
plt.show()

#generate ROC curve for out-of-sample
fpr, tpr, thresholds = roc_curve(yTest,testPredictions)
roc_auc = auc(fpr, tpr)
print( 'AUC for out-of-sample ROC curve: %f' % roc_auc)

# Plot ROC curve
plt.clf()
```

```
plt.plot(fpr, tpr, label='ROC curve (area = %0.2f)' % roc_auc)
plt.plot([0, 1], [0, 1], 'k--')
plt.xlim([0.0, 1.0])
plt.ylim([0.0, 1.0])
plt.xlabel('False Positive Rate')
plt.ylabel('True Positive Rate')
plt.title('Out-of-sample ROC rocks versus mines')
plt.legend(loc="lower right")
plt.show()__author__ = 'mike-bowles'

from Read_Fcns import list_read_rvm
import numpy as np
import random
from sklearn import datasets, linear_model
from sklearn.metrics import roc_curve, auc
import matplotlib.pyplot as plt


def confusionMatrix(predicted, actual, threshold):
    if len(predicted) != len(actual): return -1
    tp = 0.0
    fp = 0.0
    tn = 0.0
    fn = 0.0
    for i in range(len(actual)):
        if actual[i] > 0.5: #labels that are 1.0  (positive examples)
            if predicted[i] > threshold:
                tp += 1.0 #correctly predicted positive
            else:
                fn += 1.0 #incorrectly predicted negative
        else:              #labels that are 0.0 (negative examples)
            if predicted[i] < threshold:
                tn += 1.0 #correctly predicted negative
            else:
                fp += 1.0 #incorrectly predicted positive
    rtn = [tp, fn, fp, tn]
    return rtn

#use scikit learn package to perform linear regression
#read in the rocks versus mines data set from uci.edu data repository
xList, labels = list_read_rvm()

#divide attribute and labels into training and test sets (2/3 and 1/3)
indices = range(len(xList))
xListTest = [xList[i] for i in indices if i%3 == 0 ]
xListTrain = [xList[i] for i in indices if i%3 != 0 ]
labelsTest = [labels[i] for i in indices if i%3 == 0]
labelsTrain = [labels[i] for i in indices if i%3 != 0]

#form train and test data arrays
```

```
xTrain = np.array(xListTrain); yTrain = np.array(labelsTrain)
xTest = np.array(xListTest); yTest = np.array(labelsTest)

#check shapes to see what they look like
print("Shape of xTrain array", xTrain.shape)
print("Shape of yTrain array", yTrain.shape)
print("Shape of xTest array", xTest.shape)
print("Shape of yTest array", yTest.shape)

#train linear regression model
rocksVMinesModel = linear_model.LinearRegression()
rocksVMinesModel.fit(xTrain,yTrain)

#generate predictions on in-sample error
trainingPredictions = rocksVMinesModel.predict(xTrain)
print("\nSome values predicted by model", trainingPredictions[0:5], \
      trainingPredictions[-6:-1])

#generate confusion matrix for predictions on training set (in-sample
confusionMatTrain = confusionMatrix(trainingPredictions, yTrain, 0.5)
#pick threshold value and generate confusion matrix entries
tp = confusionMatTrain[0]; fn = confusionMatTrain[1]
fp = confusionMatTrain[2]; tn = confusionMatTrain[3]

print("\ntp = " + str(tp) + "\tfn = " + str(fn) + "\n" + "fp = " + \
      str(fp) + "\ttn = " + str(tn) + '\n')

#generate predictions on out-of-sample data
testPredictions = rocksVMinesModel.predict(xTest)

#generate confusion matrix from predictions on out-of-sample data
conMatTest = confusionMatrix(testPredictions, yTest, 0.5)

#pick threshold value and generate confusion matrix entries
tp = conMatTest[0]; fn = conMatTest[1]
fp = conMatTest[2]; tn = conMatTest[3]
print("tp = " + str(tp) + "\tfn = " + str(fn) + "\n" + "fp = " + \
      str(fp) + "\ttn = " + str(tn) + '\n')

#generate ROC curve for in-sample

fpr, tpr, thresholds = roc_curve(yTrain,trainingPredictions)
roc_auc = auc(fpr, tpr)
print( 'AUC for in-sample ROC curve: %f' % roc_auc)

# Plot ROC curve
plt.clf()
plt.plot(fpr, tpr, label='ROC curve (area = %0.2f)' % roc_auc)
plt.plot([0, 1], [0, 1], 'k--')
plt.xlim([0.0, 1.0])
```

```
plt.ylim([0.0, 1.0])
plt.xlabel('False Positive Rate')
plt.ylabel('True Positive Rate')
plt.title('In sample ROC rocks versus mines')
plt.legend(loc="lower right")
plt.show()

#generate ROC curve for out-of-sample
fpr, tpr, thresholds = roc_curve(yTest,testPredictions)
roc_auc = auc(fpr, tpr)
print( 'AUC for out-of-sample ROC curve: %f' % roc_auc)

# Plot ROC curve
plt.clf()
plt.plot(fpr, tpr, label='ROC curve (area = %0.2f)' % roc_auc)
plt.plot([0, 1], [0, 1], 'k--')
plt.xlim([0.0, 1.0])
plt.ylim([0.0, 1.0])
plt.xlabel('False Positive Rate')
plt.ylabel('True Positive Rate')
plt.title('Out-of-sample ROC rocks versus mines')
plt.legend(loc="lower right")
plt.show()

Printed Output:

Shape of xTrain array (138, 60)
Shape of yTrain array (138,)
Shape of xTest array (70, 60)
Shape of yTest array (70,)

Some values predicted by model [-0.10240253   0.42090698   0.38593034
0.36094537   0.31520494] [1.11094176 1.12242751 0.77626699 1.02016858
0.66338081]

tp = 68.0     fn = 6.0
fp = 7.0      tn = 57.0

tp = 28.0     fn = 9.0
fp = 9.0      tn = 24.0


AUC for in-sample ROC curve: 0.979519
```

The first section of the code reads the input data from the University of California Irvine data repository and then formats it as a list for the labels and a list of lists for the attributes. The next step is to break the data (labels and attributes) into two subsets: a test set that contains one third of the data, and a training set that contains the other two thirds. The data labeled *test* will not be used in training the classifier, but will be reserved for assessing performance after the classifier is trained. This step simulates the behavior of the classifier on new data examples after it has been deployed. Later, this chapter discusses a variety of different methods for holding out data and making estimates of performance on new data.

The classifier is trained by converting the labels M (for mine) and R (for rock) in the original data set into numeric values—1.0 corresponding to mine, and 0.0 corresponding to rock—and then using the ordinary least squares regression to fit a linear model. This is a fairly simple method to understand and to implement and will often generate very similar performance to the more sophisticated algorithms discussed later. The program in Listing 3.2 employs the linear regression class from scikit-learn to train the ordinary least squares model. Then the trained model is used to generate predictions on the training set and on the test set.

The code prints out some representative values for the predictions. The linear regression model generates numbers that are mostly in the interval between 0.0 and 1.0, but not entirely. The predictions aren't quite probabilities. They can still be used to generate predicted classifications by comparing to a threshold value. The function `confusionMatrix()` produces the values for a confusion matrix, similar to Figure 3.9. It takes the predictions, the corresponding actual values (labels), and a threshold value as input. It compares the predictions to the threshold to determine whether to assign each example to the "predicted positive" or "predicted negative" column in the confusion matrix. It uses the actual value to make the assignment to the appropriate row of the confusion matrix.

The error rates for each threshold value can be read out of the confusion matrix. The total number of errors is the sum of FPs and FNs. The example code produces confusion matrices for the in-sample data and the out-of-sample data and prints them both out. The misclassification error rate on the in-sample data is about 8 percent, and about 26 percent on the out-of-sample data. Generally, the out-of-sample performance will be worse than performance on in-sample data. It will also be more representative of the expected error on new examples.

The misclassification error changes when the thresholds are changed. Table 3.2 shows how the misclassification error rate changes as the threshold value changes. The numbers in the table are based on out-of-sample results. That will be generally true of numbers characterizing performance throughout the book. Any in-sample errors will have warning labels attached: "Warning: These are in-sample errors." If the goal is to minimize the misclassification error, the best threshold value is 0.25.

Table 3.2: Dependence of Misclassification Error on Decision Threshold

DECISION THRESHOLD	MISCLASSIFICATION ERROR RATE
0.0	28.6 percent
0.25	24.3 percent
0.5	25.7 percent
0.75	30.0 percent
1.0	38.6 percent

The best value for the threshold may be the one that minimizes the misclassification error. Sometimes, however, there's more cost associated with one type of error than with another. Suppose, for instance, that for the rocks-versus-mines problem it costs $100 to send a diver to do a visual inspection and that unexploded mines cost $1,000 in expected injuries and property damage if not removed. An FP costs $100, and an FN costs $1,000. Given these assumptions, Table 3.3 summarizes the dollar cost of mistakes for different threshold values. The higher cost of mistaking a mine for a rock (and leaving it in place to threaten health and safety) has pushed the decision threshold down to zero. That means more FNs, but they aren't as expensive. A more thorough analysis could include the costs associated with TP and TN. For example, the TP might have costs associated with removing the mine and a benefit of +$1,000 associated with its removal. If these figures are available (or can be reasonably approximated) in your problem, it behooves you to use them to derive better threshold values.

Table 3.3: Cost of Mistakes for Different Decision Thresholds

DECISION THRESHOLD	FALSE NEGATIVE COST	FALSE POSITIVE COST	TOTAL COST
0.0	1,000	1,900	2,900
0.25	3,000	1,400	4,400
0.5	9,000	900	9,900
0.75	18,000	300	18,300
1.00	26,000	100	26,100

Note that the relative cost of total FPs versus FNs depends on the proportion of positive and negative examples in the data set. The rocks-versus-mines data set has an equal number of positives and negatives (mines and rocks). That was presumably determined by an experimental protocol. The proportion of positives and negatives encountered in actual practice may differ. If the numbers are likely to be different when the system is deployed, you need to make some adjustments to account for the proportions in actual use.

The data scientist may not have the costs available but may still want a method to characterize the overall performance of the classifier instead of using the mis-classification error rate for a particular decision threshold. A common technique for doing that is called the *receiver operating characteristic* or ROC curve (http://en.wikipedia.org/wiki/Receiver_operating_characteristic).

ROC inherits its name from its original application—processing returns from a radar receiver to determine the presence or absence of hostile aircraft. The ROC curve yields a single plot that summarizes all of these different contingency tables. The ROC curve plots the true positive rate (abbreviated TPR) versus the false positive rate (FPR). TPR is the proportion of positive examples that are correctly classified as positive (see Equation 3.8). FPR is the number of FPs relative to the total number of actual negatives (see Equation 3.9). In terms of the elements of the contingency table, these are given by the following formulas:

$$TPR = \frac{TP}{TP + FN}$$

Equation 3.8: True positive rate

$$FPR = \frac{FP}{TN + FP}$$

Equation 3.9: False positive rate

As a simple thought experiment, consider using an extremely low value for the decision threshold. For a low value, every example is predicted as positive. That gives 1.0 for TPR. Because everything is classified as positive, there are no FNs (FN is 0.0). It also gives 1.0 for FPR because nothing gets classified as negative (TN is 0.0). However, when the decision threshold is set very high, TP is equal to zero, and so TPR is also zero and FP is also zero because nothing gets classified as positive. Therefore, FPR is also zero. The following two figures were drawn using the `pylab roc_curve()` and `auc()` functions. Figure 3.10 shows the ROC curve-based performance on in-sample data. Figure 3.11 shows the ROC curve based on out-of-sample data.

The ROC curve for the classifier that operates by randomly deciding rock or mine forms a diagonal line from the lower-left corner to the upper-right corner of the plot. That line is often drawn onto ROC curves as a reference point. For a perfect classifier, the ROC curve steps straight up from (0, 0) to (0, 1) and then goes straight across to (1, 1). Not surprisingly, Figure 3.10 (on in-sample data) comes closer to perfection than Figure 3.11 (on out-of-sample data). The closer that a classifier can come to hitting the upper-left corner, the better it is. If the ROC curve drops significantly below the diagonal line, it usually means that the data scientist has gotten a sign switched somewhere and should examine his code carefully.

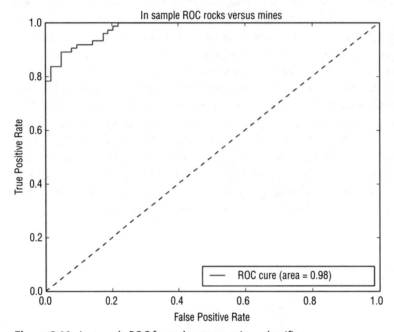

Figure 3.10: In-sample ROC for rocks-versus-mines classifier

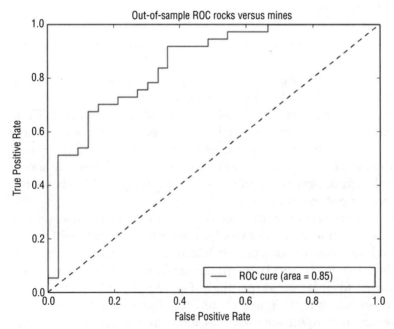

Figure 3.11: Out-of-sample ROC for rocks-versus-mines classifier

Figures 3.10 and 3.11 also show the area under the curve (AUC) numbers. AUC, as the name suggests, is the area under the ROC curve. A perfect classifier has an AUC of 1.0, and random guessing has an AUC of 0.5. AUCs for Figures 3.10 and 3.11 provide another demonstration that performance estimates based on the error on the training set (in-sample data) overestimate performance. The AUC on in-sample data is 0.98. The AUC on out-of-sample data is 0.85.

Some of the methods used for measuring binary classifier performance will also work for multiclass classifiers. Misclassification error still makes sense, and the confusion matrix also works. There are also multiclass generalizations of the ROC curve and AUC.[1]

Simulating Performance of Deployed Models

The examples from the preceding section demonstrated the need for testing performance on data not included in the training set to get a useful estimate of expected performance once a predictive model is deployed. The example broke the available labeled data into two subsets. One subset, called the *training set*, contained approximately two-thirds of the available data and was used to fitting an ordinary least squares model. The second subset, which contained the remaining third of the available data, was called the *test set* and was used only for determining performance (not used during training of the model). This is a standard procedure in machine learning.

Test set sizes range from 25 percent to 35 percent of the data, although there aren't any hard-and-fast rules about the sizes. One thing to keep in mind is that the performance of the trained model deteriorates as the size of the training data set shrinks. Taking out too much data from the training set can prove detrimental to end performance.

Another approach to holding out data is called *n-fold cross-validation*. Figure 3.12 shows schematically how a data set is divided up for training and testing with n-fold cross-validation. The set is divided into n disjointed sets of roughly equal sizes. In the figure, n is 5. Several training and testing passes are made through the data. In the first pass, the first block of data is held out for testing, and the remaining $n-1$ are used for training. In the second pass, the second block is held out for testing, and the other $n-1$ are used for training. This process is continued until all the data have been held out (five times for the five-fold example depicted in Figure 3.12).

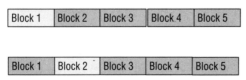

Figure 3.12: N-fold cross-validation

The n-fold cross-validation process yields an estimate of the prediction error and has several samples of the error so that it can estimate error bounds on the error. It can keep more of the data in the training set, which generally gives lower generalization errors and better final performance. For example, if the 10-fold cross-validation is chosen, then only 10 percent of the data is held out for each training pass. These features of n-fold cross-validation come at the expense of taking more training time. The approach of taking a fixed holdout set has the advantage of faster training, because it employs only one pass through the training data. Taking a fixed holdout set is probably a better choice when the training times are unbearable with n-fold cross-validation and when there's so much training data available that some extra in the holdout set won't adversely affect performance.

Another thing to keep in mind is that the sample should be representative of the whole data set. The sampling plan used in the example in the preceding section was not a random sample. It was a sample of every third data point. Spreading the samples uniformly through the data usually works fine. However, you do need to avoid sampling in a way that introduces a bias in training and test sets. For example, if you were given data that was sampled once per day and arranged in order of sampling date, then coding seven-fold cross-validation and sampling every seventh point should be avoided.

Sampling may need to be carefully controlled if the phenomenon being studied has unusual statistics. Care may have to be taken to preserve the statistical peculiarities in the test sample. Examples of this include predicting rare events like fraud or ad clicks. The events being modeled are so infrequent that random sampling may over- or under-represent them in the test set and lead to erroneous estimates of performance. Stratified sampling (http://en.wikipedia.org/ wiki/Stratified_sampling) divides the data into separate subsets that are separately sampled and then recombined. When the labels are rare events, you might need to separately sample the fraudulent examples and the legitimate examples and then combine them for the test set to match the training set and, more importantly, the new data upon which the model will be used.

After a model has been trained and tested, it is good practice to recombine the training and test data into a single set and retrain the model on the larger data set. The out-of-sample testing procedure will have already given good estimates of the expected prediction errors. That was the purpose of holding out some of the data. The model will perform better and generalize better if trained on more data. The deployed model should be trained on all the data.

This section supplied you with tools to quantify the performance of your predictive model. The next section shows you how to replace the intuitive graphical comparisons of model and problem complexity that you saw in the section "Factors Driving Algorithm Choices and Performance—Complexity and Data" with numerical comparison. This replacement makes it possible to mechanize some of the selection process.

Achieving Harmony between Model and Data

This section uses ordinary least squares (OLS) regression to illustrate several things. First, it illustrates how OLS can sometimes *overfit* a problem. Overfitting means that there's a significant discrepancy between errors on the training data and errors on the test data, such as you saw in the previous section where OLS was used to solve the rocks-versus-mines classification problem. Second, it introduces two methods for overcoming the overfit problem with OLS. These methods will cultivate your intuition and set the stage for the penalized linear regression methods that are covered in more depth in Chapter 4. In addition, the methods for overcoming overfitting have a property that is common to most modern machine learning algorithms. Modern algorithms generate a number of models of varying complexity and then use out-of-sample performance to balance model complexity, problem complexity, and data set richness and thus determine which model to deploy. This process will be used repeatedly throughout the rest of the book.

Ordinary least squares regression serves as a good prototype for machine learning algorithms in general. It's a supervised algorithm that has a training procedure and a deployment procedure. It can be overfit in some circumstances. It shares these features with other more modern function approximation algorithms. OLS is missing an important feature of modern algorithms, however. In its original formulation (the most familiar formulation), there's no means to throttle it back when it overfits. It's like having a car that only runs at full throttle (great when there's plenty of road, but tough to use in tight circumstances). Fortunately, there's been a lot of work on ordinary least squares regression since its invention more than 200 years ago by Gauss and Legendre. This section introduces two of the methods for adjusting the throttle on ordinary least squares regression. One is called *forward stepwise regression*; the other is called *ridge regression*.

Choosing a Model to Balance Problem Complexity, Model Complexity, and Data Set Size

A couple of examples will illustrate how modern machine learning techniques can be tuned to best fit a given problem and data set. The first example is a modification to ordinary least squares regression called forward stepwise regression. Here's how it works. Recall Equations 3.1 and 3.2, which define the problem being solved (see Equations 3.10 and 3.11 here, which repeat those equations).

The vector Y contains the labels. And the matrix X contains the attributes available to predict the labels.

$$Y = \begin{matrix} y_1 \\ y_2 \\ \vdots \\ y_m \end{matrix}$$

Equation 3.10: Vector of numeric labels

$$X = \begin{matrix} x_{11} & x_{12} & \cdots & x_{1n} \\ x_{21} & x_{22} & \cdots & x_{2n} \\ \vdots & \vdots & & \ddots \\ x_{m1} & x_{m2} & \cdots & x_{mn} \end{matrix}$$

Equation 3.11: Matrix of numeric attributes

If this is a regression problem, then Y is a column vector of real numbers, and the linear problem is to find a column vector of weights and a scalar 0 (see Equation 3.12).

The values for are selected so that Y is well approximated (see Equation 3.13).

$$\beta = \begin{matrix} \beta_1 \\ \beta_2 \\ \vdots \\ \beta_m \end{matrix}$$

Equation 3.12: Vector of coefficients for linear model

If the number of columns of X is the same as the number of rows of X and the columns of X are independent (not linear multiples of one another), then X can be inverted and the ~ can be replaced with =. A coefficient vector will make the linear fit the labels exactly. That's too good to be true. The problem is one of overfitting (that is, getting terrific performance on the training data that cannot be replicated on new data). In real problems, this is not a good outcome. The source of overfitting is having too many columns of data in X. The answer might be to get rid of some of the columns of X. However, getting rid of some involves deciding how many to eliminate and which ones should be eliminated. The brute-force method is called *best subset selection*.

$$Y \sim X\beta + \begin{matrix} \beta_0 \\ \beta_0 \\ \vdots \\ \beta_0 \end{matrix}$$

Equation 3.13: Approximating labels as linear function of attributes

Using Forward Stepwise Regression to Control Overfitting

The following code provides an outline of the algorithm for best subset selection. The basic idea is to impose a constraint (say, nCol) on the number of columns and then take all subsets of the columns of X that have that number of columns, perform ordinary least squares regression, identify the nCol subset that has the least out-of-sample error, increment nCol, and repeat. The process results in a list of the best choice of one-column subsets: two-column subsets up to the full matrix X (the all-column subset). It also yields the performance of each of these. Then the next step is to determine whether to deploy the one-column version, the two-column version, and so on. But that's relatively easy; just pick the one with the least errors:

```
Initialize: Out_of_sample_error = NULL
Break X and Y into test and training sets
for i in range(number of columns in X):
  for each subset of X having i+1 columns:
     fit ordinary least squares model
     Out_of_sample_error.append(least error among subsets containing
        i+1 columns)
Pick the subset corresponding to least overall error
```

The problem with best subset selection is that it requires too much calculation for even modest numbers of attributes (columns of X). For example, 10 attributes leads to $2^{10} = 1{,}000$ subsets. There are several techniques that avoid this. The following code shows the procedure for forward stepwise regression. The idea with forward stepwise regression is to start with one-column subsets and then, given the best single column, to find the best second column to append instead of evaluating all possible two-column subsets. Pseudo-code for forward stepwise regression is given here:

```
Initialize: ColumnList = NULL
Out-of-sample-error = NULL
Break X and Y into test and training sets
For number of column in X:
  For each trialColumn (column not in ColumnList):
```

```
Build submatrix of X using ColumnList + trialColumn
Train OLS on submatrix and store RSS Error on test data
ColumnList.append(trialColumn that minimizes RSS Error)
Out-of-sample-error.append(minimum RSS Error)
```

Best subset selection and forward stepwise regression have similar processes. They train a series of models (several for one column, several for two columns, and so on). They result in a parameterized family of models (all linear regression parameterized on number of columns). The models vary in complexity, and the final model is selected from the family on the basis of performance on out-of-sample error.

Listing 3.3 shows Python code implementing forward stepwise regression on the wine data set.

Listing 3.3: Forward Stepwise Regression: Wine Quality Data—fwdStepwiseWine.py

```python
__author__ = 'mike_bowles'

from Read_Fcns import list_read_wine
import numpy as np
from sklearn import datasets, linear_model
from math import sqrt
import matplotlib.pyplot as plt

def xattrSelect(x, idxSet):
    #takes X matrix and return subset containing columns in idxSet
    xOut = []
    for row in x:
        xOut.append([row[i] for i in idxSet])
    return(xOut)

#read data into iterable
names, xList,labels = list_read_wine()

#divide attributes and labels into training and test sets
indices = range(len(xList))
xListTest = [xList[i] for i in indices if i%3 == 0 ]
xListTrain = [xList[i] for i in indices if i%3 != 0 ]
labelsTest = [labels[i] for i in indices if i%3 == 0]
labelsTrain = [labels[i] for i in indices if i%3 != 0]

#build list of attributes one-at-a-time - starting with empty
attributeList = []
index = range(len(xList[1]))
indexSet = set(index)
indexSeq = []
oosError = []
```

```
for i in index:
    attSet = set(attributeList)
    #attributes not in list already
    attTrySet = indexSet - attSet
    #form into list
    attTry = [ii for ii in attTrySet]
    errorList = []
    attTemp = []
    #try each attribute not in set to see which one gives least oos error
    for iTry in attTry:
        attTemp = [] + attributeList
        attTemp.append(iTry)

        #use attTemp to form training and testing sub matrices
        xTrainTemp = xattrSelect(xListTrain, attTemp)
        xTestTemp = xattrSelect(xListTest, attTemp)

        #form into numpy arrays
        xTrain = np.array(xTrainTemp); yTrain = np.array(labelsTrain)
        xTest = np.array(xTestTemp); yTest = np.array(labelsTest)

        #use sci-kit learn linear regression
        wineQModel = linear_model.LinearRegression()
        wineQModel.fit(xTrain,yTrain)

        #use trained model to generate prediction and calculate rmsError
        rmsError = np.linalg.norm((yTest-wineQModel.predict(xTest)), 2)\
        /sqrt(len(yTest))
        errorList.append(rmsError)
        attTemp = []

    iBest = np.argmin(errorList)
    attributeList.append(attTry[iBest])
    oosError.append(errorList[iBest])

print("Out of sample error versus attribute set size" )
print(oosError)
print("\n" + "Best attribute indices")
print(attributeList)
namesList = [names[i] for i in attributeList]
print("\n" + "Best attribute names")
print(namesList)

#Plot error versus number of attributes
x = range(len(oosError))
plt.plot(x, oosError, 'k')
plt.xlabel('Number of Attributes')
plt.ylabel('Error (RMS)')
plt.show()
```

```
#Plot histogram of out of sample errors for best number of attributes
#Identify index corresponding to min value,
#retrain with the corresponding attributes
#Use resulting model to predict against out of sample data.
indexBest = oosError.index(min(oosError))
attributesBest = attributeList[1:(indexBest+1)]

#Define column-wise subsets of xListTrain and xListTest convert to numpy
xTrainTemp = xattrSelect(xListTrain, attributesBest)
xTestTemp = xattrSelect(xListTest, attributesBest)
xTrain = np.array(xTrainTemp); xTest = np.array(xTestTemp)

#train and plot error histogram
wineQModel = linear_model.LinearRegression()
wineQModel.fit(xTrain,yTrain)
errorVector = yTest-wineQModel.predict(xTest)
plt.hist(errorVector)
plt.xlabel("Bin Boundaries")
plt.ylabel("Counts")
plt.show()

#scatter plot of actual versus predicted
plt.scatter(wineQModel.predict(xTest), yTest, s=100, alpha=0.10)
plt.xlabel('Predicted Taste Score')
plt.ylabel('Actual Taste Score')
plt.show()
```

The preceding listing includes a small function to extract selected columns from the X matrix (in the form of a list of lists). Then it breaks the X matrix and the vector of labels into training and test sets. After that, the code follows the preceding algorithm description. A pass through the algorithm begins with a subset of attributes that are included in the solution. For the first pass, this subset is empty. For subsequent passes, the subset includes the attributes selected one at a time during earlier passes. Each pass selects a single new attribute to add to the subset of attributes. The attribute to be added is chosen by testing each non-included attribute to see which one results in the best performance when added to the subset. In turn, each attribute is added to the attribute subset and ordinary least squares is used to fit a linear model with the resulting attribute subset. For each attribute tested, the out-of-sample performance is measured. The tested attribute that yields the best root sum of squares (RSS) error is added to the attribute set, and the associated RSS error is captured.

Figure 3.13 plots the RMSEs as a function of the number of attributes included in the regression. The error decreases until nine attributes are included and then increases somewhat.

Listing 3.4 shows numeric output for forward stepwise regression applied to wine quality data.

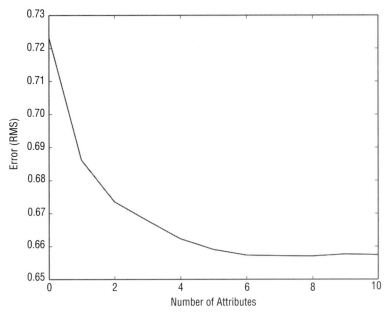

Figure 3.13: Wine quality prediction error using forward stepwise regression

Listing 3.4: Forward Stepwise Regression Output

```
Printed Output:

Out of sample error versus attribute set size
[0.7234259255116278, 0.6860993152837196, 0.6734365033420278,
0.6677033213897796, 0.6622558568522271, 0.6590004754154625,
0.6572717206143076, 0.65709058062077, 0.6569993096446137,
0.657581894004473, 0.657390986901134]

Best attribute indices
[10, 1, 9, 4, 6, 8, 5, 3, 2, 7, 0]

Best attribute names
alcohol, volatile acidity, sulphates, chlorides, total sulfur dioxide,
pH,
free sulfur dioxide, residual sugar, citric acid, density, fixed acidity
```

The first list shows the RSS error. The error decreases until the 10th element in the list, and then gets larger again. The associated column indices are shown in the next list. The last list gives the names (column headers) of the associated attributes.

Evaluating and Understanding Your Predictive Model

Several other plots are helpful in understanding the performance of a trained algorithm and can point the way to making improvements in its performance. Figure 3.14 shows a scatter plot of the true labels plotted versus the predicted labels for points in the test set. Ideally, all of the points in Figure 3.14 would lie on a 45-degree line—the line where the true labels and the predicted labels are equal. Because the real scores are integers, the scatter plot shows horizontal rows of points. When the true values take on a small number of values, it is useful to make the data points partially transparent so that the darkness can indicate the accumulation of many points in one area of the graph. Actual taste scores of 5 and 6 are reproduced fairly well. The more extreme values are not as well predicted by the system. Generally speaking, machine learning algorithms do worse at the edges of a data set.

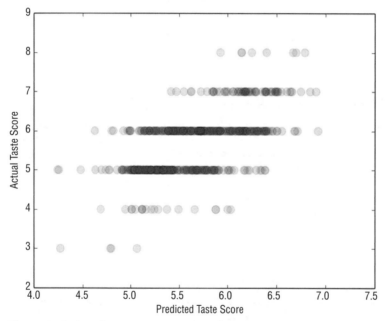

Figure 3.14: Actual taste scores versus predictions generated with forward stepwise regression

Figure 3.15 shows a histogram of the prediction error for forward stepwise prediction predicting wine taste scores. Sometimes the error histogram will have two or more discrete peaks. Perhaps it will have a small peak on the far right or far left of the graph. In that case, it may be possible to find an explanation for the different peaks in the error and to reduce the prediction error by adding a new attribute that explains the membership in one or the other of the groups of points.

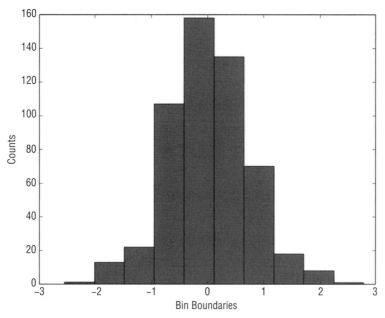

Figure 3.15: Histogram of wine taste prediction error with forward stepwise regression

You want to note several things about this output. First, let's reiterate the process. The process is to train a family of models (in this case, ordinary linear regression trained on column-wise subsets of X). The series of models is parameterized (in this case, by the number of attributes that are used in the linear model). The model to deploy is chosen to minimize the out-of-sample error. The number of attributes to be incorporated in the solution can be called a *complexity parameter*. Models with larger complexity parameters have more free parameters and are more likely to overfit the data than less-complex models.

Also note that the attributes have become ordered by their importance in predicting quality. In the list of column numbers and the associated list of attribute names, the first in the list is the first attribute chosen, the second was next, and so on. The attributes used come out in a nice ordered list. This is an important and desirable feature of a machine learning technique. Early stages of a machine learning task mostly involve hunting for (or constructing) the best set of attributes for making predictions. Having techniques to rank attributes in order of importance helps in that process. The other algorithms developed in this book will also have this property.

The last observation regards picking a model from the family that machine learning techniques generate. The more complicated the model, the less well it will generalize. It is better to err on the side of a less-complicated model. The earlier example indicates that there's very little degradation in performance between the 9th (best) model and the 10th model (a change in the 4th significant digit). Best practice would be to remove those attributes even if they were better in the 4th significant digit in order to be conservative.

Control Overfitting by Penalizing Regression Coefficients— Ridge Regression

This section describes another method for modifying ordinary least squares regression to control model complexity and to avoid overfitting. This method serves as a first introduction to penalized linear regression. You'll see more coverage of this in Chapter 4.

Ordinary least squares regression seeks to find scalar β_0 and vector β that satisfy (see Equation 3.14).

$$\beta_0^*, \beta^* = argmin_{\beta_0, \beta} \left(\frac{1}{m} \sum_{i=1}^{m} \left(y_i - \left(\beta_0 + x_i \beta \right) \right)^2 \right)$$

Equation 3.14: OLS minimization problem

The expression *argmin* means the "values of β_0 and that minimize the expression." The resulting coefficients β_0^*, β^* are the ordinary least squares solution. Best subset regression and forward stepwise regression throttle back ordinary regression by limiting the number of attributes used. That's equivalent to imposing a constraint that some of the entries in the vector β be equal to zero. Another approach is called *coefficient penalized regression*. Coefficient penalized regression accomplishes the same thing by making all the coefficients smaller instead of making some of them zero. One version of coefficient penalized linear regression is called *ridge regression*. Equation 3.15 shows the problem formulation for ridge regression.

$$\beta_0^*, \beta^* = argmin_{\beta_0, \beta} \left(\frac{1}{m} \sum_{i=1}^{m} \left(y_i - \left(\beta_0 + x_i \beta \right) \right)^2 + \alpha \beta^T \beta \right)$$

Equation 3.15: Ridge regression minimization problem

The difference between Equation 3.15 and ordinary least squares (Equation 3.14) is the addition of the $\alpha \beta^T \beta$ term. The $\beta^T \beta$ term is the square of the Euclidean norm of β (the vector of coefficients). The variable is a complexity parameter for this formulation of the problem. If $\alpha = 0$, the problem becomes ordinary least squares regression. When α becomes large, β (the vector of coefficients) approaches zero, and only the constant term β_0 is available to predict the labels y_i. Ridge regression is available in scikit-learn. Listing 3.5 shows the code for solving the wine taste regression problem using ridge regression.

Listing 3.5: Predicting Wine Taste with Ridge Regression—ridgeWine.py

```
__author__ = 'mike_bowles'

from Read_Fcns import list_read_wine
import numpy as np
```

```
from sklearn import datasets, linear_model
from math import sqrt
import matplotlib.pyplot as plt

#read data into lists
names, xList, labels = list_read_wine()

#divide attributes and labels into training and test sets
indices = range(len(xList))
xListTest = [xList[i] for i in indices if i%3 == 0 ]
xListTrain = [xList[i] for i in indices if i%3 != 0 ]
labelsTest = [labels[i] for i in indices if i%3 == 0]
labelsTrain = [labels[i] for i in indices if i%3 != 0]

xTrain = np.array(xListTrain); yTrain = np.array(labelsTrain)
xTest = np.array(xListTest); yTest = np.array(labelsTest)

alphaList = [0.1**i for i in [0,1, 2, 3, 4, 5, 6]]

rmsError = []
for alph in alphaList:
    wineRidgeModel = linear_model.Ridge(alpha=alph)
    wineRidgeModel.fit(xTrain, yTrain)
    rmsError.append(np.linalg.norm((yTest-wineRidgeModel.\
                        predict(xTest)), 2)/sqrt(len(yTest)))

print('{:18}'.format("RMS Error"), "alpha")
for i in range(len(rmsError)):
    print(rmsError[i], alphaList[i])

#plot curve of out-of-sample error versus alpha
x = range(len(rmsError))
plt.plot(x, rmsError, 'k')
plt.xlabel('-log(alpha)')
plt.ylabel('Error (RMS)')
plt.show()

#Plot histogram of out of sample errors for best alpha value and
#scatter plot of actual versus predicted
#Identify index corresponding to min value, retrain with the
#corresponding value of alpha
#Use resulting model to predict against out of sample data.
indexBest = rmsError.index(min(rmsError))
alph = alphaList[indexBest]
wineRidgeModel = linear_model.Ridge(alpha=alph)
wineRidgeModel.fit(xTrain, yTrain)
errorVector = yTest-wineRidgeModel.predict(xTest)
plt.hist(errorVector)
plt.xlabel("Bin Boundaries")
plt.ylabel("Counts")
plt.show()
```

```
plt.scatter(wineRidgeModel.predict(xTest), yTest, s=100, alpha=0.10)
plt.xlabel('Predicted Taste Score')
plt.ylabel('Actual Taste Score')
plt.show()
```

Recall that the forward stepwise regression algorithm produced a sequence of different models—the first with one attribute, the next with two attributes, and so on until the final model included all the attributes. The code for ridge regression also has a sequence of models. Instead of different numbers of attributes, the sequence of ridge regression models have different values of α—the parameter that determines the severity of the penalty on the β's. The construction of sequence of α's decreases them by powers of 10. Generally speaking, you'll want to make them decrease exponentially, not by a fixed increment. The range needs to be fairly wide and may take some experimentation to establish.

Figure 3.16 plots the RMSE as a function of the ridge complexity parameter α. The parameter is arranged from largest value on the left to smallest value on the right. It is conventional to show the least complex model on the left side of the plot and the most complex on the right side. The plot shows much the same character as with forward stepwise regression. The errors are roughly the same, but favor forward stepwise regression slightly.

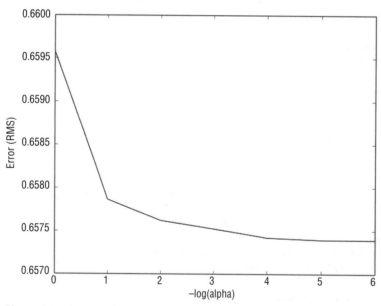

Figure 3.16: Wine quality prediction error using ridge regression

Listing 3.6 shows the output from the ridge regression. The numbers show that ridge regression has roughly the same character as forward stepwise regression. The numbers slightly favor forward stepwise regression.

Listing 3.6: Ridge Regression Output

```
RMS Error alpha
(0.65957881763424564, 1.0)
(0.65786109188085928, 0.1)
(0.65761721446402455, 0.010000000000000002)
(0.65752164826417536, 0.0010000000000000002)
(0.65741906801092931, 0.00010000000000000002)
(0.65739416288512531, 1.0000000000000003e-05)
(0.65739130871558593, 1.0000000000000004e-06)
```

Figure 3.17 shows the scatter plot of actual taste score versus predicted taste score for the ridge regression predictor trained on wine taste data. Figure 3.18 shows the histogram of prediction error.

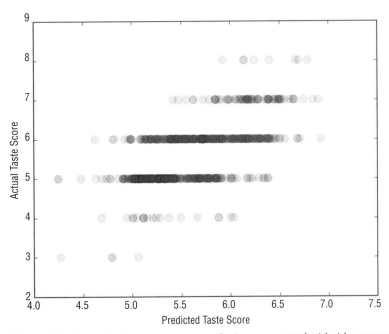

Figure 3.17: Actual taste scores versus predictions generated with ridge regression

You can apply the same general method to classification problems. The section "Measuring the Performance of Predictive Models" discussed several methods for quantifying classifier performance. The methods outlined included using misclassification error, associating economic costs to the various prediction outcomes, and using the area under the ROC curve (AUC) to quantify performance. That section built a classifier using ordinary least squares regression. Listing 3.7 shows Python code that follows that same general plan. Instead of OLS, it uses ridge regression as a regression method (with a complexity tuning parameter) for building the rocks-versus-mines classifier and uses AUC as the performance measure for the classifier. The program in Listing 3.7 is similar to the wine taste prediction with ridge regression. The big difference is that the program uses the predictions on the test data and the test labels as input to the roc_curve program from the scikit-learn package. That makes it easy to calculate the AUC for each pass through the training. These are accumulated, and the printed values are shown in Listing 3.8.

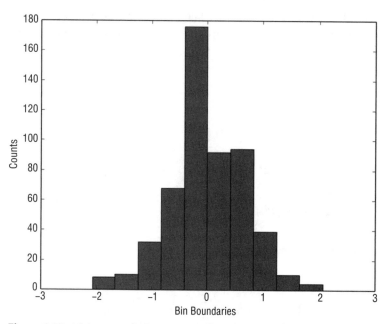

Figure 3.18: Histogram of wine taste prediction error with ridge regression

Listing 3.7: Rocks Versus Mines Using Ridge Regression—classifierRidgeRocksVMines.py

```
__author__ = 'mike_bowles'

import numpy as np
from Read_Fcns import list_read_rvm
from sklearn import datasets, linear_model
from sklearn.metrics import roc_curve, auc
import matplotlib.pyplot as plt
```

```
#read data from uci data repository
xList, labels = list_read_rvm()

#divide attribute label vector into training and test sets (2/3, 1/3)
indices = range(len(xList))
xListTest = [xList[i] for i in indices if i%3 == 0 ]
xListTrain = [xList[i] for i in indices if i%3 != 0 ]
labelsTest = [labels[i] for i in indices if i%3 == 0]
labelsTrain = [labels[i] for i in indices if i%3 != 0]

xTrain = np.array(xListTrain); yTrain = np.array(labelsTrain)
xTest = np.array(xListTest); yTest = np.array(labelsTest)

alphaList = [0.1**i for i in [-3, -2, -1, 0,1, 2, 3, 4, 5]]

aucList = []
for alph in alphaList:
    rocksVMinesRidgeModel = linear_model.Ridge(alpha=alph)
    rocksVMinesRidgeModel.fit(xTrain, yTrain)
    fpr, tpr, thresholds = roc_curve(yTest,rocksVMinesRidgeModel.\
                    predict(xTest))
    roc_auc = auc(fpr, tpr)
    aucList.append(roc_auc)


print('{:18}'.format("AUC"), "alpha")
for i in range(len(aucList)):
    print(aucList[i], alphaList[i])

#plot auc values versus alpha values
x = [-3, -2, -1, 0,1, 2, 3, 4, 5]
plt.plot(x, aucList)
plt.xlabel('-log(alpha)')
plt.ylabel('AUC')
plt.show()

#visualize the performance of the best classifier
indexBest = aucList.index(max(aucList))
alph = alphaList[indexBest]
rocksVMinesRidgeModel = linear_model.Ridge(alpha=alph)
rocksVMinesRidgeModel.fit(xTrain, yTrain)

#scatter plot of actual vs predicted
plt.scatter(rocksVMinesRidgeModel.predict(xTest), yTest, \
        s=100, alpha=0.25)
plt.xlabel("Predicted Value")
plt.ylabel("Actual Value")
plt.show()
```

Listing 3.8 shows the AUC and associated alpha (multiplier on the coefficient penalty).

Listing 3.8: Output from Classification Model for Rocks Versus Mines Using Ridge Regression

```
AUC alpha
(0.84111384111384113, 999.9999999999999)
(0.86404586404586403, 99.99999999999999)
(0.9074529074529073, 10.0)
(0.91809991809991809, 1.0)
(0.88288288288288286, 0.1)
(0.8615888615888615, 0.010000000000000002)
(0.85176085176085159, 0.0010000000000000002)
(0.85094185094185093, 0.00010000000000000002)
(0.84930384930384917, 1.0000000000000003e-05)
```

A value of AUC close to 1 means great performance. A value near 0.5 is not good. So the goal with AUC is to maximize it instead of minimizing it, as was done with MSE in the earlier examples. AUC shows a fairly sharp peak at $\alpha = 1.0$. The numbers and the plot show a fairly significant drop off in performance relative to $\alpha = 1.0$. Recall that as alpha gets smaller, the solution approaches the solution to the unconstrained linear regression problem. The drop-off in performance for values of alpha smaller than 1.0 indicates that the unconstrained solution won't perform as well as ridge regression does. In the earlier section "Measuring the Performance of Predictive Models," you saw the results for unconstrained ordinary least squares. The AUC on in-sample data was 0.98, and on out-of-sample data it was 0.85—very close to the AUC using ridge regression with a relatively small alpha (1E-5). Ridge regression results in a significant improvement in performance.

The issue here is that the attribute space for the rocks-versus-mines problem is 60 attributes wide while the full data set contains 208 rows of data. After the removal of 70 examples to be used as holdout data, 138 rows of data are available for training. That's more than twice the number of attributes, but the unconstrained (ordinary least squares) solution still overfits the data. This situation might be a good candidate for trying 10-fold cross-validation. That would result in only 20 examples (10 percent of the data set) being held out on each of the folds and might show some consequent improvement in performance. That approach comes up in Chapter 5, "Building Predictive Models Using Penalized Linear Methods."

Figure 3.19 plots the AUC as a function of the alpha parameter. That gives a visual demonstration of the value of reducing the complexity of the ordinary least squares solution by imposing a constraint on the Euclidean length of the coefficient vector.

Figure 3.20 shows the scatter plot of actual classification versus prediction for this classifier. This plot has a similar character to the scatter plot for wine prediction. Because there are a discrete number of actual outcomes, the scatter plot is composed of two horizontal rows of points.

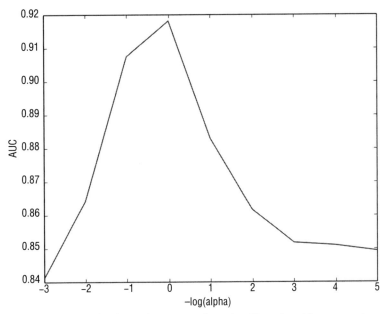

Figure 3.19: AUC for the rocks-versus-mines classifier using ridge regression

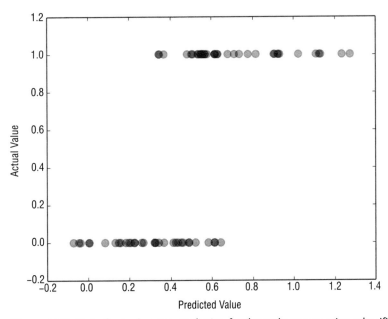

Figure 3.20: Plot of actual versus prediction for the rocks-versus-mines classifier using ridge regression

This section introduced and explored two extensions to ordinary least squares regression. These served as illustrations of the process of training and balancing a modern predictive model. In addition, these extensions help introduce the more general penalized regression methods that will be explained in Chapter 4 and used to solve a variety of problems in Chapter 5.

Using PySpark for Training Penalized Regression Models on Extremely Large Data Sets

Listing 3.9 at the end of this section demonstrates a PySpark implementation of the wine ridge regression that you saw Listing 3.5 and in the performance tables and charts that followed it. The similarities between the two help you see how accessible these techniques are to you once you've mastered the basics of using them. There are also some differences in the details that are worth pointing out and discussing.

The gross outlines of the plain Python version and the PySpark version are the same:

- Read in the data and break it into training and test sets.
- Define a list of penalty parameters (alpha) for generating models of different complexities.
- Build models for each value of alpha and determine their performance by running them on the held-out test data.

The code structure for the PySpark version was copy-pasted from the Python version.

The differences between the two can be divided into several categories. Some differences are dictated by differences in underlying code structure. For example, in the Python version a named object is specified for the wine model and the .fit() function trains it. In the PySpark version the type of model and its parameters is given a name and the .fit() function returns the trained model into a different named object. After a little practice with both of these, you'll become familiar with these minor differences in syntax.

The differences in data set sizes lead to some other differences. As one example, the PySpark version exposes a maxIter variable that controls how many passes are made through the data in order to achieve convergence to the final answer. That's because with large enough data sets the compute time can become burdensome either in time or money. That's less of an issue for the Python version. Another example is the portion of the PySpark code where the inputs are defined as specified columns from the input data set. That seems odd in the context of data like the wine data set, where the columns have already been selected for purposes of building predictive models. In many real problems the data chosen for making predictions is part of a larger data set and may be part of what you experiment with to get the best answer. If the data sets are large, it may cost too much storage space to copy them over, so PySpark lets you select columns from a larger data frame.

Difference in implementation of the algorithms can cause differences in the answers. As you can see in Figure 3.21, the overall shape of the performance versus regularization parameter curve is about the same. But there is a difference in the numbers as you can see from the printed output. The differences are small and they achieve their lowest value for the same value of the regularization parameter (which is what you're looking for).

Listing 3.9: Spark Implementation of Ridge Regression on Wine Data—linear_regression_w_ spark.py

```
__author__ = 'mike_bowles'


#Import sparksession
from pyspark.sql import SparkSession
from pyspark.ml.feature import VectorAssembler
from pyspark.ml.regression import LinearRegression
import matplotlib.pyplot as plt


spark = SparkSession.builder.appName("regress_wine_data").getOrCreate()


#read in abalone data as pandas data frame and create Spark data frame.
import pandas as pd
from pandas import DataFrame
from Read_Fcns import pd_read_wine


wine_df = pd_read_wine()


#Create spark dataframe for wine data
wine_sp_df = spark.createDataFrame(wine_df)
print('Column Names', wine_sp_df.columns, '\n\n')


vectorAssembler = VectorAssembler(inputCols = ['fixed acidity', \
    'volatile acidity', 'citric acid', 'residual sugar', 'chlorides', \
    'free sulfur dioxide', 'total sulfur dioxide', 'density', 'pH', \
                    'sulphates', 'alcohol'], outputCol = 'features')
v_wine_df = vectorAssembler.transform(wine_sp_df)
vwine_df = v_wine_df.select(['features', 'quality'])


splits = vwine_df.randomSplit([0.66, 0.34])
xTrain_sp = splits[0]
xTest_sp = splits[1]


alphaList = [0.1**i for i in [0,1, 2, 3, 4, 5, 6]]


rmsError = []
for alph in alphaList:
    wine_ridge_sp = LinearRegression(featuresCol = 'features', \
```

```
            labelCol='quality', maxIter=100, regParam=alph, \
            elasticNetParam=0.0)
        wine_ridge_sp_model = wine_ridge_sp.fit(xTrain_sp)
        test_result = wine_ridge_sp_model.evaluate(xTest_sp)
        rmsError.append(test_result.rootMeanSquaredError)

print('{:18}'.format("RMS Error"), "alpha")
for i in range(len(rmsError)):
    print(rmsError[i], alphaList[i])

#plot curve of out-of-sample error versus alpha
x = range(len(rmsError))
plt.plot(x, rmsError, 'k')
plt.xlabel('-log(alpha)')
plt.ylabel('Error (RMS)')
plt.savefig('linear_regression_w_spark.png', dpi=500)
plt.show()

Printed Output:
Column Names ['fixed acidity', 'volatile acidity', 'citric acid',
'residual sugar', 'chlorides', 'free sulfur dioxide',
'total sulfur dioxide', 'density', 'pH', 'sulphates', 'alcohol',
'quality']


RMS Error               alpha
0.6581102654673014  1.0
0.6290665424695905  0.1
0.6265318770170585  0.010000000000000002
0.6263116678129375  0.0010000000000000002
0.6262902244707693  0.00010000000000000002
0.6262880862875198  1.0000000000000003e-05
0.6262878725310369  1.0000000000000004e-06
```

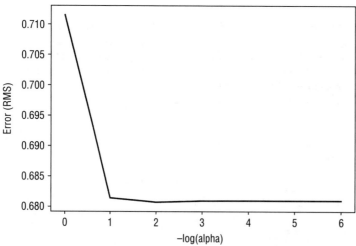

Figure 3.21: Wine quality prediction error using PySpark version of ridge regression

Summary

This chapter covered several topics that serve as a foundation for what comes later. First, the chapter provided visual demonstrations of problem complexity and model complexity and discussed how those factors and data set sizes conspire to determine predictive performance on a given problem. Easily adjusted model complexity and consequent performance measurement enable you to find the best balance of these elements for your problem. The chapter first reviewed a number of different metrics for prediction performance associated with the different problem types (regression, classification, and multiclass classification). These cover most of the problem types that arise as part of the function approximation problem. The chapter described two methods (holdout and n-fold cross-validation) for estimating performance on new data. The chapter introduced the conceptual framework wherein a machine learning technique produces a parameterized family of models of differing complexities and then selects one of these for deployment on the basis of out-of-sample performance. Several examples based on modifications of ordinary least squares regression (forward stepwise regression and ridge regression) then instantiated that conceptual framework.

You've also seen how similar the workflow is with Python and in PySpark. That should give you some confidence about being able to apply what you learn to very large data sets. Big data sets definitely add some hair pulling difficulties, but the algorithmic process for building models and tuning them is very similar.

Reference

1. David J. Hand and Robert J. Till (2001). A Simple Generalization of the Area Under the ROC Curve for Multiple Class Classification Problems. *Machine Learning*, 45(2), 171–186.

Penalized Linear Regression

As you saw in Chapter 3, "Predictive Model Building: Balancing Performance, Complexity, and Big Data," getting linear regression to work in practice requires some manipulation of the ordinary least squares algorithm. Ordinary least squares regression cannot temper its use of all the data available in an attempt to minimize the error on the training data. Chapter 3 illustrated that this situation can lead to models that perform much worse on test data than on the training data. Chapter 3 showed two extensions of ordinary least squares regression: forward stepwise regression and ridge regression. Both of these involved judiciously reducing the amount of data available to ordinary least squares and using out-of-sample error measurement to determine how much data resulted in the best performance.

Stepwise regression began by letting ordinary least squares regression use exactly one of the attribute columns for making predictions and by picking the best one. It proceeded by recursively adding a single additional column of attributes to those already being used in the model.

Ridge regression introduced a different type of constraint. Ridge regression imposed a penalty on the magnitude of the coefficients to constrict the solution. Both ridge regression and forward stepwise regression gave better than ordinary least squares (OLS) on example problems.

This chapter develops an extended family of methods for controlling the overfitting inherent in OLS. The methods discussed in this chapter are called *penalized linear regression*. Penalized linear regression covers several algorithms that operate similarly to the methods introduced in Chapter 3. Ridge regression is a specific example of a penalized linear regression algorithm. Ridge regression regulates overfitting by penalizing the sum of the regression coefficients squared. Other penalized regression algorithms use different forms of penalty. This chapter explains how the penalty method determines the nature of the solution and the type of information that is available about the solution.

Why Penalized Linear Regression Methods Are So Useful

Several properties make penalized linear regression methods outstandingly useful, including the following:

- Extremely fast model training
- Variable importance information
- Extremely fast evaluation when deployed
- Reliable performance on a wide variety of problems—particularly on attribute matrices that are not very tall compared to their width or that are sparse.
- Sparse solutions (that is, a more parsimonious model)
- A linear model may be required by regulations

   Here's what these properties mean to you as a designer of machine learning models.

Extremely Fast Coefficient Estimation

Training time matters for several reasons. One reason is that the process of building a model is iterative. You'll find that you use training as part of your feature selection and feature engineering process. You'll pick some features that seem reasonable, train a model, evaluate it on out-of-sample data, want more performance, make some changes, and try again. If the basic training gets done quickly, you don't waste so much time getting coffee while waiting for answers (and reap the health benefit of lowering your caffeine intake). This makes the development process faster. Another reason why training times matter is that you might need to retrain your models to keep them working as conditions change. If you're classifying tweets, you might need to stay on top of changes in vocabulary. If you're training to trade in financial markets, the conditions are always changing. The time taken for training, even without feature reengineering, will dictate how rapidly you can respond to changing conditions.

Variable Importance Information

Both classes of algorithms covered in this book develop variable importance information. Variable importance information consists of a ranking for each of the attributes you've chosen to base your model on. The ranking tells you how much the model values each attribute compared to others. A highly ranked attribute contributes more to the model's prediction than lesser-ranked attributes. This is crucial information for a variety of reasons. First, it helps you weed out variables during the feature engineering process. The good features will rise to the top of the list, and the not-so-good ones will sink to the bottom. Besides helping you with feature engineering, knowing what variables are driving the predictions helps you understand and explain your models to others (your boss, your customer, subject matter experts in the company, and so on). To the extent that the important attributes are what people expected it gives them confidence that the models make sense. If some of the rankings are surprises, you may gain new insights into your problem. Discussion about the relative importance can give your development group new ideas about where to look for performance improvements.

The two properties of rapid training and variable importance make penalized regression a good algorithm to try first on a new problem. These algorithms help you quickly get your arms around the problems and help you learn which features are going to be useful.

Extremely Fast Evaluation When Deployed

In some problem settings, fast evaluations are a critical performance parameter. In some electronic markets (for example, Internet ads and automated trading), whoever gets the answer first gets the business. In many other applications (for instance, spam filtering), time might be critical, although not a yes/no criterion. It is hard to beat a linear model for evaluation speed. The number of operations required for the prediction calculation is one multiply and one add for each attribute.

Reliable Performance

Reliable performance means that penalized linear methods will generate reasonable answers to problems of all different shapes and sizes. On some problems, they will equal the best performance available. In some cases, they will require a little coaxing to outperform other contenders. This chapter will talk about techniques you can use that will sometimes improve the performance of penalized linear models. Chapter 6, "Ensemble Methods," revisits this topic and explains some ways to use penalized linear regression in conjunction with ensemble methods to improve performance.

Sparse Solutions

A *sparse solution* means that many of the coefficients in the model are zero. That means that not as many multiplications and sums are required. More important, a sparse model (one with few nonzero coefficients) is easy to interpret. When some of the model coefficients' multiplying features are zero, it's easy to see what attributes are driving the predictions of your model.

Problem May Require Linear Model

The last reason for using penalized linear regression is that a linear model might be a requirement of the solution. Calculations of insurance payouts represent one example where linear models are required, where a payout formula is often part of a contract that specifies variables and their coefficients. An ensemble model that involves a thousand trees, each with a thousand parameters, would be nearly impossible to write out in English. Drug testing is another arena where regulatory apparatus requires a linear form for statistical inference.

When to Use Ensemble Methods

The prime reason for not using penalized linear regression is that you might get better performance with another technique, such as an ensemble method. As outlined in Chapter 3, ensembles perform best in complicated problems (for example, highly irregular decision surfaces) with plenty of data to resolve the problem's complexities. In addition, ensemble methods for measuring variable importance can yield more information about the relationship between attributes and predictions. For example, ensembles will give second-order (and higher) information about what pairs of variables are more important together than the sum of their individual importance. That information can actually help squeeze more performance out of penalized regression. You'll read more about that in Chapter 6.

Penalized Linear Regression: Regulating Linear Regression for Optimum Performance

As discussed in Chapter 3, this book addresses a class of problems called *function approximation*. The starting point for training a model for a function approximation problem is a data set containing a number of examples or instances. Each instance has an outcome (also called a *target, label, endpoint,* and so forth) and a number of attributes that are used to predict the outcome. Chapter 3 gave a simple illustrative example. It is repeated here in slightly modified form as Table 4.1.

Table 4.1: Example Training Set

OUTCOMES	FEATURE 1	FEATURE 2	FEATURE 3
$ Spent 2013	Gender	$ Spent 2012	Age
100	M	0.0	25
225	F	250	32
75	F	12	17

In this table, the outcomes (the amount spent in 2013) are real-valued—making this a regression problem. The gender attribute (Feature 1) is two-valued, making it a categorical (or factor) attribute. The other two attributes are numeric. The goal with a function approximation problem is to (1) build a function relating the attributes to the outcome and (2) to minimize the error in some sense. Chapter 3 discussed some of the alternative error characterizations that might be employed to quantify overall error.

Data sets of the type shown in Table 4.1 are often represented by a column vector containing the outcomes (the first column in Table 4.1) and other columns containing the attributes (the three columns of features after the first one). The attributes are what is available to predict the outcomes. Data scientists commonly refer to data structures like that in Table 4.1 as a *dataframe*. In a dataframe, the data are in a column are all of the same type: real numbers, integers, string variables, and sometimes Boolean values. You'll find dataframes in Python pandas and in PySpark (and in the R programming language). A dataframe has the same shape as a matrix, but a matrix contains elements that are all the same numeric type: real number, integer, or Boolean. A matrix cannot be a mixture of real numbers and categorical variables.

Here's an important point. Linear methods work with numeric data only. The data in Table 4.1 has non-numeric data, and therefore linear methods will not work for the data as shown. Fortunately, it is relatively simple to convert (or code) the data in Table 4.1 as numeric data. In cases where there are two different categories, as with Table 4.1 where the possibilities are either M or F, you can substitute 0.0 for M and 1.0 for F and then proceed with linear regression. You'll learn a more general technique for coding categorical attributes as numeric attributes in the section titled "Incorporating Non-Numeric Attributes into Linear Methods."

Given that the attributes are all real numbers (either in the initial problem formulation or by coding categorical attributes as real numbers), the data for a linear regression problem can be represented by two objects: Y and X, where Y

is a column vector of outcomes, and where X is a matrix of real-valued attributes. Equation 4.1 how a single capital letter Y is used to represent a column of numbers y_i.

$$Y = \begin{pmatrix} y_1 \\ y_2 \\ \vdots \\ y_n \end{pmatrix}$$

Equation 4.1: Vector of outcomes

In the example given in Table 4.1, Y is the column labeled Outcomes. Equation 4.2 shows how a single capital letter X is used to represent a matrix (rectangular grid) of numbers x_ij.

$$X = \begin{pmatrix} x_{11} & x_{12} & \cdots & x_{1m} \\ x_{21} & x_{22} & \cdots & x_{2m} \\ \vdots & \vdots & \ddots & \\ x_{n1} & x_{n2} & \cdots & x_{nm} \end{pmatrix}$$

Equation 4.2: Matrix of attributes

In the example given in Table 4.1, X is the set of columns that remains after excluding the Outcomes column.

The ith element from $Y\left(y_i\right)$ is from the same instance as the ith row of X. The ith row of X will be denoted by x_i with a single subscript and given by $x_i = \left(x_{i1}, x_{i2}, \ldots, x_{im}\right)$. The ordinary least squares regression problem is to minimize the error between the y_i and a linear function x_i, the ith row of attributes from X (that is, to find a vector of real numbers β as defined in Equation 4.3) and a scalar β_0 so that each element y_i from Y is approximated by Equation 4.4.

$$\beta = \begin{pmatrix} \beta_1 \\ \beta_2 \\ \vdots \\ \beta_m \end{pmatrix}$$

Equation 4.3: β-Vector of model coefficients

$$Prediction\ of\ y_i = x_i * \beta + \beta_0$$
$$= x_{i1} * \beta_1 + x_{i2} * \beta_2 + \ldots + x_{im} * \beta_m + \beta_0$$

Equation 4.4: Linear relation between *X* and prediction of *Y*

You might be able to find the values for the β's by using your knowledge of the subject matter. In Table 4.1, for example, you might estimate that people will spend 10% more in 2013 than in 2012, that their purchases will increase by $10 per year of age, and that even newborns will purchase $50 of books. That gives you an equation to predict book spending that looks like Equation 4.5.

$$Predicted\ \$\ Spent\ 2013 = \$50 + 1.1 * (\$\ Spent\ 2012) + \$10 * Age$$

Equation 4.5: Predicting book spending

Equation 4.5 does not use the Gender variable because it's a categorical variable. (That gets covered in "Incorporating Non-Numeric Attributes into Linear Methods" and is ignored for now.) The predictions generated by Equation 4.5 do not exactly match the Outcomes (actual number) in Table 4.1. This simple model has some error, as models usually do.

Training Linear Models: Minimizing Errors and More

Finding the values for the β's by hand is not usually the best way, although it's always a good sanity check if you can manage it. In many problems, the size of the problem or the interrelationships between the variables makes guessing the β's impossible. So, the approach taken is to find the multipliers on the attributes (the β's) by solving a minimization problem. The minimization problem is to find the values for the β's that makes the average squared error the smallest (but not zero).

Making the two sides of Equation 4.4 exactly equal usually means the model is overfit. The right side of Equation 4.4 is the predictive model you're going to train. Basically, it says that to make a prediction, you take each attribute, multiply by its corresponding beta, sum these products, and add a constant. *Training the model* means finding the numbers that make up the vector β and the constant, β_0. *Error* is defined as the difference between the actual value of y_i and the predicted value of y_i given by Equation 4.4. The average squared error is used to reduce the individual errors to a single number to be minimized. The square of the error is chosen because it's positive regardless of whether the error is positive or negative and because the square function facilitates some of the math. The formulation of the ordinary least squares regression problem is then to find β_0^*, β^* (the superscript * indicates that these are the best values for β's) that satisfy Equation 4.6.

$$\beta_0^*, \beta^* = argmin_{\beta_0, \beta} \left(\frac{1}{n} \sum_{i=1}^{n} \left(y_i - \left(x_i * \beta + \beta_0 \right) \right)^2 \right)$$

Equation 4.6: Minimization problem for OLS

The notation *argmin* means "the arguments that minimize the following expression." The sum is over rows, where a row includes the attribute values and the corresponding labels. The expression inside the $(\ )^2$ is the error between y_i and the linear function that's being used to approximate it. For the predicted $ spent on books in 2013, the expression inside the sum would be the values in the Outcome column minus the prediction calculated from Equation 4.4.

In English, Equation 4.6 says the vector beta star and the constant beta zero star are the values that minimize the expected prediction squared error—that is, the average squared error between y_i and the row of attributes predicted y_i over all data rows $(i = 1, \ldots, n)$. The minimization in Equation 4.5 yields the ordinary least squares values for this regression model. This machine learning model is a list of real numbers—the ones included in the vector β^* and the number β_0^*.

Adding a Coefficient Penalty to the OLS Formulation

The mathematical statement of the penalized linear regression problem is very similar to Equation 4.5. Ridge regression, which you saw in Chapter 3, gives an example of penalized linear regression. Ridge regression adds a penalty term to the basic ordinary least squares problem stated in Equation 4.5. The penalty term for ridge regression is shown in Equation 4.7.

$$\frac{\lambda \beta^T \beta}{2} = \frac{\lambda \left(\beta_1^2 + \beta_2^2 + \ldots + \beta_n^2 \right)}{2}$$

Equation 4.7: Penalty applied to coefficients (betas)

The OLS problem in Equation 4.6 was to choose $\beta's$ to minimize the sum of squared errors. The penalized regression problem adds the coefficient penalty in Equation 4.7 to the right-hand side of Equation 4.6. The minimization is then forced to balance the conflicting goals of minimizing the squared prediction error and the squared values of the coefficients. It is easy to minimize the sum of the squared coefficients by themselves. Just make the coefficients all zero. But that results in large prediction error. Similarly, the OLS solution minimizes the prediction errors by themselves but may result in a large coefficient penalty, depending on how large λ is.

Why does this make sense? To help develop some intuition for why this makes sense, think about the subset selection process that you saw in Chapter 3. Using subset selection eliminated overfitting by discarding some of the attributes, or equivalently by setting their coefficients to zero. Penalized regression does the same thing, but instead of reducing the coefficients of a few attributes all the way to zero like subset selection, penalized regression reduces the magnitudes of all the coefficients and thereby reduces the influence of all of the attributes. Some limiting cases will also help visualize the approach.

The parameter λ can range anywhere between 0 and plus infinity. If $\lambda = 0$, the penalty term goes away, and the problem reverts to being an ordinary least squares problem. If $\lambda \to \infty$, the penalty on the β's becomes so severe that it forces them all to zero. (Notice, however, that β_0 is not included in the penalty so the prediction becomes a constant independent of the x's.)

As you saw in the examples in Chapter 3, the ridge penalty can have a similar effect to leaving out some of the attributes. The process is to generate a whole family of solutions to the penalized version of the minimization problem shown in Equation 4.6. That meant solving the penalized minimization problem for a variety of different values of λ. Each of these solutions is then tested on out-of-sample data, and the solution that minimizes the out-of-sample error is used for making real-world predictions. Chapter 3 illustrated this sequence of steps using ridge regression.

Other Useful Coefficient Penalties—Manhattan and ElasticNet

The ridge penalty is not the only useful penalty that can be used for penalized regression. Any metric of vector length will work. You can gauge the length of a vector in a number of ways. Using different measures of length changes important properties of the solution. Ridge regression employed the metric of Euclidean geometry (that is, the sum of the *squared* β's). Another useful algorithm called Lasso regression employs the metric of the sum of the *absolute* β's or L1 metric. This metric is also known as the taxicab metric or the *Manhattan distance* because it's the distance a cab would travel being constrained to the square grid of streets in Manhattan. Lasso regression has some useful properties.

The difference between ridge regression and Lasso regression is the measure of length that each one uses for penalizing β, the vector of linear coefficients. Ridge uses squared Euclidean distance—the sum of the squares of the components of β. Lasso uses the sum of the absolute values of the components of β. The lasso penalty is given by Equation 4.8.

$$\lambda \| \beta_1 \| = \lambda \left(|\beta_1| + |\beta_2| + \ldots + |\beta_n| \right)$$

Equation 4.8: Equation for Lasso coefficient penalty

The double vertical bars are called norm bars. They are used to denote magnitude for things like vectors and operators. The subscript 1 on the right side of the norm bars denotes L_1 norm, which means the sum of absolute values.

You'll also see this written in lowercase as l_1. Norm bars with a subscript 2 mean square root of the sum of squared values—Euclidean distance. These different coefficient penalty functions cause some important and useful changes in the solutions. One of the main differences is that the Lasso coefficient vector β^* is sparse, meaning that many of the coefficients are zero for large to moderate values of λ. By contrast, the ridge regression β^* is completely populated.

Why Lasso Penalty Leads to Sparse Coefficient Vectors

Figures 4.1 and 4.2 illustrate how this sparsity property stems directly from the form of the coefficient penalty function. These figures are for a problem that has two attributes: x1 and x2.

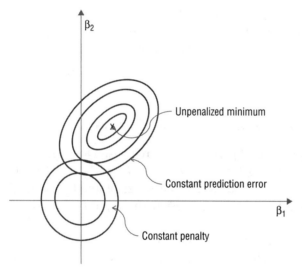

Figure 4.1: Optimum solutions with sum squared coefficient penalty

Both Figures 4.1 and 4.2 have two sets of curves. One set of curves is concentric ellipses that represent the ordinary least squares errors in Equation 4.6. The ellipses represent curves of constant sum squared error. You can think of them as being a topographic map of an elliptical depression in the ground. The error gets smaller for the more central ellipsis, just like the altitude of a depression in the ground gets smaller toward the bottom of the depression. The minimum point for the depression is marked with an x. The point x marks the ordinary least squares solution—where the solution lies if there is no coefficient penalty.

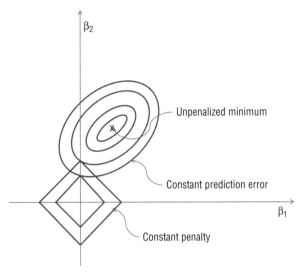

Figure 4.2: Optimum solutions with sum absolute value coefficient penalty

The other sets of curves in Figures 4.1 and 4.2 represent the coefficient penalties from Equations 4.7 and 4.8—the ridge and Lasso penalties, respectively. In Figure 4.1, the curves representing the coefficient penalty are circles centered at the origin. The set of points where the sum of the squares of β_1 and β_2 is constant defines a circle. The shape of the curves of constant penalty is determined by the nature of the distance measure being used—circles (called hypersphere or L_1 ball in higher dimensions) for sum square penalty function and diamonds (or L_1 ball) for sum of absolute values. Smaller circles (or diamonds) correspond to smaller value for the distance function. The shape is determined by the nature of the penalty function, but the value associated with each curve is determined by the non-negative parameter λ. Suppose that the two curves in Figure 4.1 correspond to sum of squares of β_1 and β_2 equal to 1.0 and 2.0 for the inner and outer circles. Then if $\lambda = 1$, the penalty associated with the two circles is 1 and 2. If $\lambda = 10$, the associated penalties are 10 and 20. The same is true of the diamonds in Figure 4.2. Increasing λ increases the penalty associated with the concentric diamonds in Figure 4.2.

The elliptical rings corresponding to the sum squares of the prediction error also get larger as the rings get farther from the unconstrained minimum, marked by an x in the figure. Minimizing the sum of these two functions, as indicated in Equation 4.7, requires a compromise somewhere in between the minimum for the prediction error and the coefficient penalty. Larger values of λ will pull the compromise closer to the minimum for the penalty (all zero coefficients). Smaller values of λ will pull the minimum closer to the unconstrained minimum prediction error (the x in Figures 4.1 and 4.2).

Here's where the distinction between sum of squared coefficient penalties and sum of absolute value penalties becomes important. The overall minimum for Equations 4.7 or 4.8 will always be at a point where the curve of constant penalty is tangent to the curve of squared prediction error. Figures 4.1 and 4.2 display two examples illustrating this tangency. The important point to make here is that in Figure 4.1 as λ changes and shifts the minimum point, the point of tangency for the sum of squares penalties (the circles) is generally a point that is not on either of the coordinate axes. Neither β_1 nor β_2 is zero. In Figure 4.2, by contrast, the point of tangency for the sum of absolute value stays stuck to the β_2-axis over a range of solutions. Along the β_2-axis, $\beta_1 = 0$.

A sparse coefficient vector is the algorithm's way of telling you that you can completely ignore some of the variables. When λ gets small enough, the best values of β_2 and β_1 will move off the β_2 axis, and both will be nonzero. The fact that a smaller penalty is required to make β_1 non-zero, gives an order to β_2 and β_1. In some sense, β_2 is more important than β_1 because it gets a nonzero coefficient for larger values of λ. Remember that these coefficients multiply attributes. If the coefficient corresponding to an attribute is zero, the algorithm is telling you that attribute is less important than the attributes that are getting nonzero coefficients. By scanning λ from large values to small ones, you can arrange all of the attributes in order of their importance. The next section shows this for a concrete problem and will show Python code that will make explicit the importance comparison between attributes as part of calculating solutions to Equation 4.8.

ElasticNet Penalty Includes Both Lasso and Ridge

Before seeing how to compute these coefficients, you need to know one more generalized statement of the penalized regression problem. This is called the ElasticNet formulation. The ElasticNet formulation of the penalized regression problem is to use an adjustable blend of the ridge penalty and the Lasso penalty. ElasticNet introduces another parameter, α, that parameterizes the fraction of the total penalty that is the ridge penalty and the fraction that is Lasso penalty. The end point $\alpha = 1$ corresponds to all Lasso penalty and no ridge penalty. The end point $\alpha = 0$ corresponds to all ridge penalty.

With the ElasticNet formulation, both λ and α must be specified to solve for the coefficients for a linear model. Usually, the approach is to pick a value for α and solve for a range of λ's. You'll see the computational reasons for that later.

In many cases, there's not a big performance difference between $\alpha = 1$ and $\alpha = 0$ or some intermediate value of α. Sometimes it will make a big difference, and it behooves you to check to a few different values of α to make sure that you're not sacrificing performance needlessly.

Solving the Penalized Linear Regression Problem

In the preceding section, you saw that determining a penalized linear regression model amounts to solving an optimization problem. A number of general-purpose numeric optimization algorithms will solve the optimization problems in Equations 4.6, 4.8, and ElasticNet, but the importance of the penalized linear regression problem has motivated researchers to develop specialized algorithms that generate solutions very rapidly. This section covers the basics of these algorithms and runs the code so that you can understand the mechanics of each algorithm. The section goes through the mechanics of two algorithms *least-angle regression,* or LARS, and glmnet. These two are chosen because they can be related to one another and to some of the methods you have already seen, such as ridge regression and forward stepwise regression. In addition, they are both very fast algorithms to train and are available as part of Python packages. Chapter 5, "Building Predictive Models Using Penalized Linear Methods," will use the Python packages incorporating these algorithms to explore example problems.

Understanding Least Angle Regression and Its Relationship to Forward Stepwise Regression

One very fast, very clever algorithm is the least-angle regression (LARS) algorithm developed by Bradley Efron, Trevor Hastie, Iain Johnstone, and Robert Tibshirani (http://en.wikipedia.org/wiki/Least-angle_regression). The LARS algorithm can be understood as a refinement to the forward stepwise algorithm that you saw in Chapter 3. The forward stepwise algorithm is summarized here:

Forward Stepwise Regression Algorithm

- Initialize all the β's equal to zero.

At each step

- Find residuals (errors) after using variables already chosen.

- Determine which unused variable best explains residuals and add it to the mix.

The LARS algorithm is very similar. The main difference with LARS is that instead of unreservedly incorporating each new attribute, it only partially incorporates them. The summary for the LARS algorithm is summarized here:

Least Angle Regression Algorithm

- Initialize all β's to zero.

At Each Step

- Determine which attribute has the largest correlation with the residuals.

- Increment that variable's coefficient by a small amount if the correlation is positive or decrement by a small amount if negative.

The LARS algorithm solves a slightly different problem from those listed earlier. However, the solutions it generates are usually the same as Lasso, and when there are differences, the differences are relatively minor. The reason for looking closely at the LARS algorithm is that it is very closely related to Lasso and to forward stepwise regression, and the LARS algorithm is easy to outline and relatively compact to code. By looking at the code for LARS, you'll get an understanding of what goes on inside more general ElasticNet solvers. More important, you'll see the issues and workarounds that accompany penalized regression solvers. Code implementing the LARS algorithm is shown in Listing 4.1.

There are three major sections to the code, described briefly here and then discussed in more detail:

- Read in the data and headers in the form of lists.

- Normalize the attributes and the labels.

- Solve for the coefficients (β_0^*, β^*) that compose the solution.

Listing 4.1: LARS Algorithm for Predicting Wine Taste—larsWine2.py

```
from Read_Fcns import list_read_wine
import numpy as np
from sklearn import datasets, linear_model
from sklearn.preprocessing import  StandardScaler

from math import sqrt
import matplotlib.pyplot as plt

#read wine data into lists
names, xList, labels = list_read_wine()

#Normalize features
xScaler = StandardScaler()
xNormalized = xScaler.fit_transform(xList)
nrows, ncols = xNormalized.shape
```

```
#Normalize labels
labelScaler = StandardScaler()
labelNormalized = labelScaler.fit_transform(np.array(labels).reshape(\
                    [-1,1]))

#initialize a vector of coefficients beta
beta = np.zeros([ncols, 1])

#initialize matrix of betas at each step
betaMat = beta.copy()

#initialize list to accumulate features as they become used
nzList = []

#number of steps and step size
nSteps = 350
stepSize = 0.004

for i in range(1, nSteps):

    #calculate residuals
    residuals = labelNormalized - np.dot(xNormalized, beta)

    #correlation between attribute columns and residual
    corr = np.mean(xNormalized * residuals, axis=0)

    #locate feature with largest magnitude correlation with residuals
    iStar = np.argmax(np.abs(corr))
    corrStar = corr[iStar]

    #increment or decrement corresponding coefficient (beta)
    #increment if corr is + decrement if it's -
    beta[iStar] += stepSize * corrStar / abs(corrStar)
    betaMat= np.concatenate( (betaMat, beta.copy()), axis=1)

    #form list of non-zero coefficients and accumulate new ones
    nzBeta = [index for index in range(ncols) if beta[index] != 0.0]
    for q in nzBeta:
        if (q in nzList) == False:
            nzList.append(q)

nameList = [names[nzList[i]] for i in range(len(nzList))]

print(betaMat.shape)
print(nameList)
for i in range(ncols):
    #plot range of beta values for each attribute
    coefCurve = betaMat[i,:].reshape([-1,])
    xaxis = range(nSteps)
    plt.plot(xaxis, coefCurve)
```

```
plt.xlabel("Steps Taken")
plt.ylabel(("Coefficient Values"))
#plt.savefig('larsWine2.png', dpi=500)
plt.show()

Printed Output:
(11, 350)
alcohol, volatile acidity, sulphates, total sulfur dioxide, chlorides,
fixed acidity, pH, free sulfur dioxide, citric acid, residual sugar,
density
```

The first step is to read headers, attribute values, and labels. Ordinary Python lists are used for these data structures.

The second step is to normalize the attributes. The normalization used is the same normalization that you saw in Chapter 2, "Understand the Problem by Understanding the Data." In Chapter 2, normalization of the attributes was used to bring attributes into commensurate scales so that they'd plot conveniently and fully occupy the same scale. Normalization is usually done as the first step in penalized linear regression for much the same reason. The attributes need to have the same scale so that the coefficient values are chosen based only on which attribute is most useful, not on the basis of which one has the most favorable scale. As an illustration, a distance attribute scaled in microns would need only a very small coefficient to make a big difference in label compared to the same attribute scaled in kilometers. Normalization is essential to getting sensible results from penalized regression.

Each step in the LARS algorithm increments one of the β's by a fixed amount. If the attributes have different scales, this fixed increment means different things to different attributes. Also, changing the scale on one of the attributes (say from miles to feet) makes the answers come out differently. For these reasons, penalized linear regression packages generally normalize using the common normalization that you saw in Chapter 2. They normalize to zero mean (by subtracting the mean) and unit standard deviation (by dividing the result by standard deviation). Packages will often give you the option of not normalizing, but I've never heard a good reason for not normalizing.

The third and final section solves for β_0^*, β^*. Because the algorithm is running on the normalized variables, there's no need for the intercept β_0^*. That would normally account for any difference between the labels and the weighted attributes. Because all the attributes have been normalized to zero mean, there's no offset between them and no purpose for β_0^*. Notice that two beta-related lists are initialized. One is called *beta* and has the same number of elements as the number of attributes—one weight for each attribute. The other is a matrix-like list of lists that will house a list of betas for each step in the LARS algorithm. This gets into a key concept with penalized linear regression and modern machine learning algorithms in general.

How LARS Generates Hundreds of Models of Varying Complexity

Modern machine learning algorithms in general, and penalized linear regression in particular, generate families of solutions, not just single solutions. Look back at Equations 4.6 and 4.8. On the left side of those equations are the β's and on the right-hand side are all numeric values that are fixed by the data available for the problem with one exception. In Equations 4.6 and 4.8, there is a parameter λ that has to be determined some other way. As was pointed out in the discussion of those equations, when $\lambda = 0$, the problems reduce to ordinary least squares regression, and when $\lambda \to \infty$, $\beta^* \to 0$. So, the β's depend on the parameter λ in the problems stated in Equations 4.6 and 4.8.

The LARS algorithm doesn't explicitly deal with λ values, but it has the same effect. The LARS algorithm starts with β's equal to zero and then adds a small increment to whichever of the β's will reduce the error the most. The small increment that's added increases the sum of absolute values of the β's by the amount of the increment. If the increment is small and if it's spent on the best of the attributes, the process has the effect of solving the minimization problem in Equation 4.8. You can trace the evolution of this process in Listing 4.1.

The basic iteration is just a few lines of code at the beginning of the for-loop iterating for nSteps. The starting point for the iteration is a value for the β's. On the first pass, those are all set to zero. On subsequent passes, they come from the result of the last pass. There are two steps in the iteration. First, the β's are used to calculate residuals. The term *residuals* means the difference between observed outcome and predicted outcome. In this case the predictive method consists of multiplying each attribute times a corresponding element from β and then summing the products. The second step is to find the correlation between each of the attributes and the residuals to determine which attribute will contribute the most to reducing the residual (error). The correlation between two variables is the product of their variations from their means normalized by their individual standard deviations.

Variables that are scaled versions of one another will have correlations of plus one or minus one depending on whether the scaling between them is positive or negative. If two variables vary independently of one another, their correlation is zero. The Wikipedia page on correlation, `http://en.wikipedia.org/wiki/Correlation_and_dependence`, gives good illustrations of variables having other degrees of correlation with one another. The list named corr contains the result of the calculation for each attribute. You may notice that strictly speaking the code omits calculation of the standard deviation of the mean, residuals, and normalized attributes. That works here because the attributes have been normalized to all have standard deviation one and because the resulting values are going to be used to find the biggest correlation, and multiplying all the values by a constant won't change that order.

Once the correlations are calculated, it's a simple matter to determine which attribute has the largest correlation with the residuals (largest in absolute value). The corresponding element from the list of $\beta's$ is incremented by a small amount. The increment is positive if the correlation is positive and negative otherwise. The new value of the $\beta's$ is then used to rerun the iteration.

The net result from the LARS algorithm are the coefficient curves shown in Figure 4.3. The way to view these is to imagine a point along the "steps taken" axis in the graph. At that point, a vertical line will pass through all the coefficient curves. The values at which the vertical line intersects the coefficient curves are the coefficients at that step in the evolution of the LARS algorithm. If 350 steps are used to generate the curves, there are 350 sets of coefficients. Each one optimizes Equation 4.8 for some value of λ. That raises the question of which one you should use. That question will be addressed shortly.

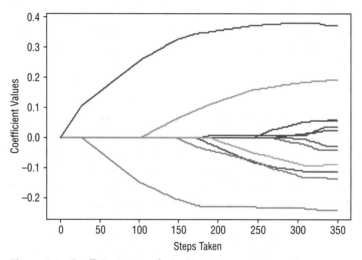

Figure 4.3: Coefficient curves for LARS regression on wine data

Notice that for the first 25 steps or so, only one of the coefficients is nonzero. This is the sparsity property that comes with Lasso regression. The coefficient that is the first to move off zero is alcohol; for a while, that's the only variable being used by LARS regression. Then a second variable comes into play. This process continues until all the variables are being used in the solution. The order in which coefficients move off zero can be used as an indication of the rank order of importance of the variables. If you had to discard a variable, you'd want to discard one that came in last rather than the one that came in first.

THE IMPORTANCE OF IMPORTANCE

This property of indicating the importance rank of the variables is an important feature of penalized regression methods. It makes them a handy tool to use early in your development process because they'll help you make decisions about what

> variables to keep and which ones to discard—a process called feature engineering. You'll see later that tree ensembles also yield measures of variable importance. Not all machine learning methods give this sort of information. You could always generate the ordering by trying all combinations of one variable, then two variables, and so on. But even with the mere 10 attributes in the wine data, it's prohibitive to make the 10 factorial training passes required to try all possible subsets.

Choosing the Best Model from the Hundreds LARS Generates

Now you've got 350 possible solutions to the problem of predicting wine taste scores from the chemical properties of the wine. How do you choose the best one? To choose which of the curves you'll use, you need to determine how each of the 350 choices performs. As discussed in Chapter 3, *performance* means performance on out-of-sample data. Chapter 3 outlined several methods for holding out data from the training process to use it to determine performance. Listing 4.2 shows the code for performing 10-fold cross-validation to determine the best set of coefficients to deploy.

Ten-fold cross-validation is the process of dividing the input data into 10 more or less equal groups, removing one of the groups from the data, training on the remainder, and then testing on the removed group. By cycling through all 10 of the groups and removing them one at a time for testing, you can develop a good estimate of the error and of the estimate's variability.

Listing 4.2: 10-Fold Cross-Validation to Determine Best Set of Coefficients—larsWineCV.py

```
__author__ = 'mike-bowles'

from Read_Fcns import list_read_wine
import numpy a np
from sklearn import datasets, linear_model
from math import sqrt
import matplotlib.pyplot as plt

#read data into iterable
names, xList, labels = list_read_wine()

#Normalize columns in x and labels
nrows = len(xList)
ncols = len(xList[0])

#read wine data into lists
names, xList, labels = list_read_wine()

#Normalize features
xScaler = StandardScaler()
```

```
xNormalized = xScaler.fit_transform(xList)
nrows, ncols = xNormalized.shape

#Normalize labels
labelScaler = StandardScaler()
labelNormalized = labelScaler.fit_transform(np.array(labels).reshape( \
                 [-1,1]))

#Build cross-validation loop to determine best coefficient values.

#number of cross validation folds
nxval = 10

#number of steps and step size
nSteps = 350
stepSize = 0.004

#initialize accumulator for errors
mean_sq_err = np.zeros([nSteps,1])

for ixval in range(nxval):
    #Define test and training index sets
    idxTest = [a for a in range(nrows) if a%nxval == ixval]
    idxTrain = [a for a in range(nrows) if a%nxval != ixval]

    #Define test and training attribute and label sets
    xTrain = xNormalized[idxTrain, :]
    xTest = xNormalized[idxTest]
    labelTrain = labelNormalized[idxTrain]
    labelTest = labelNormalized[idxTest]

    #Train LARS regression on Training Data
    nrowsTrain = len(idxTrain)
    nrowsTest = len(idxTest)

    #initialize a vector of coefficients beta
    beta = np.zeros([ncols, 1])

    for iStep in range(nSteps):
        #calculate residuals
        residuals = labelTrain - np.dot(xTrain, beta)

        #correlation between attribute columns and residual
        corr = np.mean(xTrain * residuals, axis=0)

        #locate feature w largest magnitude correlation with residuals
        iStar = np.argmax(np.abs(corr))
        corrStar = corr[iStar]

        #update coefficients
```

```
        beta[iStar] += stepSize * corrStar / abs(corrStar)

        #calculate out of sample squared errors
        err = labelTest - np.dot(xTest, beta)
        mean_sq_err[iStep,0] += np.mean(err*err) / float(nxval)

    cvCurve = mean_sq_err

    minPt = np.argmin(cvCurve)
    minMse = cvCurve[minPt]
    print("Minimum Mean Square Error", minMse)
    print("Index of Minimum Mean Square Error", minPt)

    xaxis = range(len(cvCurve))
    plt.plot(xaxis, cvCurve)

    plt.xlabel("Steps Taken")
    plt.ylabel(("Mean Square Error"))
    #plt.savefig('larsWineCV.png', dpi=500)
    plt.show()
```

Mechanizing Cross-Validation for Model Selection in Python Code

The code in Listing 4.2 begins similarly to the code in Listing 4.1. The differences become clear at the cross-validation loop that is looping nxval times. In this case nxval = 10, but it could be set to other values as well. The tradeoffs with how many folds to use are that smaller numbers of folds mean that you're training on less of the data. If you take 5 folds, then you're leaving out 20% each training pass. If you take 10 folds, you're only leaving out 10%. As you saw in Chapter 3, training on less data causes deterioration in the accuracy your algorithm will achieve. However, taking more folds means making more passes through the training process. That can be cumbersome in terms of the clock or calendar time required for training.

Just ahead of the cross-validation loop, an error list gets initialized. This error list will consist of a list of errors for each step in the evolution of the LARS algorithm. It will accumulate the errors for each step over all 10 of the cross-validation folds. Just inside the cross-validation loop, you'll see definition of training and test sets. I typically use a modulus function to define these sets unless there's some reason not to. For example, sometimes you may need to do what's called *stratified sampling*. Suppose that you're trying to build a classifier on data that are unbalanced, so there are very few of one of the classes. You want for the training sets to be representative of the full data set. You may need to segregate the data by classes so that the classes are represented in both in-sample and out-of-sample data.

You may prefer to use a random function to define training and test sets. You do need to be aware of any patterning in the data set that would interact with the sampling process adversely (that is, if observations are not exchangeable). For example, if data were taken daily during the work week, then using the modulus function with five-fold cross-validation might result in one set having all the Mondays and another having all the Tuesdays, and so on.

Accumulating Errors on Each Cross-Validation Fold and Evaluating Results

Once the training and test sets are defined along with a few constants, the iteration of the LARS algorithm begins. This is very similar to the process defined in Listing 4.1, with a couple of important differences. First, the basic iteration of the algorithm is carried out on the training set instead of the full data set and second, at each step in the iteration and for each cross-validation fold the current values of the $\beta's$ are used along with the test attributes and test labels to ascertain the error on the test set for that step. You'll see that calculation at the bottom of the cross-validation loop. Each time β is updated, it is applied to the test data, and the error is accumulated in the appropriate list in "error." It's a simple matter to then square and average each of the lists in error. This produces a curve of the mean square error (MSE) at each iteration, averaged over all 10 of the cross-validation folds.

You might worry whether the test data is being used properly. It's always important to be vigilant about letting the test data leak into the training process. There are numerous ways to trick oneself into violating this necessity. In this case, you'll notice that the test data is not used in the calculation of the increments of β. Only the training data is being used there.

Practical Considerations with Model Selection and Training Sequence

The curve of MSE versus number of steps in the LARS iteration is shown in Figure 4.4. This curve exhibits a fairly common pattern. It decreases more or less monotonically over its whole range. Strictly speaking, it does have a minimum point at around 311, as indicated in the associated printed output from the program. But the graph shows that the minimum is fairly weak, not very sharp. In some cases, this curve will have a sharp minimum at some point and will increase markedly to the right and left of the minimum. You use the result of cross-validation to determine which of the 350 solutions generated by LARS should be used for making predictions. In this case, the minimum is at step 311. The 311th set of $\beta's$ would be the coefficients to deploy. When there's any ambiguity about the best solution to deploy, it's usually best to deploy the more conservative solution. More conservative for penalized regression means the one with smaller coefficient values. By convention, out-of-sample performance is usually portrayed with the less-complex models on the left and the more-complex models on the right. Less-complex models have better generalization error; that is, they perform more predictably on new data. The more conservative model would be the one more to the left side of the out-of-sample performance graph.

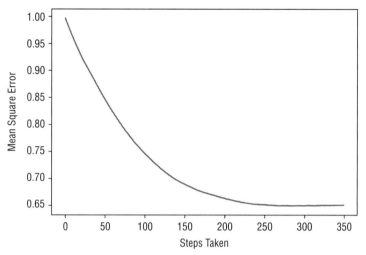

Figure 4.4: Cross-validated mean square error for LARS on wine data

This description of the LARS algorithm and of the cross-validation process has gone through training the algorithm on the whole data set first, then running cross-validation second. In practice, you'll probably first run cross-validation and then train the algorithm on the whole data set. The purpose of cross-validation is to determine what level of MSE (or other) performance you'll be able to achieve and to learn how complicated a model your data set will sustain. If you recall, Chapter 3 discussed the issues of data set size and model complexity. Cross-validation (or other process for setting aside data to get a sound estimate of performance) is how you determine the best model complexity for the model you will deploy. You determine the complexity but not the specific model (that is, not the specific set of β's). As you can see in Listing 4.2, with 10-fold cross-validation, you've actually trained 10 models, and there's no way to decide among the 10. Best practice is to train on the full data set and to use the cross-validation results to determine which of the models determine which of the models to deploy. In the example shown in Listing 4.2, cross-validation gives a minimum MSE of 0.59 at the 311th step in the training process. The coefficient curves in Figure 4.5 were trained on the full data set. The digression into cross-validation was motivated by not knowing which of the 350 sets of coefficients represented in Figure 4.5 should be deployed. Cross-validation has yielded a sound estimate of the MSE and tells us to deploy the 311th model from training on the full data set.

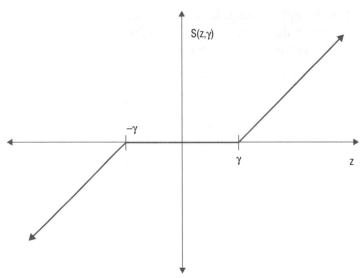

Figure 4.5: Plot of S() function

Using Glmnet: Very Fast and Very General

The glmnet algorithm was developed by Professor Jerome Friedman and his colleagues at Stanford in 2010. The glmnet algorithm solves the ElasticNet problem. Recall that the ElasticNet problem incorporates a generalization of the penalty function that includes both the Lasso penalty (sum of absolute values) and the ridge penalty (sum of squares). ElasticNet has a parameter λ that determines how heavily the coefficient penalty is penalized compared to the fit error. It also has a parameter that determines how close the penalty is to ridge ($\alpha = 0$) or Lasso ($\alpha = 1$). The glmnet algorithm yields the full coefficient curves, similar to the LARS algorithm. Whereas the LARS algorithm accumulates quanta of coefficient into the β's to drive the curves forward, the glmnet algorithm makes steady reductions in the λ's to drive the coefficient curves forward. Equation 4.9 shows the key equation from Friedman's paper—the key iterative equation for the coefficients that solve the ElasticNet equation.

$$\beta_j^{\sim} \leftarrow \frac{S\left(\frac{1}{m}\sum_{i=1}^{m}x_{ij}r_i + \beta_j^{\sim}, \lambda\alpha\right)}{1 + \lambda(1-\alpha)}$$

Equation 4.9: Coordinate-wise update for glmnet

Equation 4.9 is a combination of Equations 5 and 8 in Friedman's paper (for those of you who would like to follow the math). It looks complicated, but a little inspection will reveal some similarities and relationships to the LARS method that you saw in the last section.

Comparison of the Mechanics of Glmnet and LARS Algorithms

Equation 4.9 gives the basic update equation for the β's. The update equation for LARS was "find the attribute with the largest magnitude correlation with the residual and increment (or decrement) its coefficient by a small fixed amount." The updated Equation 4.9 is a little more involved. It has an arrow instead of an equals sign. The arrow means something like "gets mapped to." Notice that $\beta_j^{\sim}$ appears on both sides of the arrow. On the right side of the arrow is the old value of $\beta_j^{\sim}$, and on the left side (the direction the arrow points) is the new value of $\beta_j^{\sim}$. After several passes through, the iteration inferred in 4.9, $\beta_j^{\sim}$ stops changing. (More precisely, the change becomes insignificant.) Once $\beta_j^{\sim}$ stops changing, the algorithm has arrived at a solution for the given values of λ and α. It's time to move to the next point in the coefficient curve.

The first thing to notice is the expression $x_{ij}r_i$ inside the sum. The sum of $x_{ij}r_i$ over i (that is over rows of data) yields the correlation between the jth attribute and the residual. Recall that with LARS regression at each step through the algorithm each attribute was correlated against the residuals. In the LARS algorithm, those correlations were tested to see which attribute had the biggest correlation with the residual, and the coefficient corresponding to the attribute with the highest correlation was incremented. With the glmnet algorithm, the correlation is used somewhat differently.

With glmnet, the correlation between the residuals is used to calculate how much each coefficient ought to be changed in magnitude. But the result passes through the function s() before resulting in a change in $\beta_j^{\sim}$. The function s() is the Lasso coefficient shrinkage function. It is plotted in Figure 4.5. As you can see in Figure 4.5, if the first input is smaller than the second, the output is zero. If the first input is larger than the second, the output is the first input reduced in magnitude by the second. This is called a soft limiter.

Listing 4.3 shows code for the glmnet algorithm. You can see in the code how Equation 4.9, for updating the β's, is used to generate ElasticNet coefficient curves. The code in Listing 4.3 is annotated with the equation number from Friedman's paper. The paper is very accessible, and you can refer to it to get more mathematical details if you're interested.

Initializing and Iterating the Glmnet Algorithm

The iteration starts with a large value of λ. It begins with a value for λ that is large enough to make all the β's zero. You can see how to calculate the starting value for λ by reference to Equation 4.9. The function s() in Equation 4.9 gives zero for output if its first input (the correlation of $x_{ij}r_i$) is less than the second—$\lambda\alpha$. The iteration starts with all the β's equal to zero, so the residual is equal to the raw labels. The code for determining the starting lambda calculates the correlations for each of the attributes and the labels, finds the largest in magnitude, and then solves for the value of λ that makes the largest correlation just equal λα. That is the largest value of λ that results in all zero β's.

Then the iteration begins by reducing λ. This is accomplished by multiplying λ by a number slightly less than one. Friedman suggests that the multiplier be selected so that $\lambda^{100} = 0.001$. That gives a value of roughly 0.93. If the algorithm runs for a long time without converging, then the multiplier on λ needs to be made closer to 1. In Friedman's code, the mechanism for accomplishing this is to increase the number of steps from 100 to, say, 200 so that it takes 200 steps to reduce the starting λ to 0.001 of its starting value. In Listing 4.3, you've got control of the multiplier directly. The coefficient curves are shown in Figure 4.6.

Listing 4.3: Glmnet Algorithm—glmnetWine2.py

```python
__author__ = 'mike_bowles'

from Read_Fcns import list_read_wine
import numpy as np
from sklearn import datasets, linear_model
from math import sqrt
import matplotlib.pyplot as plt
from sklearn.preprocessing import StandardScaler

def S(z, gamma):
    if gamma >= abs(z):
        return 0.0
    return (z/abs(z))*(abs(z) - gamma)

#read wine data into list of attribute rows and list of labels
names, xList, labels = list_read_wine()
nrows = len(xList)
ncols = len(xList[0])

#Normalize x
xScaler = StandardScaler()
xNormalized = xScaler.fit_transform(xList)

#Normalize labels
yScaler = StandardScaler()
labelNormalized = yScaler.fit_transform(np.array(labels).reshape( \
                    [-1, 1]))

#select value for alpha parameter
alpha = 1.0

#define parameters for iteration
nSteps = 100
lamMult = 0.93 #100 steps gives reduction by factor of 1000 in

#make a pass through the data to determine value of lambda that
```

```
# just suppresses all coefficients.
xy = np.mean(xNormalized * labelNormalized, axis=0)
maxXY = np.amax(np.abs(xy))
lam = maxXY/alpha  #starting lambda value

#initialize a vector of coefficients beta
beta = np.zeros([ncols, 1])

#initialize matrix of betas at each step
betaMat = beta.copy()

#begin iteration
nzList = [] #betas ordered by entry sequence

for iStep in range(nSteps):
    #make lambda smaller so that some coefficient becomes non-zero
    lam = lam * lamMult

    deltaBeta = 100.0
    eps = 0.01
    iterStep = 0
    betaInner = beta.copy()
    while deltaBeta > eps:
        iterStep += 1
        if iterStep > 100: break

        #cycle through attributes and update one-at-a-time
        #record starting value for comparison
        betaStart = betaInner.copy()
        for iCol in range(ncols):
            residual = labelNormalized - np.dot(xNormalized, betaInner)
            xjr = np.mean(xNormalized[:, iCol].reshape([-1, 1]) * \
                    residual)
            uncBeta = xjr + betaInner[iCol]
            betaInner[iCol] = S(uncBeta[0], lam * alpha) / (1 + \
                                        lam * (1 - alpha))

        sumDiff = np.sum(np.abs(betaInner - betaStart))
        sumBeta = np.sum(np.abs(betaInner))
        deltaBeta = sumDiff/sumBeta

    print('\r', 'Step', iStep, 'Iteration', iterStep, end='')
    beta = np.array(betaInner.copy()).reshape([-1, 1])

    #add newly determined beta to list
    betaMat = np.concatenate((betaMat, beta.copy()), axis=1)

    #keep track of the order in which the betas become non-zero
    nzBeta = [index for index in range(ncols) if beta[index] != 0.0]
    for q in nzBeta:
```

```
            if (q in nzList) == False:
                nzList.append(q)

#print out the ordered list of betas
nameList = [names[nzList[i]] for i in range(len(nzList))]
print('\n\n', nameList)


nPts = betaMat.shape[1]


for i in range(ncols):
    #plot range of beta values for each attribute
    coefCurve = betaMat[i,:].reshape([-1,])
    xaxis = range(nSteps +1)
    plt.plot(xaxis, coefCurve)
plt.xlabel("Steps Taken")
plt.ylabel(("Coefficient Values"))
#plt.savefig('glmnetWine2.png', dpi=500)
plt.show()

Printed Output:
Step 99 Iteration 1

alcohol, volatile acidity, sulphates, total sulfur dioxide, chlorides,
fixed acidity, pH, free sulfur dioxide, residual sugar, citric acid,
density
```

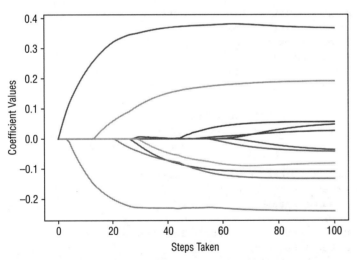

Figure 4.6: Coefficient curves for glmnet models for predicting wine taste

Figure 4.6 shows the coefficient curves generated by Listing 4.3. The curves look similar in character to those generated by LARS and shown in Figure 4.3—similar but not identical. LARS and Lasso often give the same curves, but sometimes give somewhat different results. The only way to tell which one is superior is to try them both against out-of-sample data and see which one gives the best performance.

The testing and deployment process for a Lasso model is the same as for a LARS model. Use one of the methods described in Chapter 3 for testing on out-of-sample data (n-fold cross-validation, for example). Use the results on out-of-sample data to determine the optimum model complexity. Then train on the full data set to build coefficient curves and pick the step in the coefficient curves that out-of-sample testing shows to be the optimum.

This section has gone through two solution approaches for solving the minimization problems that define penalized linear regression models. You've seen how these two methods work algorithmically, how they relate to one another and what the code looks like to implement them. This should give you a firm foundation for using the packages available in Python that implement these algorithms. It also puts you in a good position to understand various extensions to the models that will be covered in the next section and that will be used in the examples that you'll see in Chapter 5.

Extension of Linear Regression to Classification Problems

So far, the development has focused on regression problems—problems where the outcomes being predicted take real number values. How can the machinery discussed be applied to classification problems—problems where the outcomes take two (or more) discrete values like "click" or "not click"? There are several ways to extend what you've seen so far to cover classification problems.

Solving Classification Problems with Penalized Regression

For binary classification problems, you'll often get good results by coding the binary outcomes as real numbers. This simple procedure codes one of the two binary values as a 1 and the other as a 0 (or +1 and –1). With that simple arrangement, the list of labels becomes a list of real numbers. For example, the outcomes "click" and "not click" become 1.0 or 0.0. Then the algorithms already discussed can be employed. This is often a good alternative even though there are more sophisticated approaches. This simple coding approach usually trains faster than more sophisticated approaches and that can be important.

Listing 4.4 gives an example of using the method of substituting numeric 0 or 1 labels for class membership in the rocks versus mines data set. You'll recall from Chapter 2 that the rocks versus mines data set presents a classification problem. The data set comes from an experiment to determine if sonar can be used to detect unexploded mines left in the water. Various other objects besides mines will reflect the sonar's sound waves. The prediction problem is to determine whether the reflected waves come from an unexploded mine or from rocks on the sea floor.

The sonar in the experiment uses what's called a chirped waveform. A chirped waveform is one that rises (or falls) in frequency over the duration of the transmitted sonar pulse. The 60 attributes in the rocks versus mines data set are the returned pulse sampled at 60 different times, which correspond to 60 different frequencies in the chirped pulse.

Listing 4.4 demonstrates how to convert the classification labels R and M into 0.0 and 1.0 to convert the problem into an ordinary regression problem. The code then uses the LARS algorithm to build a classifier. Listing 4.4 goes through a single pass on the full data set. As discussed in the last section, you'll want to use cross-validation or some other holdout procedure to choose the optimal model complexity. Chapter 5 goes through those design steps and performance comparisons on this data set. The point here is for you to see how to apply the regression tools you've already seen to a classification problem.

Listing 4.4: Converting a Classification Problem to an Ordinary Regression Problem by Assigning Numeric Values to Binary Labels—larsRocksVMines.py

```python
__author__ = 'mike_bowles'
from Read_Fcns import list_read_rvm
from math import sqrt
import matplotlib.pyplot as plt
import numpy as np
from sklearn.preprocessing import StandardScaler

#define function for producing coef curves
def lars_coef_curves(xNormalized, labelNormalized, nSteps, stepSize):
    nrows, ncols = xNormalized.shape

    beta = np.zeros([ncols, 1])
    betaMat = beta.copy()

    for i in range(1, nSteps):

        #calculate residuals
        residuals = labelNormalized - np.dot(xNormalized, beta)

        #correlation between attribute columns and residual
        corr = np.mean(xNormalized * residuals, axis=0)

        #locate feature w largest magnitude correlation with residuals
        iStar = np.argmax(np.abs(corr))
        corrStar = corr[iStar]

        #increment or decrement corresponding coefficient (beta)
        #increment if corr is + decrement if it's -
```

```
        beta[iStar] += stepSize * corrStar / abs(corrStar)
        betaMat= np.concatenate( (betaMat, beta.copy()), axis=1)

        #form list of non-zero coefficients and accumulate new ones
        nzBeta = [index for index in range(ncols) if beta[index]\
               != 0.0]
        for q in nzBeta:
            if (q in nzList) == False:
                nzList.append(q)
    return betaMat, nzList

#read data from uci data repository
xNum, labels = list_read_rvm()

xNum = np.array(xNum)
labels = np.array(labels)

#number of rows and columns in x matrix
nrow, ncol = xNum.shape

#normalize features
xScaler = StandardScaler()
xNormalized = xScaler.fit_transform(xNum)

#Normalize labels
yScaler = StandardScaler()
labelNormalized = yScaler.fit_transform(labels.reshape([-1, 1]))

#number of steps to take
nSteps = 350
stepSize = 0.004
print('shapes', xNormalized.shape, labelNormalized.shape)

betaMat, nzList = lars_coef_curves(xNormalized, labelNormalized, \
                    nSteps, stepSize)

#make up names for columns of xNum
names = ['V' + str(i) for i in range(ncol)]
nameList = [names[nzList[i]] for i in range(len(nzList))]

print(nameList)
for i in range(ncol):
    #plot range of beta values for each attribute
    coefCurve = betaMat[i,:].reshape([-1,])
    xaxis = range(nSteps)
    plt.plot(xaxis, coefCurve)

plt.xlabel("Steps Taken")
plt.ylabel(("Coefficient Values"))
#plt.savefig('larsRocksVMines.png', dpi=500)
plt.show()
```

```
Printed Output:
shapes (208, 60) (208, 1)
'V10', 'V48', 'V44', 'V11', 'V35', 'V51', 'V20', 'V3', 'V21', 'V15',
'V43', 'V0', 'V22', 'V45', 'V53', 'V27', 'V30', 'V50', 'V58', 'V46',
'V56', 'V28', 'V39'
```

Figure 4.7 shows the coefficient curves developed by the LARS algorithm. They are similar in character to the curves you saw for the wine taste prediction problem. However, there are more curves because the rocks versus mines data set has more attributes. (The rock versus mines data has 60 attributes and 208 rows of data.) From the discussion in Chapter 3, you might expect that the optimum solution won't use all the attributes. You'll see how that tradeoff turns out in Chapter 5, which concentrates on solutions to this and other problems and comparisons between different approaches.

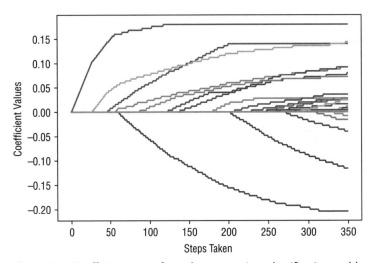

Figure 4.7: Coefficient curves for rocks versus mines classification problem solved by converting to labels

Another approach is to formulate the problem in terms of the likelihoods of the two outcomes in the problem. That leads to what's called *logistic regression*. The glmnet algorithm can be cast in that framework, and Friedman's original paper goes through the development of the logistic regression version of glmnet and of its extension to multiclass problems—problems with more than two discrete outcomes. You'll see the use of the binary and multiclass versions of the algorithm in Chapter 5.

Working with Classification Problems Having More Than Two Outcomes

Some problems require deciding among several alternatives. For example, say you show a visitor to your website several links. The visitor may click any one of the several links, click the back button, or exit the site entirely. There are several alternatives that aren't ordered like the integer wine taste scores are. A taste score of 4 naturally fits between 3 and 5, and if changing an attribute (like alcohol) makes the score go from 3 to 4, changing it some more seems likely to move the score further in the same direction. Alternative actions a site visitor will take have no such order. This is called a multiclass classification problem.

You can always handle a multiclass problem with an algorithm for binary classification. The technique is called *one versus all* or *one versus the rest*, and the names give you some idea of how the approach works. Basically you pose your multiclass problem as several binary problems. For the example, you could predict whether the visitor would leave the site or choose another option. Another binary classification problem is to predict whether the user would click the back button or take any of the rest of the options available. You'll wind up with as many binary classification problems as you have alternative outcomes. The binary classifiers all give numeric values, like the LARS classifier in Listing 4.4. The outcome that has the largest one-versus-all value is the winner. Chapter 5 implements this method for the glass data set, where there are six different possible outcomes.

Understanding Basis Expansion: Using Linear Methods on Nonlinear Problems

By their nature, linear methods assume classification and regression predictions can be expressed as a linear combination of the attributes that are available to the designer. What if you have reason to suspect that a linear model isn't enough? You can get a linear model to work with strong nonlinearities by using what's called basis expansion. The basic idea behind basis expansion is that the nonlinearities in your problem can be approximated as polynomials of the attributes (or sum of other nonlinear functions of the attributes); then you can add attributes that are powers of the original attributes and let a linear method determine the best set of coefficients for the polynomial.

To get a concrete idea of how this would work, look at the code in Listing 4.5. Listing 4.5 starts with the wine taste data set. If you recall, the linear models that were produced earlier in this chapter both found that alcohol was the most important attribute in determining wine taste. It occurs to you that the relationship might not be a straight line, but might roll off for really high alcohol content and for really low alcohol content.

Listing 4.5 shows you how to test this notion.

Listing 4.5: Basis Expansion for Wine Taste Prediction—wineBasisExpansion.py

```
__author__ = 'mike-bowles'

from Read_Fcns import list_read_wine
import matplotlib.pyplot as plt
from math import sqrt, cos, log

#read wine data
names, xList, labels = list_read_wine()

#extend the alcohol variable - the last column in that attribute matrix
xExtended = []
alchCol = len(xList[1])


for row in xList:
    newRow = list(row)
    alch = row[alchCol - 1]
    newRow.append((alch - 7) * (alch - 7)/10)
    newRow.append(5 * log(alch - 7))
    newRow.append(cos(alch))
    xExtended.append(newRow)

nrow = len(xList)
v1 = [xExtended[j][alchCol - 1] for j in range(nrow)]

for i in range(4):
    v2 = [xExtended[j][alchCol - 1 + i] for j in range(nrow)]
    plt.scatter(v1,v2)

plt.xlabel("Alcohol")
plt.ylabel(("Extension Functions of Alcohol"))
plt.show()
```

The code reads in the data as before. Right after reading in the data (and before it is normalized), the code runs through the rows of data that it's read, adds a few new elements to the row, and then appends the new expanded row to a new set of attributes. The new elements that are appended are all functions of the alcohol attribute in the original data. For example, the first new attribute is ((alch - 7) * (alch - 7)/10), where alch is the alcohol level in the row. The constants 7 and 10 were introduced so that the resulting new attributes would all plot nicely on one plot. Basically, the new attribute is alcohol squared.

The next step in the process is to take the expanded set of attributes and build a linear model using the tools already developed in this chapter (or another of the methods available for building linear models). Whatever algorithm is used for building a linear model, the model will consist of multipliers (or coefficients) for each of the attributes, including the new ones. If the functions used in the expansion are all powers of the original variable, the linear model yields coefficients in a polynomial function of the original variable. By choosing different functions for the expansion, other function series can be constructed.

Figure 4.8 illustrates the functional dependence of the new attributes (and the original attribute) on the original attribute. You can see the squared, logarithmic, and sinusoidal behavior of the selection of functions in the expansion.

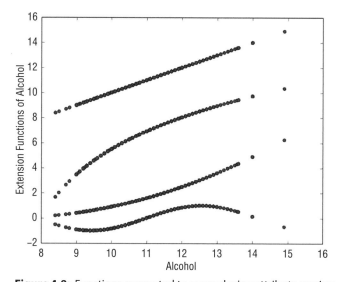

Figure 4.8: Functions generated to expand wine attribute session

Incorporating Non-Numeric Attributes into Linear Methods

Penalized linear regression (and other linear methods) require numeric attributes. What if your problem has some non-numeric attributes (also called categorical or factor attributes)? A familiar example would be a gender attribute where the possibilities are male and female. The standard method for converting categorical variables to numeric is to code them into several new columns of attribute data. If an attribute has N possible values, it gets coded into N − 1 new columns of data as follows. Identify N − 1 columns of data with N − 1 of the N attributes. In each row enter a 1 in the ith column if the row takes the ith possible value of the categorical variable. Put zeros in the other columns. If the row takes the Nth value of the categorical variable, all the entries will be zero.

Listing 4.6 shows how this technique can be applied to the abalone data set. The task with the abalone data set is to predict the age of abalone from various physical measurements.

Listing 4.6: Coding Categorical Variable for Penalized Linear Regression – Abalone Data—larsAbalone.py

```python
__author__ = 'mike_bowles'

from Read_Fcns import list_read_abalone
import matplotlib.pyplot as plt
from math import sqrt
from sklearn.preprocessing import StandardScaler

#read abalone data
xList, labels = list_read_abalone()

names = ['Sex', 'Length', 'Diameter', 'Height', 'Whole weight', \
        'Shucked weight', 'Viscera weight', 'Shell weight', 'Rings']

#code three-valued sex attribute as numeric
xCoded = []
for row in xList:
    #first code the three-valued sex variable
    codedSex = [0.0, 0.0]
    if row[0] == 'M': codedSex[0] = 1.0
    if row[0] == 'F': codedSex[1] = 1.0

    numRow = [float(row[i]) for i in range(1,len(row))]
    rowCoded = list(codedSex) + numRow
    xCoded.append(rowCoded)

namesCoded = ['Sex1', 'Sex2', 'Length', 'Diameter', 'Height', \
 'Whole weight', 'Shucked weight', 'Viscera weight', 'Shell weight', \
    'Rings']

nrows = len(xCoded)
ncols = len(xCoded[1])

#Normalize features (w coded 3-valued sex)
xScaler = StandardScaler()
xNormalized = xScaler.fit_transform(xCoded)

#Normalize labels
yScaler = StandardScaler()
labelNormalized = yScaler.fit_transform(np.array(labels).reshape(\
                    [-1, 1]))

#initialize matrix of betas at each step
betaMat = []
```

```
betaMat.append(list(beta))


#number of steps to take
nSteps = 500
stepSize = 0.01

betaMat, nzList = lars_coef_curves(xNormalized, labelNormalized, \
        nSteps, stepSize)

nameList = [namesCoded[nzList[i]] for i in range(len(nzList))]

print(nameList)
for i in range(ncols):
    #plot range of beta values for each attribute
    coefCurve = betaMat[i,:].reshape([-1,])
    xaxis = range(nSteps)
    plt.plot(xaxis, coefCurve)

plt.xlabel("Steps Taken")
plt.ylabel(("Coefficient Values"))
plt.savefig('larsAbalone.png', dpi=500)
plt.show()

Printed Output:
['Shell weight', 'Height', 'Sex2', 'Shucked weight', 'Diameter', 'Sex1',
'Whole weight', 'Viscera weight']
```

The first attribute is the gender of the abalone, which takes three values. When abalone are infants, their sex is indeterminate so the entries in the first column are M, F, and I.

The variable names associated with the columns are shown in a Python list that gets named *names*. With the abalone data set, these names don't come from the first row of data, but from a separate file on the UC Irvine website. The first variable in the list is Sex—the sex of the animal. The last variable in the list is Rings. These are shell rings that are counted by slicing the shell and counting up the rings through a microscope. The number of rings is essentially the age of the abalone. The objective of the problem is to train a regression system to predict the Rings using easier, less time-consuming and less-expensive measurements.

Coding the Sex attribute is accomplished before the attribute matrix is normalized. The process is to build two columns to represent the three possible values. The logic of the construction is that the first column has a 1 if the corresponding row is from a male (M) and zero otherwise. The second column is 1 for female (F). Both columns are zero if the example is an infant (I). The new columns that replace Sex are given the names Sex1 and Sex2.

Once this coding is accomplished, then the attribute matrix contains all numeric values, and the example proceeds as in earlier examples. It normalizes the variables to zero mean and unit standard deviation, and then it applies the LARS algorithm introduced earlier to develop coefficient curves. The printed output shows the order in which variables enter into the solution of the penalized linear regression solution. You'll observe that both the two columns coding for Sex appear in the solution.

Figure 4.9 shows the coefficient curves that result from LARS applied to this problem. Chapter 5 delves more into performance, with different approaches to this problem.

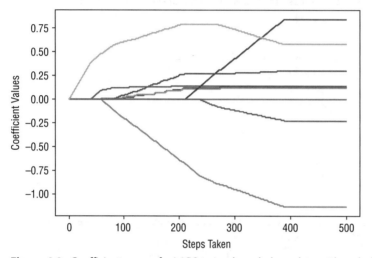

Figure 4.9: Coefficient curves for LARS trained on abalone data with coded categorical variable

This section discussed several extensions to penalized regression that broaden its utility to cover a wide class of problems. The section described a simple and frequently effective method of converting a classification problem to an ordinary regression problem. It also discussed how to convert a binary classifier into a multiclass classifier. The section went on to discuss how to model nonlinear behaviors using linear regression by adding new attributes that are nonlinear functions of the old attributes. Finally, the section showed how to turn categorical variables into real-valued variables so you can train linear algorithms on categorical variables. This method of converting categorical variables doesn't just work for linear regression. It is also useful for other linear methods such as support vector machines.

Summary

The goal of this chapter was to lay the groundwork for you to confidently understand and use the Python packages implementing the algorithms described here. The chapter described the nature of the input data set as a column vector of outcomes to be predicted and a table of attributes upon which to base the predictions. Chapter 3, the previous chapter, demonstrated that predictive models need to have their complexity tuned to get the best performance for a given problem complexity and data set size. Chapter 3 also showed some methods for introducing a tuning parameter into linear regression. This chapter built on that background and introduced several minimization problems where a tunable coefficient penalty was added to the error penalty from least squares regression. As was demonstrated, this tunable penalty on linear coefficient sizes results in suppression of the coefficients to a greater or lesser degree and thereby adds a complexity adjustment. You saw how to tune the complexity of the resulting models by using the error on out-of-sample data to achieve optimum performance.

The chapter described principles of operation for two modern algorithms for solving the penalized regression minimization problem and Python code implementing the main features of the algorithms in order for you to have a concrete instantiation of the core of the algorithms to make the principals of operation clear. The plain regression problem (numeric features and numeric targets) served as the exemplar for in-depth coverage of algorithms. The chapter showed several extensions to broaden the use cases to include binary classification problems, multiclass classification problems, problems with nonlinear relationship between attributes and outcomes, and problems with non-numeric features.

Chapter 5 will use Python packages implementing these algorithms to run through a series of examples that were chosen to exercise a variety of different problem characteristics in order to cement these ideas. Based on what you've learned in this chapter, the various parameters and methods in the Python packages will make sense for you.

References

1. Bradley Efron, Trevor Hastie, Iain Johnstone, and Robert Tibshirani (2004). "Least Angle Regression." *Annals of Statistics*, *32*(2), 407–499.

2. Jerome H. Friedman, Trevor Hastie, and Rob Tibshirani (2010). "Regularization Paths for Generalized Linear Models via Coordinate Descent." *Journal of Statistical Software*, vol. 33, issue 1, Feb 2010.

Building Predictive Models Using Penalized Linear Methods

Chapter 2 looked at a number of different data sets with an eye toward understanding the data sets, the relations between the various attributes and labels, and the nature of the problems being posed. This chapter picks up those data sets once again and runs through some case studies demonstrating the process of building predictive models by using the penalized linear methods that you saw in Chapter 4, "Penalized Linear Regression." Generally, the model building will be segmented into two or more parts.

You'll recall from Chapter 4 that model building with penalized linear regression has two steps. The first step is to run cross-validation to determine the best achievable out-of-sample performance and to identify the model that achieves it. Determining the achievable performance encompasses the hard design work, and in many of the examples in this chapter, that's the only step that will be presented. The second step is to train on the whole data set to trace out coefficient curves. The purpose of training on the whole data set is to get the best estimates of the model coefficients. But it does not change your estimate of the errors, which are the gauge of performance.

This chapter runs through a variety of different types of problems: regression problems, classification problems, problems with categorical attributes, and problems with nonlinear dependence of the labels on the attributes. It looks at basis expansion to see whether it improves the prediction performance. In each case, the objective is to work through the steps you'd take to arrive at a deployable linear model and to consider some alternative paths so that you can ensure that you're getting all the performance you can.

Python Packages for Penalized Linear Regression

The examples in Chapter 4 used Python versions of the training algorithms involved: LARS, and coordinate descent with the ElasticNet penalty. The purpose for using the Python code in Chapter 4 was to expose the workings of the algorithms to further your understanding of them. Fortunately, you don't have to code those algorithms each time you want to use them.

Scikit-learn has packages implementing Lasso, LARS, and ElasticNet regression. Using those packages has several advantages. One advantage is that using them results in fewer lines of code that you need to write and debug. Another big advantage is that they are much faster than the code in Chapter 4. The scikit-learn packages take advantage of practices like not computing correlations for attributes that aren't being used in order to cut down on the number of calculations. You'll see when you run these packages that they execute very quickly.

You can find the packages used in this chapter in `sklearn.linear_model`. The link `http://scikit-learn.org/stable/modules/classes.html#module-sklearn .linear _ model` shows a list including the models you'll see used here. Notice that several of the models come in two flavors. For example, there's a package titled `linear_model.ElasticNet` and one titled `linear_model.ElasticNetCV`. These two models correspond to the two tasks discussed at the beginning of this chapter. The Python package `linear_model.ElasticNet` is used to calculate coefficient curves on the whole data set, and `linear_model.ElasticNetCV` does the cross-validation run to produce out-of-sample estimates of performance. It's handy to have these two forms.

The same basic input objects fuel both versions (two NumPy arrays—one of attributes and one of labels). In some cases, you won't be able to use the cross-validation version because you'll need very specific control of the contents of training and test sets for each fold:

- If your problem has a categorical attribute that takes one of its values very infrequently, you may need to control sampling so that the attribute is represented evenly across the folds.

- You may also need to have access to the separate fold data to compile error statistics for your problem, if you want a different error measure from the *mean squared error* (MSE) that the CV packages deliver. You might prefer *mean absolute error* (MAE) because it better matches the penalty that you'll pay for errors in your real problem.

- Another example of needing fold-by-fold access for error statistics is when you use linear regression to solve classification problems. As discussed in Chapter 3, "Predictive Model Building: Balancing Performance, Complexity, and Big Data," standard error measures for classification problems are things such as misclassification error or *area under the ROC curve* (AUC). You'll see that case specifically in the "rocks versus mines" and "glass classification" case studies in this chapter.

You should keep a couple of things in mind as you look at these packages and begin thinking about using them. One is that some of them (but not all of them) automatically normalize the attributes before fitting a model. The second thing to be aware of is that the scikit-learn packages name variables differently from Chapter 4 and Friedman's papers. Chapter 4 used the variable λ to represent the multiplier on the coefficient penalty and used the variable α to represent the proportion of Lasso penalty versus ridge penalty in the ElasticNet penalty. The scikit-learn packages use α instead of λ and l1_ratio instead of α. The text that follows switches to the notation used in the scikit-learn packages.

SOME SCIKIT-LEARN CHANGES

The scikit-learn documentation states an intention to bring all the penalized regression packages into conformance with one another by including normalization in all of them. That is in process at the time of writing this book.

Multivariable Regression: Predicting Wine Taste

As discussed in Chapter 2, "Understand the Problem by Understanding the Data" the wine taste data set comes from the UC Irvine data repository (`http://archive.ics.uci.edu/ml/datasets/Wine+Quality`). The data set contains chemical analyses for 1,599 wines along with average taste scores given to each wine by a panel of wine tasters. The predictive problem is to predict the taste given the data on chemical composition. The chemical composition data consist of numeric measurements of 11 different chemical properties—alcohol content, pH and citric acid, and so on. Have a look at the exploration of these data in Chapter 2 or look at the UC Irvine page for the data set for more information.

Predicting the wine taste is a regression problem because the objective of the problem is to predict the quality score, which is an integer between 0 and 10. The data set only includes examples between 3 and 8. Because only integer scores are given, it is also possible to treat this problem as a multiclass classification problem. The multiclass problem would have six possible classifications (the integers from 3 to 8). It would ignore the order relation that exists among the various scores. (For example, 5 is a worse score than 6 and a better score than 4.) Regression is a more natural way to pose the problem because it preserves the order relationship.

Another way to think about how to pose the problem is to consider the different error measures that come with a regression problem versus a multiclass classification problem. The regression error function is the average squared error. When the true taste is 3, predicting a 5 contributes more to the cumulative error than predicting a 4. The error measure for the multiclass problem is the number of examples that get misclassified. With this error measure, if the true taste is 3, predicting a 5 or 4 contributes the same amount to the cumulative error. Regression seems more natural, but I don't know of a way to prove that it will give superior performance. The only way to know whether this is the best approach is to try both. In the section titled "Multiclass Classification: Classifying Crime Scene Glass Samples," you'll see how to handle multiclass classification problems. You can then come back and try the multiclass approach to see whether it does better or worse. What error measure will you use?

Building and Testing a Model to Predict Wine Taste

The first step in the process of building a model is to generate some out-of-sample performance numbers to see whether they're going to meet your performance requirements. Listing 5-1 shows the code to perform 10-fold cross-validation and plot the results. The sklearn.linear_model package LassoCV does all the work of dividing the data into cross-validation folds, running the Lasso modeling process on in-sample data for each fold, and testing performance on out-of-sample data for a range of weight penalty parameters (alpha) values. Check the sklearn documentation to see default values for the parameters required. At a minimum you'll probably want to supply the number of folds and to set normalize=True. The default is to leave the data unnormalized. The two plots in Figures 5.1 and 5.2 show the results of running the code with and without normalization. You can generate these two figures yourself by running the code in the Python notebook that you'll find in the code for this book. To see the two different versions of the curves, simply toggle the normalize parameter back and forth between 'normalize=True' and 'normalize=False'. The corresponding plot will appear in the results cell for the code.

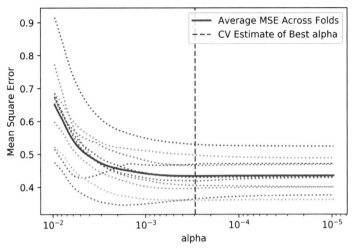

Figure 5.1: Out-of-sample error with normalized data—Lasso model on wine taste data

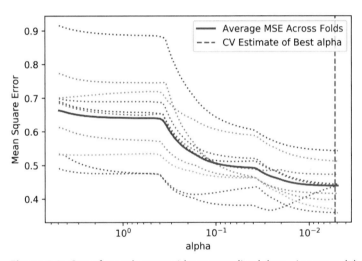

Figure 5.2: Out-of-sample error with unnormalized data—Lasso model on wine taste data

Listing 5-1: Using Cross-Validation to Estimate Out-of-Sample Error with Lasso Modeling Wine Taste—wineLassoCV.py

```
__author__ = 'mike-bowles'

from Read_Fcns import list_read_wine
import numpy
from sklearn import datasets, linear_model
from sklearn.linear_model import LassoCV
from math import sqrt
import matplotlib.pyplot as plt
```

```
#read data into iterable
names, xList, labels = list_read_wine()

#Use LassoCV class from sklearn.linear_model
#sklearn lasso class includes a normalization option, so
#normalization isn't required
#to get the unnormalized version of the curves just change
#normalize=True to normalize=False
wineModel = LassoCV(cv=10, normalize=True).fit(xList, labels)

# Display results
plt.figure()
plt.plot(wineModel.alphas_, wineModel.mse_path_, ':')
plt.plot(wineModel.alphas_, wineModel.mse_path_.mean(axis=-1),
         label='Average MSE Across Folds', linewidth=2)
plt.axvline(wineModel.alpha_, linestyle='--',
         label='CV Estimate of Best alpha')
plt.semilogx()
plt.legend()
ax = plt.gca()
ax.invert_xaxis()
plt.xlabel('alpha')
plt.ylabel('Mean Square Error')
plt.axis('tight')
#plt.savefig('wineLassoCVNormalized.png', dpi=500)
plt.show()

#print out the value of alpha that minimizes the Cv-error
print("alpha Value that Minimizes CV Error", wineModel.alpha_)
print("Minimum MSE  ", min(wineModel.mse_path_.mean(axis=-1)))
Printed Output:

Normalized Version:
alpha Value that Minimizes CV Error 0.00029358033516
Minimum MSE   0.4339376197674394

Unnormalized Version:
alpha Value that Minimizes CV Error  0.0052692947038
Minimum MSE   0.4393606730929137
```

The performance numbers in Listing 5-1 show a slight worsening of performance if the data is left unnormalized. However, the plot of CV error versus alpha in Figure 5.2 shows a radical difference from the plot in Figure 5.1. The plot has a scalloped character that's caused by the mishmash of scales that comes from leaving the X's unscaled. What happens is that the algorithm picks a large variable that requires a correspondingly small coefficient. That can happen if the variable has high correlation with Y or if the variable has low correlation with Y and a large scale. The algorithm uses a somewhat inferior variable for a few iterations until α (formerly known as λ) gets small enough to let in a better variable, at which time the error drops precipitously. The moral of the story is to normalize the X's or be wary about not normalizing them. You'll get better models that way.

Training on the Whole Data Set before Deployment

Listing 5-2 shows the code for training on the whole data set. As mentioned, the reason for training on the whole data set is to obtain the best set of coefficients for deployment. Cross-validation yields an estimate of the deployed model's performance and gives you the α value that yields the best performance. The program in Listing 5-2 does two things. It trains a model on normalized data in order to visualize coefficient curves and to assess variable importance. Variable importance uses the coefficients applied to normalized data to determine which variables are most important. But you'll probably want to have coefficients that you can apply directly to the data in its natural state. That's what you get when the normalization is done internal to the Lasso package that gets called at the end of the listing. The Lasso package, as with most of the other penalized regression packages, will accept data with its natural scaling. If you take the package's option to normalize the data, the package will internally normalize the data and calculate coefficients. It will then transform the coefficients back to what you'll want for application to the unnormalized data. You'll see those coefficients at the end of the listing. Coefficient curves relative to normalized data are shown in Figure 5.3.

Listing 5-2: Lasso Training on Full Data Set—wineLassoCoefCurves.py

```
__author__ = 'mike-bowles'

from Read_Fcns import list_read_wine
import numpy as np
from sklearn import datasets, linear_model
from sklearn.linear_model import LassoCV, lasso_path, Lasso
from sklearn.preprocessing import StandardScaler
from math import sqrt
import matplotlib.pyplot as plt

#read data
names, xList, labels = list_read_wine()

#First let's see the coefficient curves for the full data set and get a
#feel for variable importance
#For variable importance you'll need to normalize the variables before
#fitting otherwise the models will
#return coefficients relative to full scale variables which is what you
#need for applying the model
#but to determine importance you need coefficients on normalized
#features.
```

```
#lasso_path doesn't have a built-in normalize option
alphas, coefs, _ = lasso_path(StandardScaler().fit_transform(xList),
        labels,  return_models=False)

plt.xlabel('alpha')
plt.ylabel('Coefficients')
plt.semilogx(alphas,coefs.T)
plt.axis('tight')
ax = plt.gca()
ax.invert_xaxis()
plt.savefig('wineLassoCoefCurves.png', dpi=500)
plt.show()
nattr, nalpha = coefs.shape

#find coefficient ordering
nzList = []
for iAlpha in range(1,nalpha):
    coefList = list(coefs[: ,iAlpha])
    nzCoef = [index for index in range(nattr) if coefList[index]
        != 0.0]
    for q in nzCoef:
        if not(q in nzList):
            nzList.append(q)

print("Features Ordered by How Early They Enter the model:")
_ = [print(names[nzList[i]]) for i in range(len(nzList))]


#find coefficients corresponding to best alpha value = 0.00029358033
alphaStar = 0.00029358033516075065
indexLTalphaStar = [index for index in range(100) if alphas[index] >
        alphaStar]
indexStar = max(indexLTalphaStar)

#here's the set of coefficients to deploy
coefStar = list(coefs[:,indexStar])

# The coefficients on normalized attributes give another slightly
# different ordering
absCoef = [abs(a) for a in coefStar]

#sort by magnitude
coefSorted = sorted(absCoef, reverse=True)

idxCoefSize = [absCoef.index(a) for a in coefSorted if not(a == 0.0)]

print('\nFeatures ordered by coefficient size on normalized features:')
_ = [print(names[idxCoefSize[i]]) for i in range(len(idxCoefSize))]
```

```
lasso_model = linear_model.Lasso(alpha=0.00029358033516075065,
      normalize=True)
lasso_model.fit(xList, labels)

print('\nCoefficient relative to natural features (from model trained
      on normalized features)')
_ = [ print(a, '\t', b) for (a,b) in zip(names, lasso_model.coef_)]
```

```
Printed Output:
Features Ordered by How Early They Enter the Model:
"alcohol"
"volatile acidity"
"sulphates"
"total sulfur dioxide"
"chlorides"
"fixed acidity"
"pH"
"free sulfur dioxide"
"residual sugar"
"citric acid"
"density"

Features ordered by coefficient size on normalized features:
"alcohol"
"volatile acidity"
"sulphates"
"total sulfur dioxide"
"chlorides"
"pH"
"free sulfur dioxide"
"fixed acidity"
"citric acid"
"density"
"residual sugar"

Coefficient relative to natural features (from model trained on
normalized features)
"fixed acidity"            0.0
"volatile acidity"        -1.0281352611594459
"citric acid"             -0.0
"residual sugar"           0.0
"chlorides"               -1.5880563981842544
"free sulfur dioxide"      0.0014678661905409881
"total sulfur dioxide"    -0.002355585750391008
"density"                 -0.0
"pH"                      -0.3458236199282011
"sulphates"                0.7946569090063523
"alcohol"                  0.28388450021384204
```

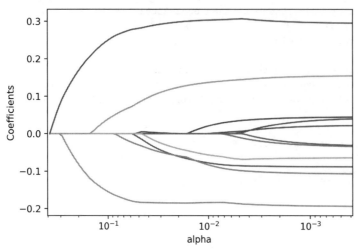

Figure 5.3: Coefficient curves for Lasso trained to predict wine quality

The printed output in Listing 5-2 shows variable importance calculated in two different ways. One way is to order the variables according to how early they become non-zero as alpha is decreased. This only makes sense with normalized data. The first variable to get a non-zero coefficient is most important, the second one is second most important, and so forth. You'll see the variables listed in that order as part of the printed output in Listing 5-2. The second way to determine variable importance is to look at the magnitude of the coefficients at the value of alpha that gave the best performance in cross-validation. Again, this ordering only makes sense with normalized variables. That list is also shown in the printed output in Listing 5-2. Generally, the two methods agree on the most important variables and their ordering. The two methods disagree on some of the less important variables. That's normal. The importance rankings further down the list are less stable. Since all of the variables will enter the model at some point, the first method gives a ranking to all of the variables. The second method uses coefficients at the best alpha value, which means that some of the coefficients may be zero.

There's an interesting quirk in the ordering. You'll see that fixed acidity is fourth from the bottom of the list generated by coefficient values, and you can see from the coefficient values that fixed acidity has a 0.0 coefficient in the model chosen by cross-validation. But fixed acidity comes in sixth from the last according to that measure of importance. Have a close look at the coefficient curves. You'll see that the coefficient for fixed acidity briefly becomes non-zero. It's the sixth variable to do so as you can see in the coefficient plots. But it returns to zero to be replaced by another free sulphur dioxide in the best set of coefficients. To see this level of detail, it might be best to run the program in a Jupyter notebook, which you can get off the book's code page. It will store the image as a high-resolution PNG file and you can blow it up to see the details.

The program has hard-coded the α value that gave the best results in cross-validation. The version in the code is the best alpha trained with normalized attributes and labels. Changing either of these to unnormalized will change the corresponding value of the best α. Changing Y to unnormalized changes it by the 1.2 factor that comes from normalizing the standard deviation to 1.0 (as discussed earlier in the context of the MSE difference between normalized and unnormalized labels). The hard-coded value of α is used to identify the vector of coefficients corresponding to the best cross-validation results.

Basis Expansion: Improving Performance by Creating New Variables from Old Ones

Chapter 4 discussed adding new attributes in the form of functions of the old attributes. The point of doing that is to see whether it results in improved performance. Listing 5-3 shows how to add two new attributes to the wine data.

Listing 5-3: Using Out-of-Sample Error to Evaluate New Attributes for Predicting Wine Quality—wineExpandedLassoCV.py

```
__author__ = 'mike-bowles'

from Read_Fcns import list_read_wine
import numpy as np
from sklearn.preprocessing import StandardScaler
from sklearn import datasets, linear_model
from sklearn.linear_model import LassoCV
from math import sqrt
import matplotlib.pyplot as plt

# read data into iterable
names, xList, labels = list_read_wine()

# append two new attributes - square of last term (alcohol) and product
# of alcohol and volatile acidity
for i in range(len(xList)):
    alcElt = xList[i][-1]
    volAcid = xList[i][1]
    temp = list(xList[i])
    temp.append(alcElt*alcElt)
    temp.append(alcElt*volAcid)
    xList[i] = list(temp)

# check the new dimensions
print('New number of attributes    ', len(xList[0]))

#add new names to variable list
names.append("alco^2")
names.append("alco*volAcid")
```

```
# Normalize columns in x and labels
# Note: be careful about normalization.  Some penalized regression
# packages include it
# and some don't.

xScaler = StandardScaler()
xNormalized = xScaler.fit_transform(xList)

# Normalize labels
yScaler = StandardScaler()
yNormalized = yScaler.fit_transform(np.array(labels).reshape([
        -1,1])).reshape([-1])

#normalized lables
Y = np.array(yNormalized)

#Normalized Xs
X = np.array(xNormalized)

#Call LassoCV from sklearn.linear_model
wineModel = LassoCV(cv=10).fit(X, Y)

# Display results

plt.figure()
plt.plot(wineModel.alphas_, wineModel.mse_path_, ':')
plt.plot(wineModel.alphas_, wineModel.mse_path_.mean(axis=-1),
        label='Average MSE Across Folds', linewidth=2)
plt.axvline(wineModel.alpha_, linestyle='--',
            label='CV Estimate of Best alpha')
plt.semilogx()
plt.legend()
ax = plt.gca()
ax.invert_xaxis()
plt.xlabel('alpha')
plt.ylabel('Mean Square Error')
plt.axis('tight')
plt.savefig('wineExpandedLassoCV.png', dpi=500)
plt.show()

#print out the value of alpha that minimizes the Cv-error
print("alpha Value that Minimizes CV Error  ",wineModel.alpha_)
print("Minimum MSE  ", min(wineModel.mse_path_.mean(axis=-1)))

Printed Output:
New number of attributes    13

alpha Value that Minimizes CV Error    0.020612103466917726
Minimum MSE    0.6666999823938234
```

The key step comes right after the attributes are read in and converted to floats. A dozen or so lines of code take each row of attributes, pull out the two variables corresponding to measures of alcohol and volatile acidity, and then append *alcohol squared* and the product *alcohol times volatile acidity*. These are chosen because it makes sense to start with variables that are more important in the solution. A thorough hunt for possible improvements might include several attempts with combinations of the top variables.

The results show that adding these new variables degrades performance slightly. A little hunting might synthesize some new variables that make a useful difference. You might run out coefficient curves for this example to see whether the new variables replaced any old ones that were important at the optimum solution. That information might lead you to remove the old variables in favor of these new synthetic ones.

Figure 5.4 shows the cross-validation error curves for Lasso trained using the expanded set of attributes. The character of the cross-validation curves doesn't show substantial difference from the curves without basis expansion.

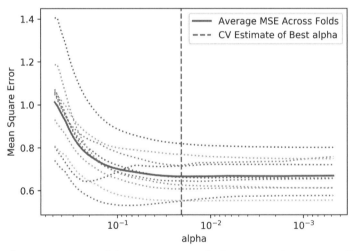

Figure 5.4: Cross-validation error curves for Lasso trained on wine quality data with expanded feature set

This section has demonstrated the use of penalized regression methods on a problem with real number outcomes—a regression problem. The next section shows the use of penalized linear regression methods on a problem where the outcomes are two-valued. The code will look similar to what you have seen in this section, and some of the techniques, like basis expansion, can be used in classification problems. The main difference is how performance is scored for a classification problem.

Binary Classification: Using Penalized Linear Regression to Detect Unexploded Mines

Chapter 4 discussed how you can use penalized linear regression for classification problems and set the process up for the rocks versus mines problem. This section gets into the details of how you would approach and solve a binary classification problem using penalized linear regression. The section incorporates the Python ElasticNet package. You'll recall from Chapter 4 that ElasticNet incorporates a more general penalty function that includes the Lasso and ridge regression penalty functions as special cases. This makes it possible to see how performance of the classifier changes as you make alterations in the penalty function. These are the steps along the path to a solution:

1. Cast the binary classification problem as a regression problem. Construct an outcome vector of real number labels by assigning 0.0 when the class outcome takes one of its two values and assigning 1.0 when it takes the other.

2. Perform cross-validation. The cross-validation becomes a little more complicated because you'll need to calculate an error quantity for each fold. Scikit-learn has some handy utilities to streamline these calculations.

The first step (outlined in Chapter 4) is to cast the binary classification problem as a regression problem by replacing the classification labels with real number labels. The rocks versus mines problem is basically to build a system using sonar to detect unexploded mines on the seabed. You'll recall from the data discovery in Chapter 2 that the data set contains digitized versions of the signals returned from rocks and from metal cylinders shaped like mines. The objective is to build a prediction system that can process the digitized signals to correctly identify whether the object is a rock or a mine. The data set consists of 208 experiments. Of the 208, 111 are mines and 97 are rocks. The data set is 61 columns wide. The first 60 columns contain the digitized sonar return. The last column contains an M or an R, depending on whether the object is in a rock or a mine. The 60 columns of numbers are the attributes for the problem. A regression problem requires numeric labels, too. An approach outlined in Chapter 4 is to build the column of numeric labels by assigning the number 1 to one of the two cases and 0 to the other. Listing 5-4 initializes an empty list called *labels* and appends a 1.0 for each M row and a 0.0 for each R row.

With numeric attributes and numeric labels, everything is in place to use the regression version of penalized linear regression. The next logical step is to perform cross-validation to get an estimate of out-of-sample performance and identify the best value of α, the penalty parameter. For this problem, doing cross-validation requires building a cross-validation loop to enclose training and testing. Why build a cross-validation loop instead of using the cross-validation package available in Python (like the one used in the wine quality example earlier in this chapter)?

The cross-validation for regression is based on MSE. That's perfectly reasonable for a regression problem, but not for a classification problem. As discussed in Chapter 3, you characterize performance differently for a classification problem than for a regression problem. Chapter 3 discussed several ways to characterize performance. One natural way is to measure the percentage of examples that are misclassified. Another way is to measure the AUC. See Chapter 3 or the Wikipedia page http://en.wikipedia.org/wiki/Receiver_operating_characteristic to refresh your memory on the AUC measure. To measure either of these requires that you have access to the predictions and labels in each of the cross-validation folds. You can't judge misclassification error from a summary of the MSE for the fold.

The cross-validation loop breaks the data into training and test sets and then calls the Python enet_path method to accomplish training on the training portion of the data. Two inputs to the routine are different from defaults. One is the l1_ratio, which is set equal to 0.8. This parameter determines what fraction of the penalty is the sum of absolute values of coefficients. The value 0.8 means that penalty function is 80 percent sum of absolute values and 20 percent sum of squares. The other nondefault parameter is fit_intercept, which is set to False. The code is using normalized labels and normalized attributes. Because all of these are zero mean, there's no need to calculate an intercept term. The intercept is required only to adjust any constant offset between the attributes and the labels. Eliminating the need for the intercept term by using normalized labels makes the calculation of predictions a little cleaner. The only downside of normalizing the labels is that it makes the MSE calculation less meaningful relative to a regression problem, but for a classification problem, you're not going to use that metric of performance anyway.

In each fold, after training is completed, the coefficients that are produced are used to generate predictions on the out-of-sample data for the fold. This is accomplished in the code by using the numpy dot function, the attributes for out-of-sample data for the fold, and the coefficients for the fold. This matrix-like multiplication of two numpy arrays leads to another two-dimensional array whose rows correspond to the rows in the out-of-sample test data for the fold and whose columns correspond to the sequence of models generated by enet_path (that is, the sequence of coefficient vectors and the corresponding sequence of α's). These matrices of predictions for each fold are concatenated (visualize stacking them atop one another), as are the out-of-sample labels. Then, at the end of the run, these compendia of the fold-by-fold out-of-sample results can be processed easily and efficiently to yield performance data for each model and to select a model complexity (α) for deployment.

Listing 5-4 generates comparisons using two metrics. The first is misclassification error. The second is area under the *receiver operating curve* (ROC). Each column from the matrix of predictions represents predictions generated for the totality of the out-of-sample data for one set of model coefficients. All the data are represented in each column since every row is held out in one (and only one) of the folds. The misclassification comparison considers the prediction data one column at a time and out-of-sample labels (called yOut in the code) accumulated fold by fold. Each prediction is compared to a fixed threshold (0.0 in this example) to determine a predicted classification. Then the predicted classification is compared to the corresponding entry in yOut to determine whether the predicted classification is correct.

Listing 5-4: Using ElasticNet Regression to Build a Binary (Two-Class) Classifier—rocksVMinesENetRegCV.py

```
__author__ = 'mike_bowles'

from Read_Fcns import list_read_rvm
from math import sqrt, fabs, exp
import matplotlib.pyplot as plt
from sklearn.preprocessing import StandardScaler
from sklearn.linear_model import enet_path
from sklearn.metrics import roc_auc_score, roc_curve
import numpy as np

#read data from uci data repository
xNum, labels = list_read_rvm()

#number of rows and columns in x matrix
nrow = len(xNum)
ncol = len(xNum[1])

#use StandardScaler to normalize data
xScaler = StandardScaler()
xNormalized = xScaler.fit_transform(xNum)

yScaler = StandardScaler()
labelsNormalized = yScaler.fit_transform(np.array(labels).
reshape([-1, 1])).reshape([-1])

#number of cross validation folds
nxval = 10


for ixval in range(nxval):
    #Define test and training index sets
    idxTest = [a for a in range(nrow) if a%nxval == ixval%nxval]
    idxTrain = [a for a in range(nrow) if a%nxval != ixval%nxval]

    #Define test and training attribute and label sets
    xTrain = numpy.array([xNormalized[r] for r in idxTrain])
    xTest = numpy.array([xNormalized[r] for r in idxTest])
```

```
    labelTrain = numpy.array([labelsNormalized[r] for r in idxTrain])
    labelTest = numpy.array([labelsNormalized[r] for r in idxTest])

    alphas, coefs, _ = enet_path(xTrain, labelTrain,l1_ratio=0.8,
fit_intercept=False, return_models=False)

    #apply coefs to test data to produce predictions and accumulate
    if ixval == 0:
        pred = numpy.dot(xTest, coefs)
        yOut = labelTest
    else:
        #accumulate predictions
        yTemp = numpy.array(yOut)
        yOut = numpy.concatenate((yTemp, labelTest), axis=0)

        #accumulate predictions
        predTemp = numpy.array(pred)
        pred = numpy.concatenate((predTemp, numpy.dot(xTest, coefs)),
axis = 0)


#calculate misclassification error
misClassRate = []
_,nPred = pred.shape
for iPred in range(1, nPred):
    predList = list(pred[:, iPred])
    errCnt = 0.0
    for irow in range(nrow):
        if (predList[irow] < 0.0) and (yOut[irow] >= 0.0):
            errCnt += 1.0
        elif (predList[irow] >= 0.0) and (yOut[irow] < 0.0):
            errCnt += 1.0
    misClassRate.append(errCnt/nrow)

#find minimum point for plot and for print
minError = min(misClassRate)
idxMin = misClassRate.index(minError)
pltAlphas = list(alphas[1:len(alphas)])

plt.figure()
plt.plot(plotAlphas, misClassRate, label='Misclassification Error Across
Folds', linewidth=2)
plt.axvline(plotAlphas[idxMin], linestyle='--',
            label='CV Estimate of Best alpha')
plt.legend()
plt.semilogx()
ax = plt.gca()
ax.invert_xaxis()
plt.xlabel('alpha')
plt.ylabel('Misclassification Error')
```

```python
plt.axis('tight')
plt.show()

#calculate AUC.
idxPos = [i for i in range(nrow) if yOut[i] > 0.0]
yOutBin = [0] * nrow
for i in idxPos: yOutBin[i] = 1

auc = []
for iPred in range(1, nPred):
    predList = list(pred[:, iPred])
    aucCalc = roc_auc_score(yOutBin, predList)
    auc.append(aucCalc)

maxAUC = max(auc)
idxMax = auc.index(maxAUC)

plt.figure()
plt.plot(plotAlphas, auc, label='AUC Across Folds', linewidth=2)
plt.axvline(plotAlphas[idxMax], linestyle='--',
            label='CV Estimate of Best alpha')
plt.legend()
plt.semilogx()
ax = plt.gca()
ax.invert_xaxis()
plt.xlabel('alpha')
plt.ylabel('Area Under the ROC Curve')
plt.axis('tight')
plt.show()


#plot best version of ROC curve
fpr, tpr, thresh = roc_curve(yOutBin, list(pred[:, idxMax]))
ctClass = [i*0.01 for i in range(101)]

plt.plot(fpr, tpr, linewidth=2)
plt.plot(ctClass, ctClass, linestyle=':')
plt.xlabel('False Positive Rate')
plt.ylabel('True Positive Rate')
plt.show()

print('Best Value of Misclassification Error = ', misClassRate[idxMin])
print('Best alpha for Misclassification Error = ', plotAlphas[idxMin])
print('')
print('Best Value for AUC = ', auc[idxMax])
print('Best alpha for AUC   = ', plotAlphas[idxMax])

print('')
print('Confusion Matrices for Different Threshold Values\n')
```

```
#pick some points along the curve to print.  There are 57 points.
#The extremes aren't useful
#Sample at 14, 28 and 42.  Use the calculated values of tpr and fpr
#along with definitions and threshold values.
#Some nomenclature (e.g. see wikkipedia "receiver operating curve")


P = len(idxPos)    #P = Positive cases
N = nrow - P       #N = Negative cases
TP = tpr[14] * P   #TP = True positives = tpr * P
FN = P - TP        #FN = False negatives = P - TP
FP = fpr[14] * N   #FP = False positives = fpr * N
TN = N - FP        #TN = True negatives = N - FP

print('Threshold Value =    ', thresh[14])
print('TP = ', TP, 'FP = ', FP)
print('FN = ', FN, 'TN = ', TN)


TP = tpr[28] * P; FN = P - TP; FP = fpr[28] * N; TN = N - FP

print('\nThreshold Value =    ', thresh[28])
print('TP = ', TP, 'FP = ', FP)
print('FN = ', FN, 'TN = ', TN)


TP = tpr[42] * P; FN = P - TP; FP = fpr[42] * N; TN = N - FP

print('\nThreshold Value =    ', thresh[42])
print('TP = ', TP, 'FP = ', FP)
print('FN = ', FN, 'TN = ', TN)

Printed Output:
Best Value of Misclassification Error =  0.22115384615384615
Best alpha for Misclassification Error =  0.017686244720179392

Best Value for AUC =  0.8686727965078481
Best alpha for AUC   =   0.020334883589342524

Confusion Matrices for Different Threshold Values

Threshold Value =     0.21560082129001007
TP =  61.00000000000001 FP =  11.0
FN =  49.99999999999999 TN =  86.0

Threshold Value =     -0.09435189216167568
TP =  89.0 FP =  23.0
FN =  22.0 TN =  74.0

Threshold Value =     -0.3223693818719528
TP =  100.0 FP =  40.0
FN =  11.0 TN =  57.0
```

The plot in Figure 5.5 shows several points that achieve the same minimum. It's good practice when you have a choice to choose the point farthest to the left on the graph of performance versus α. That's because points to the right have more tendency to be overfit. It's more conservative to choose a solution farther to the left. You'll have a better chance that the errors in deployment will match those you see in cross-validation.

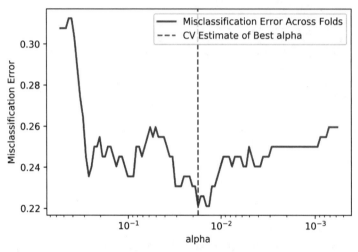

Figure 5.5: Out-of-sample classifier misclassification performance

Another way to measure the performance of your classifier is AUC. AUC has the advantage that in maximizing the AUC you wind up getting the best performance independent of where you intend to operate the system—whether you want more or less equal rates of different types of errors or you'd prefer to bias the errors toward one type. Strictly speaking, maximizing AUC does not guarantee that you'll get optimum performance at a particular error rate. Comparing the model chosen by AUC to the one chosen by minimizing overall error rate and observing the shapes of the curves help you get confidence in your solution and give you some idea about how much more performance is available with more thorough optimization.

The AUC calculations shown in Listing 5-4 use the `roc_curve` and `roc_auc_score` programs from the `sklearn.metrics` package The process for generating the AUC versus α curve is similar to the process for the misclassification error, except the column of predictions and the true values are passed to the `roc_auc_score` program to generate the AUC number. Those then get plotted in Figure 5.6. The resulting curve looks roughly like the misclassification error curve upside down—upside down because larger is better for AUC, whereas smaller is better for misclassification error. The printed output at the end of Listing 5-4 shows that the location of the optimum model based on misclassification error isn't exactly the same as the optimum model for AUC, but they're not far apart. Figure 5.7 shows the ROC plot for the classifier that maximizes AUC.

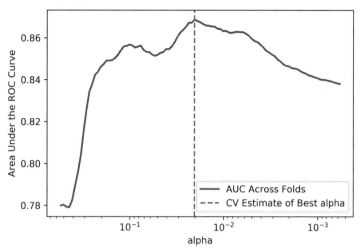

Figure 5.6: Out-of-sample classifier AUC performance

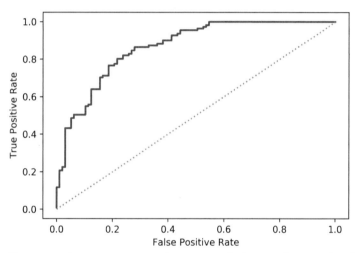

Figure 5.7: Receiver operating characteristic for best performing classifier

In your problem, some errors might be more expensive than others, causing you to want to bias the results away from the expensive errors in favor of the less expensive errors. For the rocks versus mines problem, there may be much higher expense for incorrectly classifying an unexploded mine as a rock than for classifying a rock as a mine.

One systematic way to deal with this is to use a confusion matrix, discussed in Chapter 3. It's relatively easy to build from the output of the roc _ curve program. The points on the ROC curve correspond to different values of threshold. The point (1,1) corresponds to the extreme where the threshold is set so low that all the points are classified as mines. That makes both the true positive rate and false positive rate equal one; the classifier gets all the positive points right, but it also gets all the negative points wrong. Setting the threshold higher than all the points gives the opposite corner of the plot. Getting the details on how points are shifting between the various boxes in the confusion matrix requires picking some threshold values and printing out the results. Listing 5-4 shows three values of threshold chosen from the range of threshold values at inner quartiles of the threshold values (that is, excluding the end points). Setting the threshold high results in low false positives and high false negatives. Setting the threshold low has the opposite behavior. Setting the threshold in the middle more nearly balances the two types of errors.

You could get a best value of threshold by associating costs with each type of error and finding the value of the threshold that minimizes the total cost. The three confusion matrices in the printed output can serve as an example for how this would work. If false positive and false negative both cost $1, the middle table (corresponding to a threshold value of −0.0455) gives a total cost of $46, whereas the higher threshold gives $68 and the lower threshold gives $54. However, if the cost for false positive is $10 and the cost for false negative is $1, the higher threshold gives $113, the middle gives $226, and the lower gives $504. You might want to test more threshold values at finer granularity. For this approach to work properly, you'll need to get the costs in a reasonable ballpark, and you'll need to make sure that the percentages of positive cases and negative cases match those that you'll see in real examples. The rocks versus mines examples were set up in a laboratory environment and probably don't represent the actual numbers of rocks versus mines in a harbor. That's easy enough to fix by oversampling one class or the other—that is, replicating some of the examples in one class or the other to get the proportions to match those you expect to see in deployment.

The data in the rocks versus mines training set are well balanced. That is, there are roughly the same number of positive and negative examples. In some data sets, there may be many more examples of one class or the other. For example, clicks on Internet ads are a small fraction of 1 percent of the number of times the ads are seen. You may get better training results by over-representing the less numerous examples so that the proportions are closer to equal. You can accomplish this by replicating some of the less numerous cases or removing some of the more numerous ones.

Cross-validation gives you a solid estimate of the performance that you are going to see when you deploy this system. If the performance indicated by cross-validation is not good enough, you will have to work to improve it. For example, you might try the basis expansion that was used in the section "Multivariable Regression: Predicting Wine Taste." You might also have a look at the cases giving the worst errors and see if you can discern a pattern, whether they're data-entry errors or if another variable can be added that would account for their being mistaken so badly. If the error satisfies the needs of your problem, you'll want to train a model on the whole data set for deployment. The next section runs through that process.

Build a Rocks Versus Mines Classifier for Deployment

As with the wine quality case study, the next step is to retrain the model on the full data set and pull out the coefficients corresponding to the best alpha—the one determined to minimize out-of-sample error, which is estimated in this case study by cross-validation. Listing 5-5 shows the code for accomplishing this.

Listing 5-5: Coefficient Trajectories for ElasticNet Trained on Rocks Versus Mines Data—rocksVMinesCoefCurves.py

```
__author__ = 'mike_bowles'

from Read_Fcns import list_read_rvm
from math import sqrt, fabs, exp
import matplotlib.pyplot as plt
from sklearn.preprocessing import StandardScaler
from sklearn.linear_model import enet_path
from sklearn.metrics import roc_auc_score, roc_curve
import numpy as np

#read data from uci data repository
xNum, labels = list_read_rvm()

#number of rows and columns in x matrix
nrow = len(xNum)
ncol = len(xNum[1])

#use StandardScaler to normalize data
xScaler = StandardScaler()
xNormalized = xScaler.fit_transform(xNum)

yScaler = StandardScaler()
labelsNormalized = yScaler.fit_transform(np.array(labels).
reshape([-1, 1])).reshape([-1])

#Convert normalized labels to numpy array
Y = np.array(labelsNormalized)

#Convert normalized attributes to numpy array
X = np.array(xNormalized)

alphas, coefs, _ = enet_path(X, Y,l1_ratio=0.8, fit_intercept=True,
        return_models=False)

plt.xlabel('alpha')
plt.ylabel('Coefficients')
plt.semilogx(alphas,coefs.T)
plt.axis('tight')
ax = plt.gca()
ax.invert_xaxis()
```

```
# plt.savefig('rocksVMinesCoefCurves.png', dpi=500)
plt.show()
nattr, nalpha = coefs.shape

#find coefficient ordering
nzList = []
for iAlpha in range(1,nalpha):
    coefList = list(coefs[: ,iAlpha])
    nzCoef = [index for index in range(nattr) if coefList[index]
            != 0.0]
    for q in nzCoef:
        if not(q in nzList):
            nzList.append(q)

#make up names for columns of X
names = ['V' + str(i) for i in range(ncol)]
nameList = [names[nzList[i]] for i in range(len(nzList))]
print("Attributes Ordered by How Early They Enter the Model")
print(nameList)
print('')

#find coefficients corresponding to best alpha value. alpha value
#corresponding to
#normalized X and normalized Y is 0.020334883589342503

alphaStar = 0.020334883589342503
indexLTalphaStar = [index for index in range(100) if alphas[index] >
      alphaStar]
indexStar = max(indexLTalphaStar)

#here's the set of coefficients to deploy
coefStar = list(coefs[:,indexStar])
print("Best Coefficient Values ")
print(coefStar)
print('')

#The coefficients on normalized attributes give another slightly
#different ordering

absCoef = [abs(a) for a in coefStar]

#sort by magnitude
coefSorted = sorted(absCoef, reverse=True)

idxCoefSize = [absCoef.index(a) for a in coefSorted if not(a == 0.0)]

namesList2 = [names[idxCoefSize[i]] for i in range(len(idxCoefSize))]

print("Attributes Ordered by Coef Size at Optimum alpha")
print(namesList2)
```

```
Printed Output: (output truncated run jupyter notebook in repo for
                        more)
Attributes Ordered by How Early They Enter the Model:
['V10', 'V48', 'V11', 'V44', 'V35', 'V51', 'V20', ... , 'V41', 'V40',
'V59', 'V12', 'V9', 'V18', 'V14', 'V47', 'V42']


Best Coefficient Values
[0.08225825681376615, 0.0020619887220037283, -0.11828642590855767,
... 0.06809647597425712, 0.07048886443547747, 0.0]


Attributes Ordered by Coef Size at Optimum alpha
['V48', 'V30', 'V11', 'V29', 'V35', 'V3', 'V15', ... 'V20', 'V23',
'V38', 'V55', 'V31', 'V13', 'V26', 'V4', 'V21', 'V1']
```

The code in Listing 5-5 is structured similarly to the code in Listing 5-4, except that there's no cross-validation loop. The value for alpha at which coefficients are sought is hard-coded and comes directly from the results generated by Listing 5-4. Two values of alpha were generated: one that minimized the misclassification error and one that maximized the AUC. The alpha that maximized AUC was slightly larger and slightly more conservative. It was slightly to the left of the value that minimized misclassification error and therefore slightly more conservative. The coefficients printed by the program are listed at the bottom of the code. Out of the 60 coefficients, 20-some-odd are 0. In this run (as in the cross-validation program), the `l1_ratio` variable was set to `0.8`, which typically results in more coefficients than Lasso regression, which would correspond to `l1_ratio` at `1.0`.

A couple of measures of variable importance are printed at the bottom of the listing. One is the order in which variables come into the solution as alpha is decremented downward. The other ordering is according to the magnitude of the coefficients at the optimum solution. As discussed in conjunction with the wine quality data, these orderings only make sense when the attributes are normalized. Some degree of agreement exists between these two different variable orderings, but they don't agree completely. For example, the variables V48, V11, V35, V44, and V3 appear relatively high in both lists, but V10 appears at the top of the first list and is much further down in the ordering based on coefficient size. Apparently, V10 is important when the coefficient penalty is so large that the algorithm only permits a single attribute, but when the coefficient penalty has shrunk to the point that a multitude of attributes are included, the attribute V10 levels off and drops in importance somewhat as other attributes are added to the mix.

Typically, objects give the strongest reflections for waves whose wavelength is the same order of characteristic dimensions of the object. Mines (metal cylinders) have length and diameter—relatively few and relatively long characteristic dimensions to reflect compared to rocks, which are more fractal in character and reflect a broader range of wavelengths. Because all the attribute values in the data set are positive (power levels), you might expect that the wavelengths corresponding to low frequencies would get positive coefficients and the wavelengths corresponding to high frequencies would get negative coefficients. You can see how this differencing could easily lead to overfitting the data and building a model that did extremely well on this data set but didn't generalize. The cross-validation process ensures that the model isn't overfit as long as the training data is statistically similar to what the model will see in deployment. The errors seen in cross-validation will match those in deployment to the extent that the rocks and mines encountered in deployment match the nature and proportions of those in the training data.

Figure 5.8 plots the coefficient curves for the ElasticNet regression models trained on the full rocks versus mines data set. The curves emphasize the complexity and changing nature of the relative importance of the available attributes.

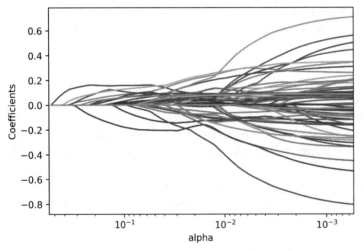

Figure 5.8: Coefficient curves for ElasticNet trained on rocks versus mines data

As mentioned in Chapter 4, an alternative to using penalized regression for classification is to use penalized logistic regression. Listing 5-5 shows code for an implementation of penalized logistic regression to build a classifier for the rocks versus mines data. The listing and the associated results highlight the similarities and differences between the two approaches. The algorithmic differences can be seen in the structure of the iteration. The logistic regression approach involves using linear functions of the attributes to calculate probabilities and likelihoods of each of the training examples being a rock or a mine. (See http://en.wikipedia.org/wiki/Logistic_ regression for more background on logistic regression and for careful derivations of the associated equations.) The algorithm for nonpenalized logistic regression is called *iteratively reweighted least squares* (IRLS). The name comes from the nature of the algorithm (see http://en.wikipedia.org/wiki/

`Iteratively_reweighted_least_squares`). It derives weights based on probability estimates for each example in the training set. Given the weights, the problem becomes a weighted least squares regression problem. The process must be iterated until the probabilities (and corresponding weights) stop changing. Basically, the IRLS for logistic regression adds another layer of iteration to the algorithm for (not logistic) penalized regression you saw in Chapter 4.

After reading in the variables and normalizing them, the program initializes weights and probabilities that are central to logistic regression and to the penalized version of it. These probabilities and weights have to be estimated along with the coefficients (β's) each time the penalty parameter decrements. You'll see the letters IRLS added to some of the variables in the code to denote that they are associated with the IRLS layer of the iteration. The iteration to estimate the probabilities is inside the loop for decrementing the λ's and wraps around the loop for iterating the coordinate descent on the β's.

The details of the update are slightly more complicated than the algorithm for plain (not logistic) penalized regression. One complication is the weights that come with IRLS. The weights and probabilities get calculated one input example at a time. Those are denoted by p and w in the code. The effects of the weights on sums of products like *attributes times residuals* and *squares of attributes* also need to be collected. Those are denoted by variables like sumWxx, which is a list containing the sum of the weights times each of the attributes squared. The other complication is that the residuals are now a function of the labels, the probabilities, and (more familiarly) the attributes and their coefficients (β's).

The code runs and produces variable ordering and coefficient curves to compare with those generated using non-logistic penalized regression. The logistic transformation makes direct comparison of the coefficients problematic because the logistic function causes a nonlinear scale change. Both plain and logistic regression (penalized and nonpenalized) generate vectors of coefficients and then multiply the (same) attributes by them and compare to a threshold. The threshold value is somewhat secondary since it can be determined subsequent to training, as was demonstrated. So, the overall scale of the β's doesn't matter as much as the magnitudes of the components relative to one another. One way to judge the relative magnitudes is to look at the order in which the two methods bring in new variables. As you can see by comparing the printed output in Listing 5-5 to the printed output in Listing 5-4, the two methods agree completely on the ordering for the first eight attributes. Of the next eight variables, seven are common to both lists, although they are ordered somewhat differently. Roughly the same is true of the next eight. There's good general agreement in the ordering between the two methods.

Another question is which one delivers better performance. Assessing that requires running cross-validation with penalized logistic regression. You have the tools and code to carry that out. The code in Listing 5-6 is not optimized for speed, but it won't take too long on the rocks versus mines problem.

Listing 5-6: Penalized Logistic Regression Trained on Rocks Versus Mines Data—rvmGlmnet2.py

```python
__author__ = 'mike_bowles'

from Read_Fcns import list_read_rvm
from math import sqrt, exp, fabs
import matplotlib.pyplot as plt
import numpy as np
from sklearn.preprocessing import StandardScaler

#define a couple of utility functions
def S(z,gamma):
    if gamma >= fabs(z):
        return 0.0
    if z > 0.0:
        return z - gamma
    else:
        return z + gamma


def Pr(b0,b,x):
    """
    :param b0: bias value
    :param b: np column matrix of coefficients
    :param x: feature matrix
    :return: column matrix of probabilities
    """
    #calculate nominal values
    sum = b0 + np.dot(x, b)
    p = (1.0/(1.0 + np.exp(-sum))).reshape([-1, 1])
    w = (p * (1.0 - p)).reshape([-1, 1])

    #treatment for extremes
    idxSmall = np.abs(p) < 1e-5
    idxLarge = np.abs(1.0 - p) < 1e-5


    p[idxSmall] = 0.0
    w[idxSmall] = 1e-5
    p[idxLarge] = 1.0
    w[idxLarge] = 1e-5
    return p, w

#read data from uci repo and arrange
xNum, labels = list_read_rvm()

nrow = len(xNum)
ncol = len(xNum[1])

alpha = 1.0
```

```
# Normalize features
xScaler = StandardScaler()
xNormalized = xScaler.fit_transform(xNum)


# Do Not Normalize labels but do calculate averages
labels = np.array(labels).reshape([-1, 1])
meanLabel = np.mean(labels)
sdLabel = np.std(labels)

# initial prob is freq of 1's
p = meanLabel
w = p * (1.0 - p)
z = (labels - p) / w
sumWxz = np.sum(w * xNormalized * z, axis=0)
maxWxz = np.amax(np.abs(sumWxz))

#starting value for lambda
lam = maxWxz / alpha



#this value of lambda corresponds to beta = list of 0's
#initialize a vector of coefficients beta
beta = np.zeros([ncol, 1])
beta0 = 0.0

#initialize matrix of betas at each step
betaMat = beta.copy()

beta0List = [0.0]


#begin iteration
nSteps = 100
lamMult = 0.93 #100 steps gives reduction by factor of 1000 in lambda
               #(recommended by authors)
nzList = []
for iStep in range(nSteps):
    #decrease lambda
    lam = lam * lamMult


    #Use incremental change in betas to control inner iteration

    #set middle loop values for betas = to outer values
    # values are used for calculating weights and probabilities
    #inner values are used for calculating penalized regression updates

    #take pass thru data to calc avg over data require for iteration
    #initilize accumulators
```

```
betaIRLS = beta.copy()
beta0IRLS = beta0
distIRLS = 100.0
#Middle loop to calc new betas w fixed IRLS wts and probs
iterIRLS = 0
while distIRLS > 0.01:
    iterIRLS += 1
    iterInner = 0

    betaInner = betaIRLS.copy()
    beta0Inner = beta0IRLS
    distInner = 100.0
    while distInner > 0.01:
        iterInner += 1
        if iterInner > 100: break
        p, w = Pr(beta0IRLS, betaIRLS, xNormalized)
        z = (labels - p) / w + beta0IRLS + np.dot(xNormalized,
                    betaIRLS)
        #cycle through attributes and update one-at-a-time
        #record starting value for comparison
        betaStart = betaInner.copy()
        for iCol in range(ncol):
            r = (z - beta0Inner - np.dot(xNormalized,
                    betaInner)).reshape([-1, 1])
            xTemp = xNormalized[:, iCol].reshape([-1, 1])
            sumWxr = np.sum(w * xTemp * r)
            sumWxx = np.sum(w * xTemp * xTemp)
            sumWr = np.sum(w * r)
            sumW = np.sum(w)
            avgWxr = sumWxr / nrow
            avgWxx = sumWxx / nrow

            beta0Inner = beta0Inner + sumWr / sumW
            uncBeta = sumWxr + sumWxx * betaInner[iCol, 0]
            betaInner[iCol, 0] = S(uncBeta, lam * alpha) / (sumWxx
                        + lam * (1.0 - alpha))

        sumDiff = np.sum(np.abs(betaInner - betaStart))
        sumBeta = np.sum(np.abs(betaInner))
        distInner = sumDiff/sumBeta

    #print(iStep, iterIRLS, iterInner)
    print('\r', 'Step', iStep, 'IRLS iteration', iterIRLS, 'Inner
                    iteration', iterInner, end='')
    #if exit inner while loop, then set betaMiddle = betaMiddle and
    #run through middle loop again.

    #Check change in betaMiddle to see if IRLS is converged
    a = np.sum(np.abs(betaIRLS - betaInner))
    b = np.sum(np.abs(betaIRLS))
```

```
            distIRLS = a / (b + 0.0001)
            dBeta = betaInner - betaIRLS
            gradStep = 1.0
            temp = betaIRLS + gradStep * dBeta
            betaIRLS = temp

        beta = betaIRLS.copy()
        beta0 = beta0IRLS
        betaMat = np.concatenate((betaMat, beta.copy()), axis=1)
        beta0List.append(beta0)

        nzBeta = [index for index in range(ncol) if beta[index] != 0.0]
        for q in nzBeta:
            if not(q in nzList):
                nzList.append(q)

#make up names for columns of xNum
names = ['V' + str(i) for i in range(ncol)]
nameList = [names[nzList[i]] for i in range(len(nzList))]

print('\n', nameList)
for i in range(ncol):
    #plot range of beta values for each attribute
    nSteps = betaMat.shape[1]
    coefCurve = betaMat[i, :].reshape([-1, 1])
    xaxis = range(nSteps)
    plt.plot(xaxis, coefCurve)

plt.xlabel("Steps Taken")
plt.ylabel("Coefficient Values")
plt.savefig('rocksVMinesGlmnet2.png', dpi=500)
plt.show()
```

Figure 5.9 shows the coefficient curves for rocks versus mines using penalized logistic regression. As noted, the scale of the coefficients is different from plain penalized regression because of the logistic function difference between the two methods. Ordinary regression attempts to fit a straight line to targets that are 0.0 and 1.0. Logistic regression attempts to predict probabilities of class membership by fitting a straight line to the "log odds ratio." Suppose p is the predicted probability that an example corresponds to the mines class. Then the odds ratio is the ratio $\frac{p}{1-p}$. The log odds ratio is the natural log of the odds ratio. Whereas p ranges from 0 to 1, the log odds ratio of p ranges from minus infinity to plus infinity. The cases where the log odd is very large and positive corresponds to cases where the prediction is very certain that the case belongs to the mines class. Ones that are large negative numbers correspond to the rocks class.

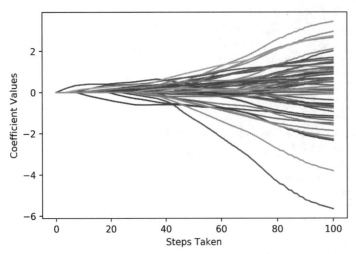

Figure 5.9: Coefficient curves for ElasticNet penalized logistic regression trained on rocks versus mines data

Because the two methods are predicting vastly different quantities, the scale on the predictions is much different and the coefficients are correspondingly different. But as the printed output from the two programs indicates, the order in which the variables appear in the solution is very similar, and the coefficient curves show that the signs are the same for the first several attributes that enter the solution.

Multiclass Classification: Classifying Crime Scene Glass Samples

The rocks versus mines problem that you saw in the last section is called a binary classification problem because the labels and predictions take one of two possible values. (Did the sonar return being processed come from reflections off a rock or a mine?) If labels and predictions can take more than two values, the problem is called a multiclass classification problem. This section uses penalized linear regression for the problem of classifying glass samples. As described more fully in Chapter 2, the glass data set consists of 9 physical chemistry measurements (refractive index and measurements of chemical composition) on 214 samples of 6 different types of glass. The problem is to use the physical chemistry measurements to determine which of the six types a given sample represents. The application for this is forensic analysis of crime and accident scenes. The data set comes from the UCI data repository, and the web page for the data set references a paper that uses support vector machines to solve this same problem. After looking at the code for solving this problem, this section will compare performance with the support vector machine approach.

Listing 5-7 shows code for solving this problem.

Listing 5-7: Multiclass Classification with Penalized Linear Regression: Classifying Crime Scene Glass Samples—glassENetRegCV.py

```
__author__ = 'mike-bowles'

from Read_Fcns import list_read_glass
from math import sqrt, fabs, exp, log
import matplotlib.pyplot as plt
from sklearn.preprocessing import StandardScaler
from sklearn.linear_model import LogisticRegressionCV
import numpy as np

#define custom cv folds
def custom_cv_folds(X, nFolds):
    n = X.shape[0]
    i = 0
    while i < nFolds:
        idxTest = np.array([it for it in range(n) if it%nFolds == i])
        idxTrain = np.array([it for it in range(n) if it not in idxTest])
        yield idxTrain, idxTest
        i += 1

#read in glass data
names, xNum, labels, yOneVAll = list_read_glass()

#use StandardScaler to normalize data
xScaler = StandardScaler()
xNormalized = xScaler.fit_transform(xNum)

#define custom x-val folds to insure labels are balanced across folds
custom_cv = custom_cv_folds(xNormalized, 9)

glassModel = LogisticRegressionCV(Cs=20,
            cv=custom_cv,
            multi_class='ovr').fit(xNormalized, labels)

#Note - LogisticRegressionCV uses inverse the usual reg param.
Cs = np.array(glassModel.Cs_)

#Average accuracy for each label across cross-validation folds
keys = list(glassModel.scores_.keys())
xvalScores = np.zeros([len(Cs), len(keys)])
for ikey in range(len(keys)):
    key = keys[ikey]
    xvalScores[:, ikey] = np.average(np.transpose(np.array(glassModel.
                        scores_[key])), axis=1)
```

```
# Display results
plt.figure()
plt.plot(Cs, xvalScores, ':')
plt.plot(Cs, xvalScores.mean(axis=1),
         label='Average accuracy for each glass type', linewidth=2)

plt.semilogx()
plt.legend()
ax = plt.gca()

plt.xlabel('C')
plt.ylabel('Average Accuracy')
plt.axis('tight')
plt.savefig('glassMulticlassLogisticRegression.png', dpi=500)
plt.show()

#print val alpha that minimizes the Cv-error for each glass type
print("C values that maximize accuracy for each type \n",glassModel.C_)
print("Maximum Accuracy for each type \n", np.amax(xvalScores, axis=0))

Printed Output:
C values that maximize accuracy for each type
 [4.28133240e+00 5.45559478e+02 1.00000000e-04 3.35981829e-02
 2.97635144e+01 5.45559478e+02]

Maximum Accuracy for each type
 [0.784219   0.69746377 0.92049114 0.94404187 0.98611111 0.97181965]
```

Have a look at the labels for the glass data. You'll see that the labels consist of integer glass types. Each row has an integer reflecting the type of glass associated with the row of chemical measurements. This is just the form that the sklearn logistic regression packages want: a single column with some unique identifier for each different class.

The features get normalized, but as with the glmnet code in the previous section, logistic regression doesn't use the labels in a way that would benefit from normalization.

Figure 5.10 shows cross-validation error for each of the glass classes as a function of the penalty parameter C. For this sklearn logistic regression package the penalty parameter is not like we've seen elsewhere. It's the inverse of the usual penalty parameter. C gets bigger going from left to right. A large value of C corresponds to less weight on the penalty. The best value of the regularization parameter C differs from one type of glass to another. Choose the value that gives the best overall performance for your problem. That will depend on the value you place on performance for each of the classes.

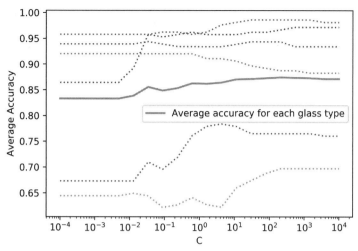

Figure 5.10: Misclassification error rates using penalized linear regression for glass classification

Figure 5.10 shows a plot of the misclassification error rate versus the number of decrementing steps that the penalty parameter has undergone. The plot shows a marked improvement at the minimum from the simplest model at the left-hand edge of the plot. The worst performing class comes in at roughly 70% accuracy or 30% error rate. You might try basis expansion to improve the results. You'll see some other approaches in the next chapters dealing with ensemble methods.

Linear Regression and Classification Using PySpark

This section will repeat several of the problems you've already seen, but will use PySpark, which means that the code examples you'll see can be run on hundreds or thousands of processors simultaneously. This will allow you to build models on enormous data sets. The section will go through a variety of examples in order to show you how to tackle regression, binary classification, and multiclass classification problems using PySpark mllib packages. You'll see a variety of algorithms and analytic techniques with which you're already familiar: penalized regression, variable normalization, cross-validation, and so forth.

Some of the computation sequences with PySpark may seem a little odd at first. Since PySpark is designed to work with data that's spread over multiple machines, it uses transformations on the data that can be done one row of data at a time, wherever the data may be stored and processed. You'll see how this operates, and with a little practice, these manipulations will become familiar tools for you.

The four problems you'll see in this section are predicting wine taste, classifying sonar targets as rocks or mines, predicting the number of rings in abalone shells, and identifying the type of glass from its chemical composition. These problems are chosen to exercise several features in PySpark that you'll want to understand. We'll talk about the features each problem highlights as we get into each problem.

Using PySpark to Predict Wine Taste

Using PySpark to tackle the wine taste prediction problem was introduced in Chapter 3 in the section titled "Using PySpark for Training Penalized Regression Models on Extremely Large Data Sets." This section will add the functionality for normalizing the variable before building the model so that the coefficients can be used to indicate variable importance. The purpose of the section in Chapter 3 was to show the simplicity and similarity of PySpark code to the sklearn Python code. This section will discuss each of the operations in the PySpark code. Listing 5-8 shows the code for using normalized features to predict wine taste.

Listing 5-8: Determining Variable Importance in Wine Taste Prediction Using PySpark Penalized Regression—wine_variable_importance_spark.py

```python
__author__ = 'mike_bowles'

#Import sparksession
from pyspark.sql import SparkSession
from pyspark.ml.feature import VectorAssembler
from pyspark.ml.regression import LinearRegression
import matplotlib.pyplot as plt
from pyspark.ml.feature import StandardScaler
import pandas as pd
from pandas import DataFrame
from Read_Fcns import pd_read_wine

spark = SparkSession.builder.appName("regress_wine_data").getOrCreate()

#read in abalone data as pandas data frame and create Spark data frame.
wine_df = pd_read_wine()

#Create spark dataframe for wine data
wine_sp_df = spark.createDataFrame(wine_df)
print('Column Names for initial data frame\n', wine_sp_df.columns,
        '\n\n')

vectorAssembler = VectorAssembler(inputCols = ['fixed acidity', \
    'volatile acidity', 'citric acid', 'residual sugar', 'chlorides', \
    'free sulfur dioxide', 'total sulfur dioxide', 'density', 'pH', \
                    'sulphates', 'alcohol'], outputCol = 'features')
v_wine_df = vectorAssembler.transform(wine_sp_df)
```

```
#invoke StandardScaler on features
scaler = StandardScaler(inputCol="features",
    outputCol="scaledFeatures")
scalerModel = scaler.fit(v_wine_df)

# Normalize each feature to have unit standard deviation.
scaledData = scalerModel.transform(v_wine_df)

# scaledData has individual original features as well as
# vectorized versions of original and scaled features
scaledData.show()

vwine_df = scaledData.select(['scaledFeatures', 'quality'])

splits = vwine_df.randomSplit([0.66, 0.34])
xTrain_sp = splits[0]
xTest_sp = splits[1]

# list of alphas larger => smaller, & empty lists for to store results
alphaList = [0.1**i for i in [0,1, 2, 3, 4, 5, 6]]
wt_list = []
intercept_list = []
rmsError = []

for alph in alphaList:
    wine_ridge_sp = LinearRegression(featuresCol = "scaledFeatures", \
        labelCol='quality', maxIter=100, regParam=alph, \
        elasticNetParam=0.0)
    wine_ridge_sp_model = wine_ridge_sp.fit(xTrain_sp)
    test_result = wine_ridge_sp_model.evaluate(xTest_sp)

    rmsError.append(test_result.rootMeanSquaredError)
    coef = wine_ridge_sp_model.coefficients.toArray()
    wt_list.append(coef)
    intercept_list.append(wine_ridge_sp_model.intercept)

print('{:18}'.format("RMS Error"), "alpha")
for i in range(len(rmsError)):
    print(rmsError[i], alphaList[i])

# order the attributes according to largest coefficient mag for alpha
# showing best performance (index=2)

len_coef = len(wt_list[0])
ordered_idx = sorted(zip(range(len_coef), wt_list[2]), key=lambda x:
                     -abs(x[1]))
print('\n\nAttributes ordered by coef magnitude----------')
[print(wine_sp_df.columns) for (a,b) in ordered_idx]
```

```
#plot curve of out-of-sample error versus alpha
x = range(len(rmsError))
plt.plot(x, rmsError, 'k')
plt.xlabel('-log(alpha)')
plt.ylabel('Error (RMS)')
plt.savefig('linear_regression_w_spark.png', dpi=500)
plt.show()

Printed Output:
Column names for initial data frame
 ['fixed acidity', 'volatile acidity', 'citric acid', 'residual sugar',
'chlorides', 'free sulfur dioxide', 'total sulfur dioxide', 'density',
'pH', 'sulphates', 'alcohol', 'quality']

Column names for transformed data set
[fixed acidity, volatile acidity, citric acid, residual sugar,
chlorides, free sulfur dioxide, total sulfur dioxide, density,
pH, sulphates, alcohol, quality, features, scaledFeatures]

Note: Printout of data frame can be seen by running Ch5 code notebook
in this book's code repo

RMS Error          alpha
0.6464799847389207 1.0
0.6173125740380354 0.1
0.6174096728881342 0.010000000000000002
0.6178333051859206 0.0010000000000000002
0.6178884012227639 0.00010000000000000002
0.6178940680418457 1.0000000000000003e-05
0.617894636333235 1.0000000000000004e-06

Attributes ordered by coef magnitude----------
alcohol
volatile acidity
sulphates
total sulfur dioxide
chlorides
pH
free sulfur dioxide
density
citric acid
residual sugar
fixed acidity
```

The first step in the process is to launch a SparkSession. This one is given the name "regress_wine_data". The second step is to read the data set into a pandas data frame and then to turn that into a PySpark data frame. Recall that a data frame is a rectangular array of data similar to a matrix with the difference that a particular data frame column may not be the same data type as another column. A data frame column could be string variables such as the label column in the rocks versus mines data, where the labels are M and R to denote mine or rock. In a matrix the variables are all the same type, typically real numbers. Data frames are very useful for handling statistical data, because data sets are rarely all real numbers. Python and PySpark have both incorporated data frames for this reason.

The next operation in the PySpark code is the `VectorAssembler`. This needs some explanation. PySpark adopts the premise that the input examples to a machine learning problem can get characterized as a row vector of real-valued features and an associated label. For the wine data, the features are all real numbers, so they naturally fit this premise and the labels are all single real-number taste scores. Labels also fit the premise. You may be thinking about the abalone data where the sex attribute takes values M, F, and I, or the classification problems you've seen where the labels are not real numbers. Later sections will show how to transform those cases to fit this premise.

In general, the data that you'll use to train your model may be a few columns from a much larger data frame. So, the first step is to assemble the vector of real numbers that will be used for making predictions. For the wine data, that's as simple as putting the column headers for the desired feature columns into a list of string variables. That's what you'll see in the function call to the `Vector-Assembler`. The variable `inputCols` is set equal to a list of feature names. The `outputCol` variable in the `VectorAssembler` is set equal to a name you choose to give to the column of row vectors that will be the feature matrix. You'll see the output name "features" used frequently. Conceptually, PySpark is going to keep track of a column of row vectors called `features`. Later examples will show you some samples of these column entries (i.e., sample rows from the feature matrix).

Now that the `VectorAssembler` is defined, the next step is to apply this transformation to the original data frame and assign it to a new data frame. The new data frame will be almost identical to the old one, except that it will have a new column named `features` added.

The next step is to normalize the features. A couple of steps are required. First is to instantiate a `StandardScaler()` function (named `scaler` in the code) and define input and output columns. The input column is `features`, the column of row vectors defined earlier. The second step is to call `scaler.fit()` on the data set after `VectorAssembler`, so that there is a `features` column to operate on. The `fit()` function will transform each of the individual features in the `features` column to zero mean and variance of one. In Chapter 2, Listing 2.11, you saw that the normalization operation requires running through each column to determine its mean and standard deviation and then subtracting the mean and dividing deviation. The `fit()` function calculates the mean and standard deviation and the `transform()` function does the subtract and divide. The result of these operations is shown in the output section of Listing 5-8. The column headers in the final `scaledData` data frame shows columns for `features` and `scaledFeatures`. The output shown does not include any of the actual feature values. The output is too cumbersome to print in page format. You can generate the output by running the Jupyter Notebook, which you can find in the code repository for the book.

Now that the data is scaled, the rest of the process for fitting an ElasticNet penalized linear model is fairly straightforward: first, define train-test splits, and then select a range of penalty parameters. Penalty parameters are generated as powers of 0.1. The ElasticNet parameter is chosen as 0.0, which gives ridge regression. After running through the process, the table of out-of-sample MSE indicates that the penalty parameter with an index of 2 is the best choice. (Notice that this value wiggles around a little depending on the random train-test split.) The coefficients have all been stored so the set corresponding to index 2 is used to order the features and the result is printed (Figure 5.11).

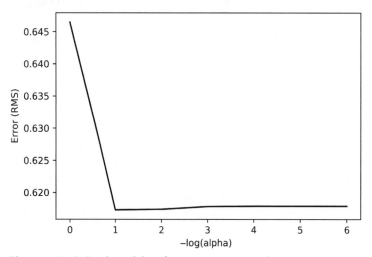

Figure 5.11: PySpark model performance versus regularization parameter

The general flow of the model-building process in this example should be familiar from the Python examples you've seen so far. The new element is the mechanics and syntax of doing these familiar operations with PySpark. The example here implemented feature normalization, partly because it's a process you might want to use and partly to illustrate how the process of performing a sequence of transformations on the data works with PySpark. The next section will go through our basic binary classification example: rocks versus mines.

Logistic Regression with PySpark: Rocks Versus Mines

This section will go through a process very similar to the one you saw in the previous section. It will include the `VectorAssembler` to generate the `features` column, etc. There will be several differences. It will use the `LogisticRegression` package instead of the `LinearRegression` package. It will use the `StringIndexer` to convert the M and R from the rocks versus mine problem into classification labels that PySpark `LogisticRegression` needs. Lastly, the code here will use the PySpark Pipeline framework to accomplish the sequence of transformations required. In the previous example, the transformations were applied one at a time, the resulting data frame named, and then used in the next step. That can get somewhat repetitive. The Pipeline framework makes a neater process.

The first steps are as before: start a PySpark session, read the data into a pandas data frame, convert it to a PySpark data frame, and generate a list of column names that will be the features to hand to `VectorAssembler`. Then comes the `StringIndexer`.

The `StringIndexer` operates on the label column, V60. It converts the M and R to 0 and 1. The `StringIndexer` operates on string values. It determines how many unique values there are and assigns index numbers starting at 0 for the most numerous value and continues down the list in order of most numerous to least. In this case, the two classes have the same size populations.

Using the Pipeline framework requires defining a sequence of "stages" that define the sequence of steps. These stages get accumulated in a list. The first operation in the list is an instantiation of the `StringIndexer` called `label_string_idx` in Listing 5-9. The second is an instantiation of the `VectorAssembler` that has assembled the feature columns V0 to V59.

Next, `pipeline` is created as an instance of the `Pipeline` class. It has a `fit()` applied in order to learn the string indexing. If normalization were included, that would also get done as part of the fit. The fitted model is called `pipelineModel` and is then used to transform the input data. The columns selected for the final data frame are printed as a schema and the printed output shows the labels from the string indexer, vectorized features, and the original variables truncated for brevity. You can get the whole list by running the Jupyter Notebook in this book's code repository.

The next steps are largely self-explanatory. The `maxIter` argument in `LogisticRegression` is a new element. Logistic regression is usually solved by an iterative process where the results improve as the iteration progresses. Each iteration requires making a pass through the entire data set. With a data set large enough to require using PySpark, that could take more time than you want to spend. So, dial the number of iterations up with a little care. You might try a few passes with it at 10 and then increase it by a factor of two to see if that gives you a significant improvement in classification performance. Keep an eye on your cloud computing expense during this process.

Listing 5-9: Code to Train PySpark Model for Rocks Versus Mines Problem—rocksVMines_spark.py

```
__author__ = 'mike_bowles'

#Import sparksession
from pyspark.sql import SparkSession
```

```python
from pyspark.ml.feature import VectorAssembler
import matplotlib.pyplot as plt
from pyspark.ml.feature import OneHotEncoderEstimator, StringIndexer,
                                VectorAssembler
from pyspark.ml.classification import LogisticRegression
import pandas as pd
from pandas import DataFrame
from Read_Fcns import pd_read_rvm
from pyspark.ml import Pipeline
from pyspark.ml.evaluation import BinaryClassificationEvaluator


spark = SparkSession.builder.appName("log_regress_rvm").getOrCreate()

#read in abalone data as pandas data frame and create Spark data frame.
rvm_df = pd_read_rvm()

#Create spark dataframe for wine data
rvm_sp_df = spark.createDataFrame(rvm_df)
print('Column Names', rvm_sp_df.columns, '\n\n')


cols = rvm_sp_df.columns

assembler_inputs = ['V0', 'V1', 'V2', 'V3', 'V4', 'V5', 'V6', 'V7',
'V8', 'V9', 'V10', 'V11', 'V12', 'V13', 'V14', 'V15', 'V16', 'V17',
'V18', 'V19', 'V20', 'V21', 'V22', 'V23', 'V24', 'V25', 'V26',
'V27', 'V28', 'V29', 'V30', 'V31', 'V32', 'V33', 'V34', 'V35',
'V36', 'V37', 'V38', 'V39', 'V40', 'V41', 'V42', 'V43', 'V44',
'V45', 'V46', 'V47', 'V48', 'V49', 'V50', 'V51', 'V52', 'V53',
'V54', 'V55', 'V56', 'V57', 'V58', 'V59']

label_string_idx = StringIndexer(inputCol = 'V60', outputCol = 'label')
stages = [label_string_idx]

assembler = VectorAssembler(inputCols=assembler_inputs,
outputCol="features")
stages += [assembler]

pipeline = Pipeline(stages = stages)
pipelineModel = pipeline.fit(rvm_sp_df)
df = pipelineModel.transform(rvm_sp_df)
selectedCols = ['label', 'features'] + cols
df = df.select(selectedCols)
df.printSchema()

train, test = df.randomSplit([0.7, 0.3], seed = 2018)
print("Training Dataset Count: " + str(train.count()))
print("Test Dataset Count: " + str(test.count()))
lr = LogisticRegression(featuresCol = 'features', labelCol = 'label',
            maxIter=10)
lrModel = lr.fit(train)
```

```
import matplotlib.pyplot as plt
import numpy as np

coefs = np.sort(lrModel.coefficients)

plt.plot(coefs)
plt.ylabel('Coefficient Value')
plt.xlabel('Order')
plt.title('Ordered Coefficients')
plt.savefig('RVM_Ordered_coef.png', dpi=500)
plt.show()

trainingSummary = lrModel.summary

roc = trainingSummary.roc.toPandas()
plt.plot(roc['FPR'],roc['TPR'])
plt.ylabel('False Positive Rate')
plt.xlabel('True Positive Rate')
plt.title('ROC Curve')
plt.savefig('rvm_AUC_spark.png', dpi=500)
plt.show()

print('AUC on training data: ', trainingSummary.areaUnderROC)

predictions = lrModel.transform(test)
predictions.select('rawPrediction', 'prediction',
        'probability').show(10)

evaluator = BinaryClassificationEvaluator()
print('Area Under ROC for test data:', evaluator.evaluate(predictions))

Printed Output:
Column Names ['V0', 'V1', 'V2', ...  'V58', 'V59', 'V60']
root
 |-- label: double (nullable = false)
 |-- features: vector (nullable = true)
 |-- V0: double (nullable = true)
 |-- V1: double (nullable = true)
 |-- V2: double (nullable = true)
 |-- V3: double (nullable = true)
 |-- V4: double (nullable = true)
 |-- V5: double (nullable = true)
 |-- V6: double (nullable = true)
 |-- V7: double (nullable = true)
 |-- V8: double (nullable = true)

Training Dataset Count: 146
Test Dataset Count: 62
+-------------------+----------+-------------------+
|      rawPrediction|prediction|        probability|
+-------------------+----------+-------------------+
```

```
| [2.26719814662696...|      0.0|[0.90612372329706...|
| [-0.5790337888769...|      1.0|[0.35915494912187...|
| [-2.0218815259206...|      1.0|[0.11692457719563...|
| [-4.4709894959055...|      1.0|[0.01130669112437...|
| [-1.6387815219325...|      1.0|[0.16263092929058...|
| [-3.7082566096388...|      1.0|[0.02393338222852...|
| [-6.6240100794511...|      1.0|[0.00132633299300...|
| [0.16127279447651...|      0.0|[0.54023103925663...|
| [3.80688871531552...|      0.0|[0.97826568007947...|
| [-3.4453630613992...|      1.0|[0.03090744405746...|
+--------------------+---------+--------------------+
only showing top 10 rows

Area Under ROC for test data: 0.8250000000000002
```

Figure 5.12 shows the coefficients generated by logistic regression. The coefficients have been ordered from smallest to largest in order to better visualize the range of values. Ordering by feature number may also be useful, particularly in a case like this where the order corresponds to the sonar frequencies that increase continuously from v0 to v59. Test your understanding of the code by making the changes required to plot the curves without ordering by magnitude.

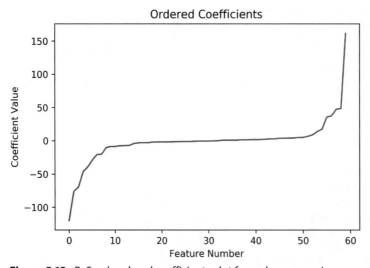

Figure 5.12: PySpark ordered coefficients plot for rocks versus mines

Figure 5.13 shows the ROC curve for the PySpark logistic regression model. The performance looks reasonably good as is corroborated by the AUC printed along with some specific predictions

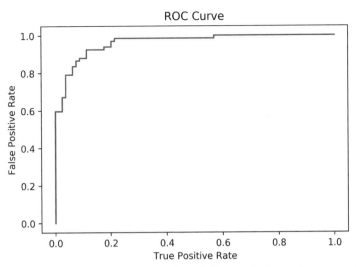

Figure 5.13: ROC curve for PySpark model for predicting rocks versus mines

This section has shown how to use PySpark logistic regression and introduced the PySpark Pipeline framework to doing the required data transformations. Pipeline results in a fairly neat and orderly arrangement of the code and saves you having to dream up new data frame names for all the intermediate steps. The next section will show you how to use the string indexer to encode categorical features. It's just a bit different from using string indexer on labels.

Incorporating Categorical Variables in a PySpark Model: Predicting Abalone Rings

This section will show how to build a regression model for the abalone problem. The only tricky part of doing regression on the abalone data is that the sex variable takes three values, since immature abalone don't have a sex. That only develops when they mature. So, the sex variable takes three possible values—M, F, and I (for indeterminate or immature). We have two complicating factors to sort out.

One is that the categorical variable (sex) first gets indexed. The string indexer learns that there are three values. With labels, the indexer output could be used directly, but that won't work for a feature. If we just put 0, 1, 2 in a column to indicate M, F, or I, then the algorithm will infer that there's an order relationship between the values (1 > 0, 2 > 1, etc.).

In Listing 5-10, each value for the categorical variable (sex) was given its own column. The column for M would have a one for the male examples and a zero for the others. That's called *one-hot encoding*. In PySpark, a one-hot encoder following the string indexer will perform this transformation.

> **NOTE** In large problems you may encounter categorical variables that have a vast number of different values. I worked on predicting health care outcomes using data that included names of drugs being given to patients. The list has several hundred thousand unique values. Usually it won't work to add hundreds of thousands of new columns to your feature matrix. In those cases, you can try several things to cut down. One thing would be to look at the statistics on how many of the values (say, a particular drug) actually appear in the data set. Chances are that many will be relatively rare. You can either throw out those rows of data or you can aggregate all of the rare cases into a single group. Another approach might be to move to a more comprehensive category. With the drug example, use only the drug name and not the dose.

The second complication is that the columns that get one-hot encoded should be left out of the data that is passed to the regression algorithm. The original variable gets replaced by a row vector. In this case a row vector has two variables, one for each possible sex minus one, since one of the variable values (say, M) can be represented by all zeros. Listing 5-10 goes through the following process. It segregates the features into those that are categorical and those that are numeric. For each of the categorical variables, it runs the string indexer and the one-hot encoder transformations and then includes the vectors from that process alongside the numeric variables as input to the vector assembly process. Then the process is a familiar regression process.

Listing 5.10: One-Hot Encoding Categorical Features: Abalone Data—abalone_data_spark.py

```
__author__ = 'mike_bowles'

#Import sparksession
from pyspark.sql import SparkSession
from pyspark.ml.feature import VectorAssembler
from pyspark.ml.regression import LinearRegression
import matplotlib.pyplot as plt
from pyspark.ml.feature import StandardScaler
from pyspark.ml.feature import OneHotEncoderEstimator, StringIndexer,
                              VectorAssembler
from pyspark.ml import Pipeline
import pandas as pd
from pandas import DataFrame
from Read_Fcns import pd_read_abalone
from pyspark.ml.evaluation import RegressionEvaluator

spark =
  SparkSession.builder.appName("abalone_regression").getOrCreate()

#read in abalone data as pandas data frame and create Spark data frame.
abalone_df = pd_read_abalone()
abalone_sp_df = spark.createDataFrame(abalone_df)
print('Column Names', abalone_df.columns, '\n\n')
```

```
cols = abalone_sp_df.columns
abalone_sp_df.printSchema()

numeric_cols = ['Length', 'Diameter', 'Height', 'Whole weight',
                'Shucked weight', 'Viscera weight', 'Shell weight']

stringIndexer = StringIndexer(inputCol = "Sex", outputCol = "SexIndex")
encoder = OneHotEncoderEstimator(inputCols=
[stringIndexer.getOutputCol()], outputCols=["SexClassVec"])
stages =[stringIndexer, encoder]

assembler_inputs = ["SexClassVec"] + numeric_cols

assembler = VectorAssembler(inputCols=assembler_inputs,
outputCol="features")
stages += [assembler]

pipeline = Pipeline(stages = stages)
pipelineModel = pipeline.fit(abalone_sp_df)
df = pipelineModel.transform(abalone_sp_df)
selectedCols = ['features'] + cols
df = df.select(selectedCols)
df.printSchema()

pd.DataFrame(df.take(4), columns=df.columns).transpose()

train, test = df.randomSplit([0.7, 0.3], seed = 2018)
print("Training Dataset Count: ", train.count())
print("Test Dataset Count: ", test.count())

lr = LinearRegression(featuresCol = 'features', labelCol='Rings',
            maxIter=10, regParam=0.003, elasticNetParam=0.8)
lr_model = lr.fit(train)
print("Coefficients: ", lr_model.coefficients)
print("Intercept: ", lr_model.intercept)

trainingSummary = lr_model.summary
print("RMSE: ", trainingSummary.rootMeanSquaredError)
print("R Squared on training data:", trainingSummary.r2)

lr_predictions = lr_model.transform(test)
lr_predictions.select("prediction","Rings","features").show(5)

from pyspark.ml.evaluation import RegressionEvaluator
lr_evaluator = RegressionEvaluator(predictionCol="prediction", \
                labelCol="Rings",metricName="r2")
print("R Squared on test data:" , lr_evaluator.evaluate(lr_predictions))

Printed Output:
Column Names Index(['Sex', 'Length', 'Diameter', 'Height',
```

```
'Whole weight', 'Shucked weight', 'Viscera weight', 'Shell weight',
'Rings'], dtype='object')

root
 |-- Sex: string (nullable = true)
 |-- Length: double (nullable = true)
 |-- Diameter: double (nullable = true)
 |-- Height: double (nullable = true)
 |-- Whole weight: double (nullable = true)
 |-- Shucked weight: double (nullable = true)
 |-- Viscera weight: double (nullable = true)
 |-- Shell weight: double (nullable = true)
 |-- Rings: long (nullable = true)

root
 |-- features: vector (nullable = true)
 |-- Sex: string (nullable = true)
 |-- Length: double (nullable = true)
 |-- Diameter: double (nullable = true)
 |-- Height: double (nullable = true)
 |-- Whole weight: double (nullable = true)
 |-- Shucked weight: double (nullable = true)
 |-- Viscera weight: double (nullable = true)
 |-- Shell weight: double (nullable = true)
 |-- Rings: long (nullable = true)
```

features	---row of attribute vectors - run notebook for more			
	0	1	2	3
Sex	M	M	F	M
Length	0.455	0.35	0.53	0.44
Diameter	0.365	0.265	0.42	0.365
Height	0.095	0.09	0.135	0.125
Whole weight	0.514	0.2255	0.677	0.516
Shucked weight	0.2245	0.0995	0.2565	0.2155
Viscera weight	0.101	0.0485	0.1415	0.114
Shell weight	0.15	0.07	0.21	0.155
Rings	15	7	9	10

```
Training Dataset Count: 2924
Test Dataset Count: 1253

Coefficients:  [-0.306360840416938, -1.5588226677602282,
 2.9172381109536025, 4.568071822665666, 32.918696234090376,-
0.09751444851762599, -7.477249822177075, -4.238501196414483,
12.00722955259035]
Intercept:  3.2080030819683936
RMSE:  2.2246864543509055
R Squared on training data: 0.5023819644971068
```

```
+-----------------+-----+--------------------+
|       prediction|Rings|            features|
+-----------------+-----+--------------------+
|8.126455982607062|    6|[0.0,0.0,0.345,0....|
|8.301277100910529|    5|[0.0,0.0,0.36,0.2...|
|9.238211710278332|   12|[0.0,0.0,0.415,0....|
|9.930756998402277|    9|[0.0,0.0,0.445,0....|
|9.987207321370438|    9|[0.0,0.0,0.45,0.3...|
+-----------------+-----+--------------------+
only showing top 5 rows
R Squared on test data = 0.424898
```

Multiclass Logistic Regression with Meta Parameter Optimization

This section introduces several new elements. One is using the string indexer to transform labels in a multiclass problem. Another is using PySpark logistic regression for a multiclass problem. These are modest steps from what you've seen already. Another new element is using parametric grid search to determine the best values for meta parameters like the ElasticNet parameter and the regularization parameters.

The basic coding for this multiclass problem (Listing 5-11) looks the same as for the binary classification problem in Listing 5-9. It works for labels to be represented in a single column, indicating the number assigned them by the string indexer.

The parameter search is accomplished by using `CrossValidator` and the `ParameterGridBuilder`. The code shows how to supply values to search for the regularization parameter and the ElasticNet parameters. Then at the end, the best values (determined by cross-validation results) are read out. The search does result in an improvement.

Listing 5.11: Code to Build and Optimize PySpark Model for Classifying Glass—glass_log_regress_spark.py

```python
__author__ = 'mike_bowles'

#Import sparksession
from pyspark.sql import SparkSession
from pyspark.ml.feature import VectorAssembler
from pyspark.ml.classification import LogisticRegression
import matplotlib.pyplot as plt
from pyspark.ml import Pipeline
from pyspark.ml.feature import OneHotEncoder, StringIndexer,
VectorAssembler
import pandas as pd
from pandas import DataFrame
```

```
from Read_Fcns import pd_read_glass
from pyspark.ml.tuning import ParamGridBuilder, CrossValidator
from pyspark.ml.evaluation import MulticlassClassificationEvaluator


spark = SparkSession.builder.appName("glass_mc_log_regress").
getOrCreate()

# read glass data into pandas data frame and create spark df
glass_df = pd_read_glass()

#Create spark dataframe for glass data
glass_sp_df = spark.createDataFrame(glass_df)

cols = glass_sp_df.columns
print('Column Names', cols, '\n\n')

glass_sp_df.printSchema()

pd.DataFrame(glass_sp_df.take(5), columns=glass_sp_df.columns).
transpose()

feature_cols = ['RI', 'Na', 'Mg', 'Al', 'Si', 'K', 'Ca', 'Ba', 'Fe']

label_stringIdx = StringIndexer(inputCol = "Type", outputCol = "label")
assembler = VectorAssembler(inputCols=feature_cols,
outputCol='features')
pipeline = Pipeline(stages=[assembler, label_stringIdx])

pipelineFit = pipeline.fit(glass_sp_df)
dataset = pipelineFit.transform(glass_sp_df)

#have a look at the dataset
dataset.show(5)

#train test split
trainingData, testData = dataset.randomSplit([0.7, 0.3], seed = 1011)

#select model p
lr = LogisticRegression(maxIter=20, regParam=0.003, elasticNetParam=0.5)
lrModel = lr.fit(trainingData)

predictions = lrModel.transform(testData)

evaluator = MulticlassClassificationEvaluator(predictionCol
                  ="prediction")
print(evaluator.evaluate(predictions))

# search for best parameter values
paramGrid = (ParamGridBuilder()
```

```
        .addGrid(lr.regParam, [0.003, 0.03, 0.3])
        .addGrid(lr.elasticNetParam, [0.0, 0.2, 0.4, 0.6])
        .build())

# 5-fold CrossValidator
cv = CrossValidator(estimator=lr, \
                    estimatorParamMaps=paramGrid, \
                    evaluator=evaluator, \
                    numFolds=5)

cvModel = cv.fit(trainingData)

predictions = cvModel.transform(testData)
# Evaluate best model
evaluator = MulticlassClassificationEvaluator(predictionCol=
"prediction")
print(evaluator.evaluate(predictions))

print( 'Best Param (regParam): ', cvModel.bestModel.
_java_obj.getRegParam())
print('Best Param (elasticNetParam): ',
cvModel.bestModel._java_obj.getElasticNetParam())
```

This section has demonstrated a multiclass classification problem using PySpark and has demonstrated how to use `ParameterGridBuilder` and cross-validation to determine best values for meta parameters.

Summary

This chapter demonstrated the use of penalized regression along with a number of general tools for predictive modeling. The chapter showed several different types of problems that you'll frequently encounter. These include regression, binary classification, and multiclass classification. The chapter used Python packages incarnating various different flavors of penalized regression for these tasks. In addition, the chapter illustrated the use of several tools that you may need in order to solve the modeling problems that you encounter. These include techniques for coding factor variables as numeric, for using a binary classifier to solve multiclass classification problems, and for extending linear methods to predict nonlinear relationships between attributes and outcomes.

The chapter also demonstrated a variety of ways to quantify performance for your predictive models. Regression problems are easiest to quantify because their errors can naturally be expressed in real number terms. Classification problems can be more involved. You saw classification performance quantified as misclassification error rates, area under the receiver operating curve, and economic costs. You should pick the method that comes closest to measuring performance in terms of your actual objectives (business objectives, science objectives, and so forth).

The chapter then went through a number of different problem setups (multi-class, categorical variables, regression, classification) and showed how to build solutions using PySpark. In addition, the chapter covered a collection of tools for building models and evaluating their performance. You'll see many of these same tools again in Chapter 6, where we'll use them with ensemble models.

References

1. P. Cortez, A. Cerdeira, F. Almeida, T. Matos, and J. Reis. (2009). "Modeling Wine Preferences by Data Mining from Physicochemical Properties." Decision Support Systems, Elsevier, 47(4):547–553.

2. T. Hastie, R. Tibshirani, and J. Friedman. (2009). *The Elements of Statistical Learning: Data Mining, Inference, and Prediction*. 2nd ed. Springer-Verlag, New York.

3. J. Friedman, T. Hastie, and R. Tibshirani. (2010). "Regularization Paths for Generalized Linear Models via Coordinate Descent." *Journal of Statistical Software*, 33(1).

4. K. Bache and M. Lichman. (2013). UCI Machine Learning Repository. Irvine, CA: University of California, School of Information and Computer Science. http://archive.ics.uci.edu/ml.

Ensemble Methods

Ensemble methods stem from the observation that multiple models give better performance than a single model if the models are somewhat independent of one another. A classifier that will give you the correct result 55% of the time is only mediocre, but if you've got 100 classifiers that are correct 55% of the time, the probability that the majority of them are right jumps to 82%. (Google "cumulative binomial probability" and try some numbers yourself.)

One way to get a variety of models that are somewhat independent from one another is to use different machine learning algorithms. For example, you can build models with support vector machines, linear regression, k nearest neighbors, binary decision trees, and so on. But it's difficult to get a very long list of models that way. And, besides, it's tedious because the different models all have different parameters that need to be tweaked separately and may have different requirements on the input data. So, the models need to be coded separately. That's not going to work for generating hundreds or thousands of models (which you'll be doing soon).

Therefore, the key with ensemble methods is to develop an algorithmic approach to generate numerous, somewhat independent models that will then be combined into an ensemble. In this chapter you learn how the most popular methods accomplish this. The chapter teaches you the mechanics of the most popular ensemble methods. It outlines the basic structure of the algorithms and demonstrates the algorithms in Python code to give you a firm understanding of their workings.

Ensemble methods employ a hierarchy of two algorithms. The low-level algorithm is called a *base learner.* The base learner is a single machine learning algorithm that gets used for all of the models that will get aggregated into an ensemble. This chapter will primarily use binary decision trees as base learners. The upper-level algorithm manipulates the inputs to the base learners so that the models they generate are somewhat independent. How can the same algorithm generate different models? Several upper-level algorithms are widely used. They go by the names *bagging, boosting,* and *random forest.* (Strictly speaking, random forest is a combination of an upper-level algorithm and particular modification to binary decision trees. You will see more detail on that in the section "Random Forests").

A number of different algorithms could conceivably be used as base learners—binary decision trees, support vector machines, and so on—but as a practical matter binary decision trees are the most widely used. They are the base learners in the open source and commercial packages that you'll be able to use in your projects. The ensembles are collections of hundreds or thousands of binary decision trees, and many of the properties of these ensembles are ones they inherit from binary decision trees. So, this chapter begins with an introduction to binary decision trees.

Binary Decision Trees

Binary decision trees operate by subjecting attributes to a series of binary (yes/no) decisions. Each decision leads to one of two possibilities: it leads to another decision or it leads to a prediction. An example of a trained tree will help cement the idea. You'll learn how training works after understanding the result of training.

Listing 6-1 shows the code to use scikit-learn's `DecisionTreeRegressor` package to build a binary decision tree for the wine quality data. Figure 6.1 depicts the trained tree produced by Listing 6-1.

> **NOTE**   In order to run the code in Listing 6-1, you will need to install `graphviz` and `pydottable`. The easiest way is to use conda to do the installations. You can find notes for installing these by searching on "conda install graphviz" (for example).

Listing 6-1: Building a Decision Tree to Predict Wine Quality—wineTree.py

```
__author__ = 'mike-bowles'

import numpy
from sklearn import tree
from sklearn.tree import DecisionTreeRegressor
from sklearn.tree import export_graphviz
from sklearn.externals.six import StringIO
```

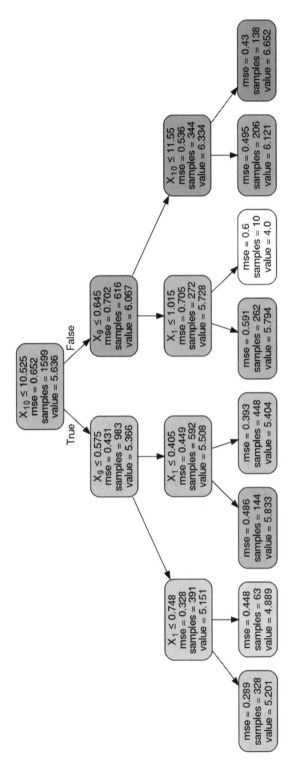

Figure 6.1: Decision tree for determining wine quality

```
from IPython.display import Image
from math import sqrt
import matplotlib.pyplot as plot
from Read_Fcns import list_read_wine
import pydotplus

#read data into iterable
names, xList, labels = list_read_wine()

wineTree = DecisionTreeRegressor(max_depth=3)
wineTree.fit(xList, labels)

f = StringIO()
export_graphviz(wineTree, out_file=f, filled=True, rounded=True,
        special_characters=True)
graph = pydotplus.graph_from_dot_data(f.getvalue())
Image(graph.create_png())
#Note: You'll need to install pydotplus to draw this graph.
# conda install -c conda-forge pydotplus
```

Figure 6.1 shows the series of decisions produced as an outcome of the training on the wine quality data. The block diagram of the trained tree shows a number of boxes, which are called *nodes* in decision tree parlance. There are two types of nodes: nodes can either pose a yes/no question of the data, or they can be terminal nodes that assign a prediction to examples that end up in them. Terminal nodes are often referred to as *leaf* nodes. In Figure 6.1, the terminal nodes are the nodes at the bottom of the figure that have no branches or further decision nodes below them.

How a Binary Decision Tree Generates Predictions

When an observation or row is passed to a nonterminal node, the row answers the node's question. If it answers yes, the row of attributes is passed to the leaf node below and to the left of the current node. If the row answers no, the row of attributes is passed to the leaf node below and to the right of the current node. The process continues recursively until the row arrives at a terminal (that is, leaf) node, where a prediction value is assigned to the row. The value assigned by the leaf node is the mean of the outcomes of the all the training observations that wound up in the leaf node.

While in this tree the second decision regards the variable X[9] in both branches of the tree, the two decisions can be about different attributes. (For example, see the third layer of decisions.)

Look at the top node, known as the *root* node. That node poses the question X[10] <= 10.525. In binary decision trees, important variables are split on early (or near the top of the tree), so the decision tree deems variable X[10], or alcohol content, important. In this respect, it agrees with the penalized linear regression in Chapter 5, "Building Predictive Models Using Penalized Linear Methods," which also deemed alcohol content most important in determining wine quality.

The tree in Figure 6.1 is said to have a depth of 3. The depth of a tree is defined as the number of decisions that must be made down the longest path through the tree. The discussion of training in the section "Tree Training Equals Split Point Selection" will show you that there's no reason that all the paths to the terminal nodes must be the same length (as they are in Figure 6.1).

You now have an idea what a trained tree looks like and you have seen how to how to use a trained tree to make predictions. Now you'll see how a tree gets trained.

How to Train a Binary Decision Tree

The easiest way to see how a tree gets trained is to look at a simple example. Listing 6-2 shows an example of predicting a real-number label given a real-number attribute. The data set for this is created in the code (so-called synthetic data). The basic idea is that the single attribute x has 100 equally spaced values between –0.5 and +0.5. The vector of labels y is equal to the vector of features x, with some random noise added.

Listing 6-2: Training a Decision Tree for Simple Regression Problem—simpleTree.py

```
__author__ = 'mike-bowles'

import numpy as np
import matplotlib.pyplot as plt
from sklearn import tree
from sklearn.tree import DecisionTreeRegressor
from sklearn.externals.six import StringIO
from sklearn.tree import export_graphviz
from IPython.display import Image
import pydotplus

#Build a simple data set with y = x + random
nPoints = 100

#x values for plotting
x = np.linspace(-0.5, 0.5, nPoints)
tree_depth = 2

#y (labels) has random noise added to x-value
#set seed
np.random.seed(1)
y = x + np.random.randn(nPoints) * 0.1

plt.plot(x,y)
plt.axis('tight')
plt.xlabel('x')
```

```
plt.ylabel('y')
plt.title('Labels (y) versus Feature (x)')
plt.savefig('Labels_versus_attribute_visualization_ex.png', dpi=500)
plt.show()

x_feat = x.reshape([-1,1])
simpleTree = DecisionTreeRegressor(max_depth=tree_depth)
simpleTree.fit(x_feat, y)

#draw the tree -- this block needs to be run in its own cell
f = StringIO()
export_graphviz(simpleTree, out_file=f, filled=True, rounded=True,
        special_characters=True)
graph = pydotplus.graph_from_dot_data(f.getvalue())
Image(graph.create_png())


#compare prediction from tree with true values

yHat  = simpleTree.predict(x_feat)

plt.figure()
plt.plot(x, y, label='True y')
plt.plot(x, yHat, label='Tree Prediction ', linestyle='--')
plt.legend(bbox_to_anchor=(1,0.2))
plt.axis('tight')
plt.xlabel('x')
plt.ylabel('Predicted and Actual Values')
plt.title('Comparison of Actual to Prediction - depth =
 ' +str(tree_depth))
plt.savefig('simpleTreeActuaVPrediction_'  + str(tree_depth) +'.png',
            dpi=500)
plt.show()

#draw the tree
f = StringIO()
export_graphviz(simpleTree, out_file=f, filled=True, rounded=True,
      special_characters=True)
graph = pydotplus.graph_from_dot_data(f.getvalue())
Image(graph.create_png())


#split point calculations - try every possible split point to find the
#best one
sse = []
xMin = []
for i in range(1, nPoints):
    #divide y-array into points on left and right of split point
    lh_array = y[0:i]
    rh_array = y[i:]
```

```
#calculate averages on each side
lhAvg = np.average(lh_array)
rhAvg = np.average(rh_array)

#calculate sum square error on left, right and total
lhSse = np.sum((lh_array - lhAvg) * (lh_array - lhAvg))
rhSse = np.sum((rh_array - rhAvg) * (rh_array - rhAvg))

#add sum of left and right to list of errors

sse.append(lhSse + rhSse)
```

```
plt.plot(x[1:], sse)
plt.xlabel('x Split Point Value')
plt.ylabel('Sum Squared Error')
plt.title('Sum Squared Error vs Split Point Location')
plt.savefig('Error_vs_split_pt_location.png', dpi=500)
plt.show()
```

Figure 6.2 plots the labels y versus the single attribute x. As you'd expect, y roughly follows x but with some randomness.

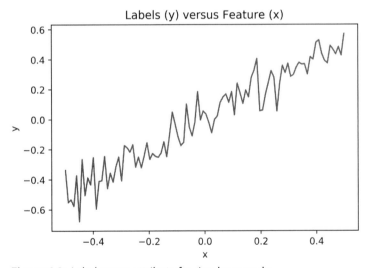

Figure 6.2: Label versus attribute for simple example

Tree Training Equals Split Point Selection

The first step in Listing 6-2 is to run scikit-learn's regression tree package with a depth of 1 specified. The results of that process are shown plotted in Figure 6.3. Figure 6.3 shows the block diagram for a depth 1 tree. Depth 1 trees are also called *stumps*. The single decision at the root node is to compare the attribute value with –0.071. This number is called the *split point* because it splits the data into two groups. The two boxes that emanate from the decision indicate that 43 of the 100 input examples go down the left leg of the tree, and the remaining 57 examples go down the right leg. If the attribute is less than the split point, the prediction from the tree is what's indicated as value in the block diagram— roughly –0.3.

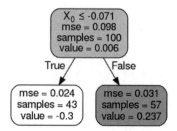

Figure 6.3: Block diagram of depth 1 tree for simple problem

How Split Point Selection Affects Predictions

Another way to view the trained tree is to see how its predictions compare with the true value of the labels. Because the simple synthetic problem has a single attribute only, the plot of the prediction generated by the trained tree alongside the actual values begins to give an idea about how the training of this simple tree was accomplished. The predicted values shown in Figure 6.4 follow a simple recipe. The prediction is a step function of the attribute. The step occurs at the split point.

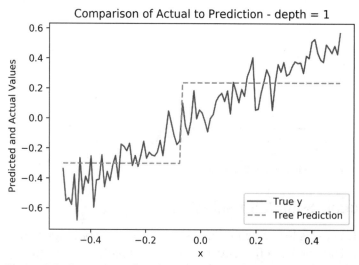

Figure 6.4: Comparison of predictions and actual values versus attribute for simple example

Algorithm for Selecting Split Points

Only three quantities are required to specify this simple tree: the split point value and the values assigned to the prediction if it falls into either of the two possible groups of points. Arriving at those quantities is accomplished during training of the tree. Here's how that works. The tree is trained to minimize the squared error of its predictions. Suppose first that the split point is given. Once the split point is given, the values assigned to the two groups are also determined. The average of each group is the single quantity that minimizes the mean squared error. That only leaves the question of how the split point is determined. Listing 6-2 has a small section of code that goes through the process of determining the split. The process is to try every possible split point. This is accomplished by dividing the data into two groups, approximating each group by its average, and then calculating the resulting sum squared error.

Figure 6.5 shows how the sum squared error varies as a function of the split point location. Training a decision tree entails exhaustively searching all possible split points to determine which one minimizes the sum squared error. As you can see, there's a well-defined minimum at roughly the midpoint of the data set. You can also see that there is some random variation due to the noise introduced. You might also imagine that with more data some of the randomness would smooth out. You'll see that demonstrated in the section on bagging later in this chapter.

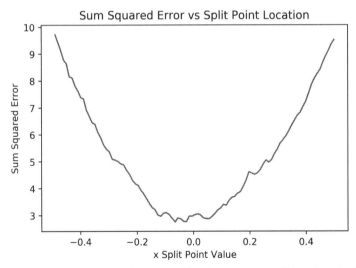

Figure 6.5: Sum squared error resulting from every possible split point location

Multivariable Tree Training—Which Attribute to Split?

What if the problem has more than one attribute? Then the algorithm checks all possible split points for all the attributes to see which split point gives the best sum squared error for each attribute and then which attributes give the overall minimum.

This split point calculation is where all the computation cycles go in training a decision tree—and, by extension, where they go in training ensembles of trees. If the attribute being split doesn't have any repeat values, there's a split point to check for every data point (minus one).

As the data set gets larger, the number of split point calculations grows in direct proportion to the size of the data set. The split points that are checked can also get ridiculously close together. Algorithms designed to run on very large data sets allow split point checking to be considerably coarser than the raw granularity of the data. An approach to this is spelled out in "PLANET: Massively Parallel Learning of Tree Ensembles with MapReduce," which outlines the approach taken by engineers at Google to build a decision tree algorithm on large data sets. As mentioned in the paper, they wanted the decision tree algorithm so that they could implement gradient boosting (one of the ensemble algorithms you'll learn about later in this chapter).

Recursive Splitting for More Tree Depth

Listing 6-2 shows what happens to the prediction curve as the tree depth increases from 1 to 2. The resulting prediction curves are shown in Figure 6.6, and the block diagram for the tree is shown in Figure 6.7. Instead of having a single step, the prediction curve now has three steps. The second set of split points is determined in the same manner as the first one. Each node in the tree deals with the subset of points determined by the splits above it. The split point for each node is determined to minimize the sum squared error in the two nodes below. The curve in Figure 6.6 approximates the actual curve with a finer stair-step function. More tree depth results in finer steps and higher fidelity to the training data. Will that continue indefinitely?

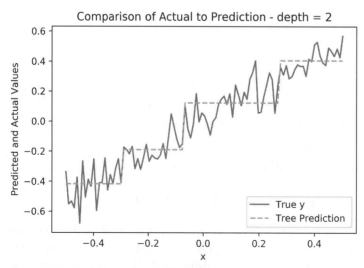

Figure 6.6: Prediction using depth 2 tree

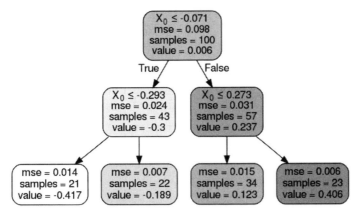

Figure 6.7: Block diagram for depth 2 tree

As splitting continues, the number of examples in the deepest nodes decreases. This can cause the splitting to terminate before the specified depth is reached. If there is only one example in a node, splitting certainly cannot continue. Tree training algorithms usually have a parameter to allow you to control how small a population will be split. Small populations in the nodes can lead to high variance in the resulting predictions.

Overfitting Binary Trees

The previous section showed how to train a binary decision tree of any depth. Is it possible to overfit a binary tree? This section discusses how to measure and regulate overfitting with binary trees. The mechanisms for overfitting binary trees are different from what you saw in Chapter 4, "Penalized Linear Regression," and Chapter 5, but you will see some similarities in the symptoms and how to measure overfitting. You will see that binary trees have parameters (tree depth and minimum leaf node size, for example) that can be used to regulate model complexity, similar to the process you saw in Chapters 4 and 5.

Measuring Overfit with Binary Trees

Figure 6.8 shows what happens when the tree depth is increased to 6. In Figure 6.8, it's hard to see the difference between the true value and the prediction. The prediction follows almost every zig and zag. That begins to suggest that the model is overfitting the data. The way the data were generated indicates that the best possible prediction would be for the prediction to equal the attribute value. The noise that was added to the attribute is unpredictable, and yet the prediction is following the noise-driven deviations of the label from the attribute. Synthetic data afford the luxury of knowing the correct answer.

Another way to look at overfitting with a binary tree is to consider the number of terminal nodes in the tree compared to the amount of data available. The tree

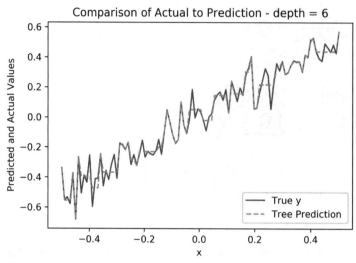

Figure 6.8: Prediction using depth 6 tree

that generated the prediction shown in Figure 6.8 was depth 6. That means that it has 64 terminal nodes (2^6). There are 100 points in the dataset. That means a lot of the points are the sole occupants of a terminal node, so their predicted value exactly matches their observed value. No wonder the graph of the prediction is matching the wiggles due to noise.

Balancing Binary Tree Complexity for Best Performance

In real problems, cross-validation can be performed to control overfitting. Listing 6-3 shows 10-fold cross-validation run on trees of a variety of depths

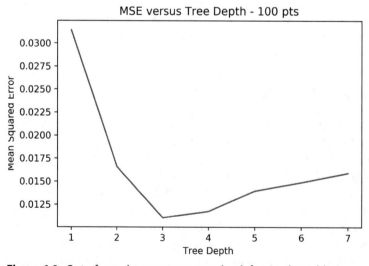

Figure 6.9: Out-of-sample error versus tree depth for simple problem

for this simple problem. The code listing shows two loops. The outer one defines the tree depth for the inner cross-validation loop. The inner loop divides the data up and makes 10 passes to calculate out of sample errors. The mean squared error (MSE) results for each depth are plotted in Figure 6.9.

Listing 6-3: Cross-Validation at a Range of Tree Depths—simpleTreeCV.py

```
__author__ = 'mike-bowles'

import numpy as np
import matplotlib.pyplot as plt
from sklearn import tree
from sklearn.tree import DecisionTreeRegressor


#Build a simple data set with y = x + random
nPoints = 1000

#x values for plotting
x = np.linspace(-0.5, 0.5, nPoints)
x_feat = x.reshape([-1,1])

#y (labels) has random noise added to x-value
#set seed
np.random.seed(1)
y = x + np.random.randn(nPoints) * 0.1

#perform 10-fold x-val to see what tree depth works best.
nrow = nPoints
depthList = [1, 2, 3, 4, 5, 6, 7]
xvalMSE = []
nxval = 10

for iDepth in depthList:

    #build x-val loop to fit tree and evaluate on out of sample data
    oosMSE = 0.0
    for ixval in range(nxval):

        #Define test and training index sets
        idxTest = [a for a in range(nrow) if a%nxval == ixval%nxval]
        idxTrain = [a for a in range(nrow) if a%nxval != ixval%nxval]

        #Define test and training attribute and label sets
        xTrain = x_feat[idxTrain]
        xTest = x_feat[idxTest]
        yTrain = y[idxTrain]
        yTest = y[idxTest]

        #train trees of various depths and accumulate test errors
        treeModel = DecisionTreeRegressor(max_depth=iDepth)
        treeModel.fit(xTrain, yTrain)
```

```
treePrediction = treeModel.predict(xTest)
error = yTest - treePrediction

oosMSE += np.average(error * error) / nxval

#average the squared errors and accumulate by tree depth

xvalMSE.append(oosMSE)

plt.plot(depthList, xvalMSE)
plt.axis('tight')
plt.xlabel('Tree Depth' )
plt.ylabel('Mean Squared Error')
plt.title('MSE versus Tree Depth - '+ str(nPoints) + ' pts')
plt.savefig('CV_Perf_vs_Tree_depth-' + str(nPoints) +  '.png', dpi=500)
plt.show()
```

Tree depth is one way to regulate the complexity of a binary tree model. It has a similar effect to the coefficient penalty in the penalized regression model in Chapter 4 and Chapter 5. More tree depth makes it possible for the model to extract more complicated behaviors from the data at the cost of additional complexity. Figure 6.8 shows that depth 3 gives the best MSE performance for the synthetic problem from Listing 6-2. That depth makes the best trade-off between reproducing the underlying relationships and overfitting the problem.

Recall from Chapter 3, "Predictive Model Building: Balancing Performance, Complexity, and Big Data," that the optimum model complexity is a function of the data set size. This synthetic data problem offers an opportunity to demonstrate how that works. Figure 6.10 shows how the optimum model complexity and performance change if the number of data points is increased to 1000.

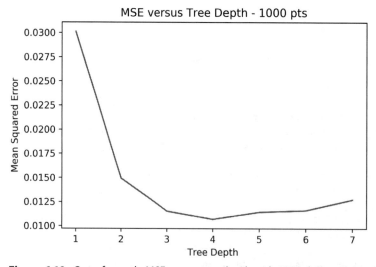

Figure 6.10: Out-of-sample MSE versus tree depth with 1000 data points

You can run the plot for yourself by changing the variable `nPoints` in Listing 6-3 to `1000`. Two things happen as a result of adding more data. For one thing, the best tree depth increases from 3 to 4. The added data supports a more complicated model. For another thing, the MSE drops slightly. The added depth permits finer steps in the stair-step approximation of the real model. The added fidelity of the model is what excites people about really large data sets.

Modifications for Classification and Categorical Features

For you to have a complete picture of how decision trees are trained, we have a couple of other details to discuss. One is this: How does this work for a classification problem? The earlier criteria used to judge splits—MSE—makes sense only for regression problems. As you've seen elsewhere in the book, classification problems have different figures of merit than regression problems. Several figures of merit can be used with classification problems to judge splits in place of MSE. One that you're already familiar with is misclassification error. The other two commonly used measures are Gini impurity measure and information gain. For more information on these, see `http://en.wikipedia.org/wiki/Decision_tree_learning#Gini_impurity`. These other two measures have somewhat different properties from misclassification error, but aren't conceptually different.

The last detail is how trees can be trained on attributes that are categorical instead of being numeric. The (nonterminal) nodes in the tree pose a yes/no question. For numeric variables, the question is in the form of whether the given attribute is less than a parameter. Splitting a categorical variable into two subsets consists of trying every possible division of the categories into two sets. If the categories are A, B, and C, the possible splits are A in the first group and B and C in the second, B in the first group and A and C in the second, and so forth. Some mathematical results simplify the process in some circumstances.

This section furnished some background on binary decision trees. On their own, binary decision trees are a legitimate prediction tool and worthy of study, but the main purpose of outlining them here is as background for ensemble methods, which incorporate hordes of binary decision trees. You will see that some of the issues that come up using an individual tree (multiple parameters to adjust, structural instability, and overfitting for large trees) will recede into the background when the hundreds or thousands of these trees are combined. That was the intent behind the development of ensemble methods, which are remarkably robust, easy to train, and accurate. The next sections discuss the three main ensemble methods one at a time.

Bootstrap Aggregation: "Bagging"

Bootstrap aggregation was developed by Leo Breiman. This method starts with picking a base learner. The method will be implemented here using binary decision trees as the base learners. You'll see as we go through the method that other machine learning algorithms could be used as base learners. Binary decision trees are a logical choice because they naturally model problems with complicated decision boundaries, but binary decision trees can exhibit excessive performance variance. Variance can be overcome by combining a multitude of tree-based models.

How Does the Bagging Algorithm Work?

The bootstrap aggregation algorithm uses what is called a *bootstrap* sample. The bootstrap sample is often used for generating sample statistics from a modest data set. A (nonparametric) bootstrap sample is a random selection of several elements from the data set with replacement (that is, a bootstrap sample can contain multiple copies of a row from the original data). Bootstrap aggregation takes several bootstrapped samples from the training data set and then trains a base learner on each of these samples. The resulting models are averaged in regression problems. For classification problems, the models can either be averaged or probabilities can be developed based on the percentages of different classes. Listing 6-4 shows code for the bagging algorithm applied to the synthetic problem introduced at the beginning of the chapter.

The code holds out 30% of the data for measuring out-of-sample performance instead of using cross-validation. The parameter numTreesMax determines the maximum number of trees that will be included in the ensemble. The code builds models from the first tree, the first two trees, the first three trees, and so on, up to numTreesMax trees, to see how the accuracy depends on the number of trees included in the ensemble. The code stores the trained models in a list and stores the predictions on the data that were held out for out-of-sample error testing.

Listing 6-4: Bootstrap Aggregation Algorithm—simpleBagging.py

```
__author__ = 'mike-bowles'

import numpy as np
import matplotlib.pyplot as plt
from sklearn import tree
from sklearn.tree import DecisionTreeRegressor
from math import floor
from numpy.random import choice


#Build a simple data set with y = x + random
nPoints = 1000

#x values for plotting
x = np.linspace(-0.5, 0.5, nPoints)
x_feat = x.reshape([-1,1])
```

```
#y (labels) has random noise added to x-value
#set seed
np.random.seed(1)
y = x + np.random.randn(nPoints) * 0.1

#take fixed test set 30% of sample
indices = list(range(nPoints))
nSample = int(nPoints * 0.30)
idxTest = choice(indices, nSample, replace=False)
idxTest.sort()
idxTrain = [idx for idx in indices if not(idx in idxTest)]

#Define test and training attribute and label sets
xTrain = x_feat[idxTrain]
xTest = x_feat[idxTest]
yTrain = y[idxTrain]
yTest = y[idxTest]
idx_Train = list(range(len(xTrain)))

#train a series of models on random subsets of the training data
#collect models in a list and check error of composite as list grows

#maximum number of models to generate
numTreesMax = 20

#tree depth - typically at the high end
treeDepth = 1

#initialize a list to hold models
modelList = []
predList = []

#number of samples to draw for stochastic bagging
nBagSamples = int(len(xTrain) * 0.5)

for iTrees in range(numTreesMax):
    #take bag sample and define train sets
    idxBag = choice(idx_Train, nBagSamples, replace=True)
    xTrainBag = xTrain[idxBag]
    yTrainBag = yTrain[idxBag]

    modelList.append(DecisionTreeRegressor(max_depth=treeDepth))
    modelList[-1].fit(xTrainBag, yTrainBag)

    #make prediction with latest model and add to list of predictions
    latestPrediction = modelList[-1].predict(xTest)
    predList.append(latestPrediction)
```

```
#build cumulative prediction from first "n" models
mse = []
allPredictions = []

for iModels in range(len(modelList)):

    prediction_i = np.zeros_like(predList[0])
    for i in range(iModels):
        prediction_i += predList[i] / float(iModels + 1)

    allPredictions.append(prediction_i)
    errors = yTest - prediction_i
    mse.append(np.average(errors * errors))

nModels = [i + 1 for i in range(numTreesMax)]

plt.plot(nModels,mse)
plt.axis('tight')
plt.xlabel('Number of Models in Ensemble')
plt.ylabel('Mean Squared Error')
plt.ylim((0.0, max(mse)))
plt.title('MSE vs Number of Trees in Ensemble - Depth =
 ' +str(treeDepth))
plt.savefig('bagging_mse_vs_nTrees_' + str(treeDepth) + '.png', dpi=500)
plt.show()

plotList = [0, 9, 19]
for iPlot in plotList:
    plt.plot(xTest, allPredictions[iPlot], label=str(iPlot))
plt.plot(xTest, yTest, linestyle="--")
plt.legend()
plt.axis('tight')
plt.xlabel('x value')
plt.ylabel('Predictions')
plt.title('Shape of prediction curves - Depth = ' + str(treeDepth))
plt.savefig('bagging_response_curve_vs_nTrees_' + str(treeDepth) +
 '.png', dpi=500)
plt.show()

print('Minimum MSE')
print(min(mse))

Printed Output:

With treeDepth = 1
Minimum MSE
0.0277111866174121

With treeDepth = 5
Minimum MSE
0.012089941293578658
```

The code produces two plots. One plot shows how the MSE changes as more trees are included in the ensemble. The second plot shows how the predictions from the first tree, the average of the first 10 trees, and the average of the first 20 trees, compare. The comparison plot is similar to the plot of the prediction curve relative to the actual labels as functions of the single attribute.

Figure 6.11 shows how the MSE varies as the number of trees is increased. The error more or less levels out at around 0.025. This isn't a particularly good model. The noise that was added had a standard deviation of 0.1. The very best MSE a predictive algorithm could generate is the square of that standard deviation, or 0.01. The single binary tree that was trained earlier in the chapter was getting close to 0.01. Why is this more sophisticated algorithm underperforming?

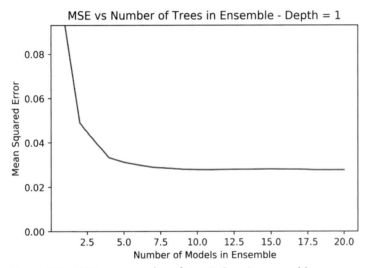

Figure 6.11: MSE versus number of trees in Bagging ensemble

Bagging Performance—Bias Versus Variance

A look at Figure 6.12 gives some insight into the problem and raises a point that is important to illustrate because it's relevant to other problems too. Figure 6.12 shows the single tree prediction, the 10-tree prediction, and the 20-tree prediction. The prediction from the single tree is easy to discern because there's a single step. The 10- and 20-tree predictions superpose a number of slightly different trees, so they have a series of finer steps that are in the neighborhood of the single step taken by the first tree. The steps of the multiple trees aren't all in exactly the same spot because they are trained on different samples of the data, and that leads to some randomness in the split points. But that randomness only jiggles the split points in a relatively small neighborhood near the center of the graph. So, the resulting ensemble doesn't see much variety because all the trees in the ensemble roughly agree about where the single split point should go.

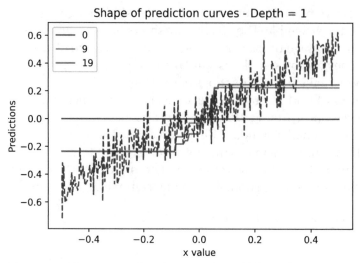

Figure 6.12: Comparison of prediction and actual label as functions of attribute

Two types of errors exist: bias and variance. Consider trying to fit a wiggly curve with a straight line. Getting more data can reduce the effect of noise in the data being used for fitting, but more data will not make a straight line into a wiggly curve. Errors that do not get smaller as more data points are added are called *bias errors*. Fitting depth 1 trees to the synthetic problem suffers from a bias error. All the split points are chosen near the center of the data, and the model accuracy suffers at the edges of the data.

The bias error with depth 1 trees comes from the basic model being too simple and sharing a common limitation. Bagging reduces variance between models. But with depth 1 trees, it gets a bias error, which can't be averaged. The way to overcome this problem is to use trees with more depth.

Figure 6.13 shows the curve of MSE versus number of trees in the ensemble for depth 5 trees. The MSE with depth 5 trees is somewhat smaller than 0.01 (probably due to randomness in the noise data), clearly much better performance than with depth 1 trees.

Figure 6.14 shows plots for the prediction based on the first tree, the first 10 trees, and the first 20 trees. The single tree prediction stands out from the others because it has a number of sharp spikes where it's making severe errors. In other words, it has a high variance. The other single trees undoubtedly show similar performance. But when they're average, the variance is reduced; the curve representing the prediction from the bagging algorithm is much smoother and closer to the true answer.

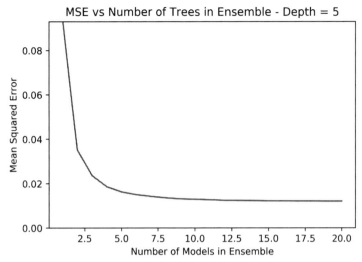

Figure 6.13: MSE versus number of trees with depth 5 trees

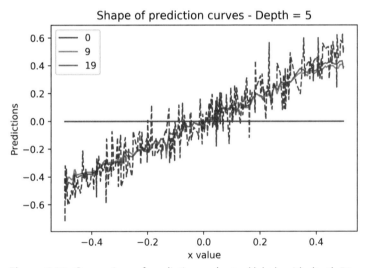

Figure 6.14: Comparison of prediction and actual labels with depth 5 trees

How Bagging Behaves on Multivariable Problem

Listing 6-5 shows the application of the bagging algorithm for the task of predicting wine quality. The wine example demonstrates some of the same principles as you saw with the synthetic data. These are best seen in Figures 6.15 through 6.17, which come from running Listing 6-4 with different parameter settings.

Listing 6-5: Predicting Wine Quality with Bagging—wineBagging.py

```python
__author__ = 'mike-bowles'

import numpy as np
from sklearn import tree
from sklearn.tree import DecisionTreeRegressor
from numpy.random import choice
from math import sqrt
import matplotlib.pyplot as plt

from Read_Fcns import list_read_wine

#read data into iterable
names, xList, labels = list_read_wine()
xArray = np.array(xList)
yArray = np.array(labels)

nrows = len(xList)
ncols = len(xList[0])


#take fixed test set 30% of sample
indices = list(range(nrows))
nSample = int(nrows * 0.30)
idxTest = choice(indices, nSample, replace=False)
idxTrain = [idx for idx in indices if not(idx in idxTest)]

#Define test and training attribute and label sets
xTrain = xArray[idxTrain]
xTest = xArray[idxTest]
yTrain = yArray[idxTrain]
yTest = yArray[idxTest]
idx_Train = list(range(len(xTrain)))

#train a series of models on random subsets of the training data
#collect models in a list and check error of composite as list grows

#maximum number of models to generate
numTreesMax = 100

#tree depth - typically at the high end
treeDepth = 12

#initialize a list to hold models
modelList = []
predList = []

#number of samples to draw for stochastic bagging
nBagSamples = int(len(xTrain) * 0.5)
```

```
for iTrees in range(numTreesMax):
    idxBag = choice(range(len(xTrain)), nBagSamples, replace=True)
    xTrainBag = xTrain[idxBag]
    yTrainBag = yTrain[idxBag]

    modelList.append(DecisionTreeRegressor(max_depth=treeDepth))
    modelList[-1].fit(xTrainBag, yTrainBag)

    #make prediction with latest model and add to list of predictions
    latestPrediction = modelList[-1].predict(xTest)
    predList.append(latestPrediction)


#build cumulative prediction from first "n" models
#build cumulative prediction from first "n" models
rmse = []
allPredictions = []

for iModels in range(len(modelList)):

    prediction_i = np.zeros_like(predList[0])
    for i in range(iModels):
        prediction_i += predList[i] / float(iModels + 1)

    allPredictions.append(prediction_i)
    errors = yTest - prediction_i
    rmse.append(sqrt(np.average(errors * errors)))


nModels = [i + 1 for i in range(numTreesMax)]


plt.plot(nModels,rmse)
plt.axis('tight')
plt.xlabel('Number of Tree Models in Ensemble')
plt.ylabel('Root Mean Squared Error')
plt.ylim((0.0, max(rmse)))
plt.title('RMS Error vs Ensemble Size - Depth = ' + str(treeDepth))
plt.savefig('bagging_wine_' + str(treeDepth) + '.png', dpi=500)
plt.show()

print('With Tree Depth = ', treeDepth)
print('With Number of Trees = ', numTreesMax)
print('Minimum RMSE = ', min(rmse))

Printed Output:

With Tree Depth =  1
With Number of Trees =  30
Minimum RMSE =  0.7440534935904853
```

```
With Tree Depth =   5
With Number of Trees =   30
Minimum RMSE =   0.6540549863025144

With Tree Depth =   12
With Number of Trees =   100
Minimum RMSE =   0.5727542363996668
```

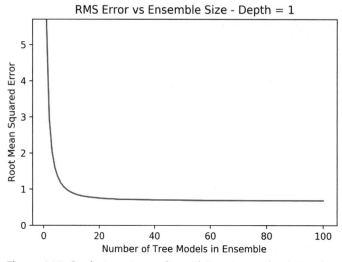

Figure 6.15: Predicting wine quality with Bagging on depth 1 trees

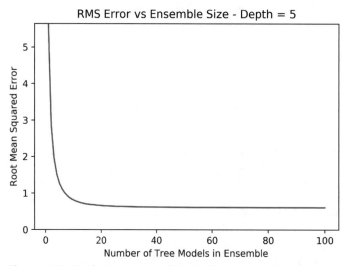

Figure 6.16: Predicting wine quality with Bagging on depth 5 trees

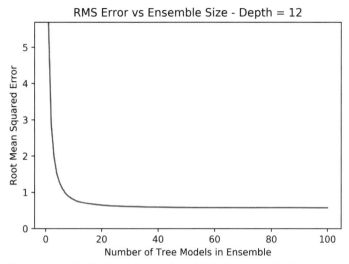

Figure 6.17: Predicting wine quality with Bagging on depth 12 trees

Figure 6.15 shows how MSE changes as more trees are included in the bagging ensemble. The ensemble of stumps (depth 1 trees) on the wine quality data shows negligible improvement in MSE over the single tree. The lack of improvement on the wine data is much more dramatic than with the synthetic data. This might be true for a couple of reasons. One possibility is that the errors at the edges of the data are more significant with the wine quality data than with the synthetic data. Another possibility is that interaction between variables is more important with the wine data.

The synthetic data had only one variable, so no interaction between variables was possible. The wine data has multiple attributes, and so it's possible that the attributes in combination are more important than the sum of their individual contributions. If you stumble while walking, it won't likely be important. If you walk along the edge of a cliff, it won't likely be important. But if you stumble while walking along the edge of a cliff, it could be important. The two conditions need to be considered together. A depth 1 tree can only consider solitary attributes and therefore cannot account for strong interactions between variables.

Bagging Needs Tree Depth for Performance

Figure 6.16 shows how the MSE depends on number of trees when the trees all have depth 5. The Bagging ensemble shows clear improvement as more trees are added. The resulting performance is much better than that achieved by Bagging depth 1 trees. The improvement suggests that perhaps even more tree depth would yield further improvement.

Figure 6.17 shows MSE versus number of trees in the Bagging ensemble when the trees are depth 12. In addition to employing deeper trees, the ensemble runs 100 trees rather than 30 to get a better picture of how much performance improvement is available by training larger numbers of trees for the Bagging ensemble. Figure 6.17 shows the lowest MSE of the three runs.

Summary of Bagging

Now you have seen a first example of an ensemble method. Bagging clearly demonstrates the two-level hierarchy common to ensemble methods. Properly speaking, bagging is the higher-level algorithm defining a series of subproblems to be solved by base learners and then averaging their predictions. The individual problems making up a bagging ensemble are derived by taking random bootstrap samples of the original training data. Bagging reduces the variance exhibited by individual binary trees. For bagging to work properly, the trees in a bagging ensemble need to be grown to sufficient depth.

Bagging serves as a good introduction to ensemble methods because it is relatively easy to understand and because it is relatively easy to demonstrate its variance reduction properties. The next two algorithms covered are gradient boosting and random forests. They take different approaches to building ensembles and exhibit some advantages over bagging. Most of the current practitioners I know use either gradient boosting or random forests first and do not regularly use bagging.

Gradient Boosting

Gradient boosting was developed by Stanford professor Jerome Friedman, who also developed the coordinate descent algorithm used to solve the ElasticNet problem (in Chapters 4 and 5). Gradient boosting develops an ensemble of tree-based models by training each of the trees in the ensemble on different labels and then combining the trees. For a regression problem where the objective is to minimize MSE, each successive tree is trained on the errors left over by the collection of earlier trees. For the derivation of the algorithm, see the "References" section at the end of this chapter. The easiest way to see how gradient boosting works is to look at some code implementing the algorithm.

Basic Principle of Gradient Boosting Algorithm

Listing 6-6 details the gradient boosting algorithm for the synthetic problem introduced earlier in this chapter. The early part of the code uses the process from earlier to build the synthetic data set.

Listing 6-6: Gradient Boosting for Simple Problem—simpleGBM.py

```
__author__ = 'mike-bowles'

import numpy as np
import matplotlib.pyplot as plt
from sklearn import tree
from sklearn.tree import DecisionTreeRegressor
from math import floor
from numpy.random import choice

#Build a simple data set with y = x + random
nPoints = 1000

#x values for plotting
x = np.linspace(-0.5, 0.5, nPoints)
x_feat = x.reshape([-1,1])

#y (labels) has random noise added to x-value
#set seed
np.random.seed(1)
y = x + np.random.randn(nPoints) * 0.1

#take fixed test set 30% of sample
indices = list(range(nPoints))
nSample = int(nPoints * 0.30)
idxTest = choice(indices, nSample, replace=False)
idxTest.sort()
idxTrain = [idx for idx in indices if not(idx in idxTest)]

#Define test and training attribute and label sets
xTrain = x_feat[idxTrain]
xTest = x_feat[idxTest]
yTrain = y[idxTrain]
yTest = y[idxTest]
idx_Train = list(range(len(xTrain)))

#train a series of models on random subsets of the training data
#collect models in a list and check error of composite as list grows

#maximum number of models to generate
numTreesMax = 30

#tree depth - typically at the high end
treeDepth = 5

#initialize a list to hold models
modelList = []
predList = []
eps = 0.3
```

```
#initialize residuals to be the labels y
residuals = yTrain

for iTrees in range(numTreesMax):

    modelList.append(DecisionTreeRegressor(max_depth=treeDepth))
    modelList[-1].fit(xTrain, residuals)

    #make prediction with latest model and add to list of predictions
    latestInSamplePrediction = modelList[-1].predict(xTrain)

    #use new predictions to update residuals
    residuals -=  eps * latestInSamplePrediction

    latestOutSamplePrediction = modelList[-1].predict(xTest)
    predList.append(latestOutSamplePrediction)


#build cumulative prediction from first "n" models
mse = []
allPredictions = []
for iModels in range(len(modelList)):

    #add the first "iModels" of the predictions and multiply by eps
    prediction_i = np.zeros_like(predList[0])
    for i in range(iModels):
        prediction_i += predList[i] * eps

    allPredictions.append(prediction_i)
    errors = yTest - prediction_i
    mse.append(np.average(errors * errors))

nModels = [i + 1 for i in range(len(modelList))]

plt.plot(nModels,mse)
plt.axis('tight')
plt.xlabel('Number of Models in Ensemble')
plt.ylabel('Mean Squared Error')
plt.title('Error vs Ensemble Size - Depth = ' + str(treeDepth))
plt.savefig('simple_gbm_error_vs_trees_' + str(treeDepth) + str(eps) +
 '.png', dpi=500)
plt.ylim((0.0, max(mse)))
plt.show()

plotList = [0, 3, 29]
lineType = [':', '-.', '--']
plt.figure()
for i in range(len(plotList)):
    iPlot = plotList[i]
    textLegend = 'Prediction with ' + str(iPlot + 1) + ' Trees'
    plt.plot(xTest, allPredictions[iPlot], label = textLegend,
```

```
    linestyle = lineType[i])
 plt.plot(xTest, yTest, label='True y Value', alpha=0.25)
 plt.legend(bbox_to_anchor=(1,0.3))
 plt.axis('tight')
 plt.xlabel('x value')
 plt.ylabel('Predictions')
 plt.title('Actual vs Predictions - Depth= ' + str(treeDepth))
 plt.savefig('simple_gbm_real_vs_pred_' +str(treeDepth) + str(eps) +
         '.png', dpi=500)
 plt.show()
```

Parameter Settings for Gradient Boosting

The first thing that looks unfamiliar is the comment about setting the depth parameter for the individual trees being trained in a gradient boosting ensemble. Gradient boosting differs from bagging and random forests in that it can reduce bias in addition to reducing variance. Gradient boosting has the useful property that it will often perform as well as low MSE values with stumps as with deeper trees. With gradient boosting, tree depth is only required to the extent that there's a significant interaction between variables. Performance improvement from increasing tree depth serves as a gauge of variable interaction in your problem.

The next thing that looks a little different is the definition of a variable called eps. This variable is a step size control of the sort that you may be familiar with from optimization problems. Gradient boosting takes gradient descent steps and, as with other gradient descent processes, if the steps are too large the optimization can diverge instead of converging. If the step size is too small, the process can take too many iterations. After generating some results, the chapter will talk about how to tune eps, the step size.

The next unfamiliar element of the code is the definition of a variable called residuals. The term *residuals* is commonly used to denote prediction errors (that is, observed values minus predicted values). The gradient boosting algorithm will make a series of refinements to its predictions of the labels. At each step along the way, the residuals will get recalculated. At the beginning of the process, gradient boosting initializes predictions to null (or zero) values so that the residuals are equal to the observed labels.

How Gradient Boosting Iterates toward a Predictive Model

The loop on iTrees begins by training a tree using the attributes, but training on the residuals instead of the labels. Only for the first pass are the raw labels used for training targets. Subsequent passes take the predictions generated by training and subtract eps of them from the residuals before training. As mentioned, the subtraction of the residuals amount to a gradient descent and the reason for multiplying by the step size control parameter `eps` is to make sure that the iterative process converges. The code uses a fixed holdout set to measure out-of-sample performance and then plots the MSE as a function of the number of trees trained, and also plots the function showing predicted values versus the single attribute.

Getting the Best Performance from Gradient Boosting

The first pair of plots (see Figures 6.18 and 6.19) shows the MSE versus number of trees and the plot of the prediction functions with eps = 0.1 and treeDepth = 1. Figure 6.18 shows that the error decreases smoothly and reaches roughly 0.014 after training 30 trees, and the MSE is heading down, indicating that it could be reduced further by training still more trees.

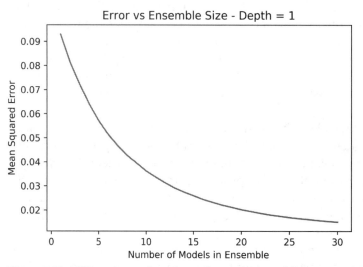

Figure 6.18: MSE versus number of trees for synthetic problem—eps = 0.1, treeDepth = 1

Figure 6.19 shows the prediction versus attribute value for three gradient boosting models—one that only trains one tree, one that trains 15 trees, and one that trains 30 trees. The model incorporating a single tree looks like a diminished version of the tree models that you saw in the introductory section about decision trees. As described, it is indeed a single depth 1 tree trained on the labels and then multiplied by 0.1—the value of `eps`. Things get more interesting with the model built on 10 trees. That model makes a nice approximation to the correct answer—a straight line at 45 degrees on the graph. The model incorporating 10 trees correctly predicts roughly half of the range right and predicts the right and left sides as constant. The model incorporating 30 trees gets a little further toward good approximation all the way to the edges of the data. This is distinct from the behavior that bagging showed with using stumps.

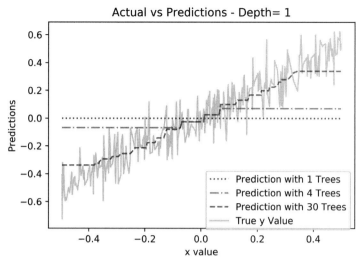

Figure 6.19: Gradient boosting predictions versus attribute value problem—eps = 0.1, treeDepth = 1

Bagging couldn't get beyond the bias error inherent in using shallow trees to build predictions for a number of problems not much different from one another. Gradient boosting starts in the same manner, but as it begins to reduce the errors in the middle of the data, it begins to pay more attention to the areas where it's making mistakes. That moves the split points out into the regions where there are mistakes. That process leads to a nice approximation without needing tree depth to get it.

What happens as the parameters controlling the training are changed? Figures 6.20 and 6.21 show how the picture changes if trees are of depth 5. The MSE

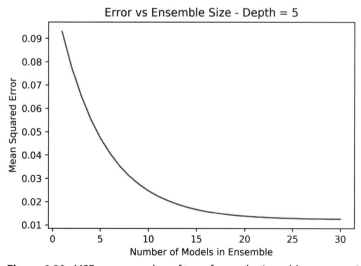

Figure 6.20: MSE versus number of trees for synthetic problem—eps = 0.1, treeDepth = 5

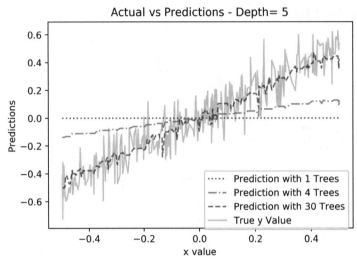

Figure 6.21: Gradient boosting predictions versus attribute value problem—eps = 0.1, treeDepth = 5

plot in Figure 6.20 shows a similar smooth reduction in MSE as the number of trees increases. The MSE value gets very close to perfection (0.01) after training 30 depth 5 trees—lower than with depth 1 trees. What the plot doesn't show is training time. Each level in a tree takes about the same time to train. At each layer, all the possible split points have to be compared for MSE. A depth 5 tree takes five times as long as five depth 1 trees. A fair comparison would be to see what error the depth 1 trees reached after 150 trees compared to depth 5 trees after 30.

Figure 6.21 clearly reflects the deeper trees being used to build the gradient boosting ensemble. Even the first prediction based on a single tree shows some structure all across the range of the attribute. The models based on 15 trees and 30 trees still exhibit higher levels of error at the edges of the data.

Figures 6.22 and 6.23 show what happens as the step size parameter eps is increased. Figure 6.22 shows behavior that's characteristic of too large a step size parameter (named eps here). The graph of MSE versus the number of trees decreases sharply but then increases again toward the right side. The minimum is on the left side of the graph, near the one-third point. You want to adjust eps so that the minimum is at or near the right edge of the graph. That usually gives better performance.

The picture of the predictions as a function of the attribute shows more spiky diversions from the correct 45% line than either of the versions using *eps=0.1*. Overall, the version with depth 1 trees is the best behaved. It looks like training more trees might improve the performance at the edges of the depth 1 model and lead to the best answer for gradient boosting.

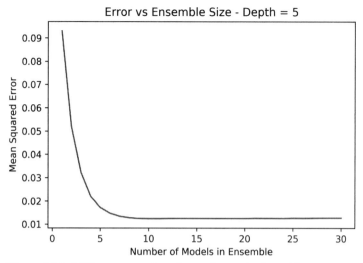

Figure 6.22: MSE versus number of trees for synthetic problem—eps = 0.3, treeDepth = 5

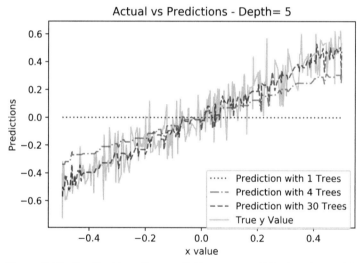

Figure 6.23: Gradient boosting predictions versus attribute value problem—eps = 0.3, treeDepth = 5

Gradient Boosting on a Multivariable Problem

Listing 6-7 shows application of gradient boosting to the task of predicting wine quality. With the exception using the wine data set for input, the code in Listing 6-6 is very similar to the code used on the simple synthetic data set.

Listing 6-7: Gradient Boosting for Predicting Wine Quality—wineGBM.py

```python
__author__ = 'mike-bowles'

import numpy as np
from sklearn import tree
from sklearn.tree import DecisionTreeRegressor
from numpy.random import choice
from math import sqrt
import matplotlib.pyplot as plt

#read data into iterable
from Read_Fcns import list_read_wine

#read data into iterable
names, xList, labels = list_read_wine()
xArray = np.array(xList)
yArray = np.array(labels)

nrows = len(xList)
ncols = len(xList[0])

#take fixed test set 30% of sample
indices = list(range(nrows))
nSample = int(nrows * 0.30)
idxTest = choice(indices, nSample, replace=False)
idxTrain = [idx for idx in indices if not(idx in idxTest)]

#Define test and training attribute and label sets
xTrain = xArray[idxTrain]
xTest = xArray[idxTest]
yTrain = yArray[idxTrain]
yTest = yArray[idxTest]
idx_Train = list(range(len(xTrain)))

#train a series of models on random subsets of the training data
#collect models in a list and check error of composite as list grows

#maximum number of models to generate
numTreesMax = 100

#tree depth - typically at the high end
treeDepth = 3

#initialize a list to hold models
modelList = []
predList = []
eps = 0.1

#initialize residuals to be the labels y
residuals = list(yTrain)
```

```
for iTrees in range(numTreesMax):

    modelList.append(DecisionTreeRegressor(max_depth=treeDepth))
    modelList[-1].fit(xTrain, residuals)

    #make prediction with latest model and add to list of predictions
    latestInSamplePrediction = modelList[-1].predict(xTrain)

    #use new predictions to update residuals
    residuals -= eps * latestInSamplePrediction

    latestOutSamplePrediction = modelList[-1].predict(xTest)
    predList.append(latestOutSamplePrediction)


#build cumulative prediction from first "n" models
rmse = []
allPredictions = []
for iModels in range(len(modelList)):

    #add the first "iModels" of the predictions and multiply by eps
    prediction_i = np.zeros_like(predList[0])
    for i in range(iModels):
        prediction_i += predList[i] * eps

    allPredictions.append(prediction_i)
    errors = yTest - prediction_i
    rmse.append(sqrt(np.average(errors * errors)))


nModels = [i + 1 for i in range(len(modelList))]

plt.plot(nModels,rmse)
plt.axis('tight')
plt.xlabel('Number of Trees in Ensemble')
plt.ylabel('Root Mean Squared Error')
plt.title('Error vs Ensemble Size for GBM')
plt.savefig('gbm_wine_error_vs_nTrees.png', dpi=500)
plt.ylim((0.0, max(rmse)))
plt.show()

print('Minimum RMSE = ', min(rmse))

Printed Output:
Minimum RMSE =  0.603455179638897
```

The parameter selections shown in the code are for 30 depth 5 trees and *eps=0.1*. This parameter set yields MSE of roughly 0.4. That's about 10% worse than the performance bagging got on the same problem. Try adjusting the number of trees, eps, the step size parameter, and the tree depth to see whether you can get better results.

The curve of MSE versus number of trees looks fairly flat at the right edge (see Figure 6.24). It might still be possible to get some more performance by adding more trees to the ensemble. The other possible approaches to squeezing out a little more performance would be to tweak the tree depth or step size parameter.

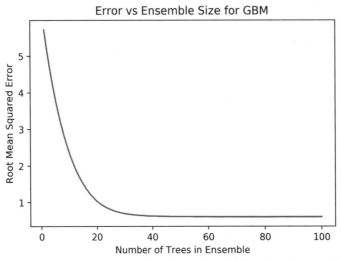

Figure 6.24: MSE versus number of trees for gradient boosting model of wine quality

Summary for Gradient Boosting

This section has shown how gradient boosting operates and demonstrated how to control its behavior to get the best performance. The section talked about the effect of changing step size, tree depth, and number of trees. You've seen how gradient boosting avoids the bias errors that bagging experienced with shallow trees. The basic difference in principle between bagging and boosting is that boosting constantly monitors its cumulative error and uses that residual for subsequent training. That difference accounts for gradient boosting only needing tree depth when there's significant interaction among the various attributes in the problem.

Random Forests

The random forests algorithm was developed by the late Berkeley professor Leo Breiman and Adele Cutler. Random forests generates its sequence of models by training them on subsets of the data. The subsets are drawn at random from the full training set. One way in which the subset is selected is to randomly sample rows with replacement in the same manner as Breiman's bootstrap aggregation algorithm. The other random element is that the training sets for the individual trees in the random forest's ensemble don't incorporate all the attributes, but take a random subset of the attributes also. Listing 6-8 approximates random forests using Python `DecisionTreeRegression`.

Listing 6-8: Bagging with Random Attribute Selection—wineRF.py

```
__author__ = 'mike-bowles'

import numpy as np
from sklearn import tree
from sklearn.tree import DecisionTreeRegressor
from numpy.random import choice
from math import sqrt
import matplotlib.pyplot as plt
from Read_Fcns import list_read_wine

#read data into iterable
names, xList, labels = list_read_wine()
xArray = np.array(xList)
yArray = np.array(labels)

nrows = len(xList)
ncols = len(xList[0])

#take fixed test set 30% of sample
indices = list(range(nrows))
nSample = int(nrows * 0.30)
idxTest = choice(indices, nSample, replace=False)
idxTrain = [idx for idx in indices if not(idx in idxTest)]

#Define test and training attribute and label sets
xTrain = xArray[idxTrain]
xTest = xArray[idxTest]
yTrain = yArray[idxTrain]
yTest = yArray[idxTest]
idx_Train = list(range(len(xTrain)))

#train a series of models on random subsets of the training data
#collect models in a list and check error of composite as list grows

#maximum number of models to generate
numTreesMax = 30

#tree depth - typically at the high end
treeDepth = 12

#pick how many attributes will be used in each model.
# authors recommend 1/3 for regression problem
nAttr = 4

#initialize a list to hold models
modelList = []
indexList = []
predList = []
n_bag = int(0.5 * len(yTrain))
```

```
for iTrees in range(numTreesMax):

    modelList.append(DecisionTreeRegressor(max_depth=treeDepth))

    #take random sample of attributes
    idx_attr = choice(list(range(ncols)), nAttr, replace=False)

    #take a random sample of training rows - bagging
    idx_bag = choice(idx_Train, n_bag, replace=True)


    #build training set
    xRfTrain = xTrain[idx_bag, ]
    xRfTrain = xRfTrain[:, idx_attr]
    yRfTrain = yTrain[idx_bag]

    modelList[-1].fit(xRfTrain, yRfTrain)

    #restrict xTest to attributes selected for training
    xRfTest = xTest[:,idx_attr]

    latestOutSamplePrediction = modelList[-1].predict(xRfTest)
    predList.append(latestOutSamplePrediction)


#build cumulative prediction from first "n" models
rmse = []
allPredictions = []

for iModels in range(len(modelList)):

    prediction_i = np.zeros_like(predList[0])
    for i in range(iModels):
        prediction_i += predList[i] / float(iModels + 1)

    allPredictions.append(prediction_i)
    errors = yTest - prediction_i
    rmse.append(sqrt(np.average(errors * errors)))

nModels = [i + 1 for i in range(len(modelList))]

plt.plot(nModels,rmse)
plt.axis('tight')
plt.xlabel('Number of Trees in Ensemble')
plt.ylabel('Root Mean Squared Error')
plt.title('Random Forest RMSE - Depth = ' + str(treeDepth))
plt.savefig('rf_wine_depth_' + str(treeDepth) + '.png', dpi=500)
plt.ylim((0.0, max(rmse)))
plt.show()
```

```
print('Number of trees = ', numTreesMax)
print('Tree depth = ', treeDepth)
print('Minimum RMSE = ', min(rmse))

Printed Output:

Number of trees =   30
Tree depth =   1
Minimum RMSE =   0.7554878119435257

Number of trees =   5
Tree depth =   30
Minimum RMSE =   0.6924346211106107

Number of trees =   12
Tree depth =   30
Minimum RMSE =   0.6396042882586701
```

Random Forests: Bagging Plus Random Attribute Subsets

The example shown in Listing 6-5 trains on the wine quality data set. The simple single-attribute example that was used earlier to illustrate bagging and gradient boosting algorithms won't work with random forests. That example had only one attribute. It does not make sense to take a random draw of a single item. The code in Listing 6-5 looks a lot like the code for bagging. The only difference between the two that shows up before the loop on iTrees is the specification of a variable called nAttr. The random draw on the attributes needs to know how many attributes to select. The authors of the original paper recommend one third the number of attributes for a regression problem (and the square root of the number of attributes for a classification problem). Inside the iTrees loop, there's a random sample on rows of the attribute matrix—just like with bagging. There's also a random draw without replacement on the columns of the attribute matrix (or what would be rows and columns if the list of lists were converted to a numpy array). Then a tree gets trained and used to make a prediction on the out-of-sample data.

There is a difference between what's implemented in Listing 6-5 and the random forests algorithm. The algorithm in Listing 6-5 takes a random subset of the attributes and trains a tree with that subset. Breiman's original version of the random forest algorithm takes a different random set of attributes for each node in the tree. To implement Breiman's original version of the algorithm requires access to the innards of the tree growing algorithm. The example, nonetheless, gives a feel for how the algorithm operates. Some people argue that there's not much advantage to make the random draw on attributes at every node.

Random Forests Performance Drivers

Figures 6.25 through 6.27 show how the addition of random attribute selection affects the curves of MSE versus the number of trees included in the ensemble. Figure 6.25 shows the result when the individual trees are depth 1 trees. The picture is very similar to bagging in that the ensemble doesn't improve performance very much. Depth 1 trees mostly cause bias error, not variance error. Bias can't be averaged away.

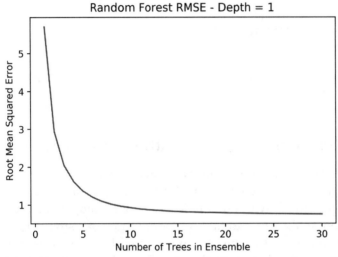

Figure 6.25: MSE versus number of trees for bagging + random attribute selection—Depth 1 trees

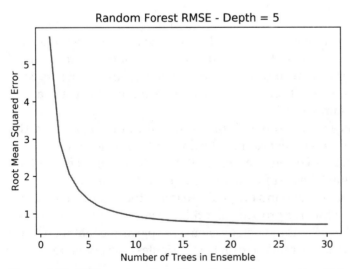

Figure 6.26: MSE versus number of trees for bagging + random attribute selection—Depth 5 trees

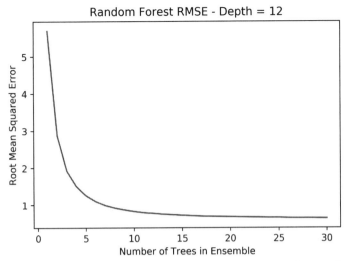

Figure 6.27: MSE versus number of trees for bagging + random attribute selection—Depth 12 trees

Figure 6.26 shows the MSE curve using depth 5 trees. Now the variance reduction with bagging plus random attribute selection begins to show some performance. The improvement with this combination gets similar performance to other methods demonstrated.

Figure 6.27 shows that a little more performance is available by using depth—12 trees.

Random Forests Summary

Random forests is a combination of bagging and a random attribute selection modification to the binary tree base learners. These differences may not seem substantial, but they give random forests different performance characteristics from bagging and gradient boosting. Some results suggest that random forest has an advantage with wide sparse attribute spaces such as occur in text mining problems. Random forest is a little easier to parallelize than gradient boosting because the individual base learners can be trained independently of one another, whereas with gradient boosting each base learner needs the results from the ones before it.

Differences like these mean that you may want to try both random forests in addition to gradient boosting, if you need to wring as much performance as possible from your data.

Summary

This chapter gave you some background on basic ensemble algorithms. It explained that ensemble methods consisted of a hierarchy of two algorithms. Ensemble methods train hundreds or thousands of the low-level algorithms called *base learners*. The higher-level algorithm controls the training of the base learners in order that their models turn out somewhat independent from one another so that combining them will reduce the variance of the combination. For bagging, the higher-level algorithm is to take bootstrap samples of the training set and train base learners on these samples. For gradient boosting, the higher-level algorithm at each stage takes a sample of the input data and trains a base learner on it. With gradient boosting, the target used to train each base learner is the error from the accumulation of all the earlier base learners. Random forest is a combination of bagging as a higher-level algorithm and base learners that are modified versions of binary decision trees. The base learners with random forests are binary trees where, at each node, the split point decisions are restricted to a random sample of the available attributes instead of considering all the attributes in each split. The packages available for doing gradient boosting in Python permit you to use random forest base learners with gradient boosting. You will see that use in the next chapter, "Building Ensemble Methods with Python."

The chapter coded each of the high-level algorithms and showed a facsimile of the random forest's base learners. The purpose for coding these is for you to gain an understanding of the mechanisms at work in each of the algorithms. The idea behind that is that you will better understand the options, input variables, nominal starting values, and so on for the Python packages for these algorithms. The next chapter uses available Python packages to generate solutions to some of the problems you've seen solved by penalized linear regression.

References

1. Panda Biswanath, Joshua S. Herbach, Sugato Basu, and Roberto J. Bayardo. (2009). "PLANET: Massively Parallel Learning of Tree Ensembles with MapReduce." Proceedings of the 35th International Conference on Very Large Data Bases. Retrieved from `http://research.google.com/pubs/pub36296.html`.

2. Leo Breiman. (September, 1994). "Bagging Predictors." Technical Report No. 421. Department of Statistics, UC Berkeley. Retrieved from `http://statistics.berkeley.edu/sites/default/files/tech-reports/421.pdf`.

3. Leo Breiman. (2001). "Random Forests. *Machine Learning*," 45:5–32. Retrieved from `https://www.stat.berkeley.edu/~breiman/random forest2001.pdf`.

4. J.H. Friedman. (2001). "Greedy Function Approximation: A Gradient Boosting Machine." *Annals of Statistics*, 29(5):1189–1232. Retrieved from `http://statweb.stanford.edu/~jhf/ftp/trebst.pdf`.

5. J.H. Friedman. (2002). "Stochastic Gradient Boosting." *Computational Statistics and Data Analysis*, 38(4):367–378. Retrieved from `http://statweb.stanford.edu/~jhf/ftp/stobst.pdf`.

## CHAPTER 7

Building Ensemble Models
with Python

This chapter uses several available Python packages to build predictive models using the ensemble algorithms that you saw in Chapter 6, "Ensemble Methods." The problems used to illustrate them were introduced in Chapter 2, "Understand the Problem by Understanding the Data." You saw in Chapter 5, "Building Predictive Models Using Penalized Linear Methods," how to build predictive models for them using penalized linear regression. This chapter uses ensemble methods to solve the same problems. That will enable you to compare the algorithms and the available Python packages in terms of how easy the packages are to use, what kinds of accuracy is achievable with ensemble methods versus penalized linear regression, how the training times compare, and so on. The end of the chapter shows some summary comparisons of the various algorithms with which you've become familiar.

Solving Regression Problems with Python Ensemble Packages

The next several sections demonstrate the application of available Python packages for building ensemble models. You will see the things you learned in Chapter 6 in action. The methods explained in Chapter 6 will be used on the series of problems explored in Chapter 2, and then used to demonstrate the application of penalized linear regression in Chapter 5. Using the same problems makes it possible to compare the algorithms covered here along several dimensions, including raw performance, training time, and ease of use. The chapter also covers the available Python packages. The background given in Chapter 6 helps you understand why the Python packages are structured the way they are and helps you see how to get the most from these methods. This section goes through a variety of different problem types, beginning with regression problems.

Using Gradient Boosting to Predict Wine Taste

As you saw in Chapter 6, gradient boosting takes an error-minimization approach to building an ensemble of trees, instead of the variance-reduction approach that Bagging and Random Forest take. Because gradient boosting incorporates binary trees as its base learners, it shares some tree-related parameters. However, because gradient boosting takes steps directed by the gradient, you'll also see parameters such as step size. In addition, gradient boosting's error-minimization approach will lead to different rationales and choices for setting tree depth. There's also a surprise variable that allows you to build models that are a hybrid between random forest and gradient boosting. You can use the gradient boosting error-minimization structure while employing the random forest random attribute selection for base learners.

Gradient boosting is arguably the hottest algorithm for making predictions on structured data sets such as we've been exploring. Structured data sets are basically data sets that can be arranged in a table like a pandas data frame or a numpy array. My friend Anthony Goldbloom, founder and CEO of Kaggle, has run hundreds of machine learning competitions. Anthony told me that gradient boosting has won more competitions on structured data than any other algorithm. The favored version is a package called XGBoost, although the Microsoft package LightGBM is also a competitive package. Both of these are well maintained and actively updated.

XGBoost can be installed with an anaconda install. You can find the most current conda install instructions by searching on "anaconda install xgboost." That makes the installation straightforward. You can similarly find a conda install for LightGBM. We'll focus on XGBoost here.

The package documentation for both of these is very high quality. For XGBoost just search on "'xgboost python api" (XGBoost is available in several different languages).

The next section provides an introduction to the XGBoost package.

Using the Class Constructor for GradientBoostingRegressor

To reach the documentation for the Python version of XGBoost, search on "xgboost python api." Look at the section titled "Python API Reference." In that section you'll find "Core Data Structure." That defines a specialized input data structure that XGBoost uses for memory and speed optimization. You'll see a function called `DMatrix()` that accepts features and labels as numpy arrays and returns the required data structures. The code examples in the next section (Listing 7-1) will show you how easy this is to use.

Next come descriptions of the learning API and scikit-learn APIs that define training functions, cross-validated training, and scikit-learn-like regressor and classifier classes. For these you'll need to supply values for a variety of parameters that will control the training process. You'll find answers to just about any question you have by searching on the question.

The following list describes the parameters and methods that you'll want to be familiar with and give some comment on the choices and tradeoffs for them where appropriate. You'll need to know these to get started (there's a longer list in the documentation):

- `max_depth` *(int)*—Maximum tree depth for base learners.
- `learning_rate` *(float)*—Boosting learning rate.
- `n_estimators` *(int)*—Number of trees to fit.
- `verbosity` *(int)*—The degree of verbosity. Valid values are 0 (silent) to 3 (debug).
- `objective` *(string or callable)*—Specify the learning task and the corresponding learning objective. This is basically the loss function that's being minimized in the course or training. For regression problems the usual choice is `'reg:squarederror'`; for binary classification it's `'binary:logistic'`. Other choices are outlined in the "learning parameters" section of the documentation.
- `booster` *(string)*—Specify which booster to use: `gbtree`, `gblinear`, or `dart`. You'll only see `gbtree` used here, but I encourage you to try some of the others.
- `n_jobs` *(int)*—Number of parallel threads used to run XGBoost (replaces `nthread`).
- `subsample` *(float)*—Fraction of the data to be sampled for use tree by tree.

    The next three parameters turn the trees in the ensemble into random forest trees, by randomly picking a subset of features for each tree, level, or node.

- `colsample_bytree` *(float)*—Subsample ratio of columns when constructing each tree.
- `colsample_bylevel` *(float)*—Subsample ratio of columns for each level.
- `colsample_bynode` *(float)*—Subsample ratio of columns for each split.
- `reg_alpha` *(float* [xgb's `alpha`])—L1 regularization term on weights.

- ▪ reg_lambda (float [xgb's lambda])—L2 regularization term on weights.

- ▪ seed (int)—Random number seed. (Deprecated, please use random_state.)

- ▪ random_state (int)—Random number seed (replaces seed).

Modeling with XGBoost proceeds by instantiating XGBRegressor or XGB-Classifier and supplying parameter values that will define the training and evaluation process. Then you'll call a series of class functions on the object. The ones you'll see regularly here include fit(), which will cause training and associated output to happen; predict(), which will generate predictions using the trained model; and feature_importances(), which will give estimates of feature importances. Those will be enough to get you started.

Getting the parameters set for gradient boosting can be a little bewildering for a new user. The following list suggests a sequence of parameter settings and adjustments for gradient boosting:

1. Start with default settings, except set subsample=0.5. Train a model and look at the curve of out-of-sample (OOS) performance versus the number of trees in the ensemble. After the first and subsequent runs, look at the shape of the OOS performance curve.

2. If the OOS performance is improving rapidly at the right end of the graph, either increase n_estimators or increase learning_rate.

3. If the OOS performance is deteriorating rapidly at the right end of the graph, decrease learning_rate.

4. Once the OOS performance curve improves over its whole length (or only deteriorates very slightly) and levels out at the right side of the graph, try altering max_depth and max_features.

Using GradientBoostingRegressor to Implement a Regression Model

Listing 7-1 shows what's required to build a gradient boosting model for the wine quality data set.

Listing 7-1: Build a Gradient Boosting Model to Predict Wine Quality—wine_gbm.py

```
__author__ = 'mike_bowles'

import numpy as np
from sklearn.metrics import mean_squared_error
from Read_Fcns import list_read_wine
from math import sqrt
import matplotlib.pyplot as plt
import xgboost as xgb

# Read wine quality data from UCI website
names, xList, labels = list_read_wine()
```

```python
names = [x.replace('\"', '') for x in names]
print(names)

nrows = len(xList)
ncols = len(xList[0])

X = np.array(xList)
y = np.array(labels)

n_fold = 5

idx_array = np.array(range(len(y))).reshape([-1, 1])
params = {"objective":"reg:linear",
        'colsample_bytree': 0.4,
        'learning_rate': 0.02,
        'n_estimators': 500,
        'max_depth': 4,
        'alpha': 10,
        'verbosity':1}

reg_model = xgb.XGBRegressor(**params)
results_list = []
for i_fold in range(n_fold):
    idx_test = idx_array[np.mod(idx_array, n_fold) == i_fold]
    idx_train = idx_array[np.mod(idx_array, n_fold) != i_fold]
    x_test = X[idx_test]
    y_test= y[idx_test]
    x_train = X[idx_train]
    y_train = y[idx_train]

    reg_model.fit(x_train, y_train, eval_set=[(x_train, y_train),
        (x_test, y_test)], eval_metric='rmse', verbose=False)
    results_list.append(reg_model.evals_result())

train_err = [eval['validation_0']['rmse'] for eval in results_list]
test_err = [eval['validation_1']['rmse'] for eval in results_list]

train_err_array = np.array(train_err)
test_err_array = np.array(test_err)

train_avg = np.mean(train_err_array, axis = 0)
test_avg = np.mean(test_err_array, axis = 0)

print('Final training rmse', train_avg[-5:])
print('Final test rmse', test_avg[-5:])

plt.plot(train_avg)
plt.plot(test_avg)
plt.xlabel('Number of Trees in Ensemble')
plt.ylabel('RMSE')
plt.title('Train and Test Errors')
```

```
plt.savefig('wineXGB_train_test_rmse.png', dpi=500)
plt.show()

#retrain on full set for importance calc
data_matrix = xgb.DMatrix(data=X, label=y, feature_names=names[0:-1])
params = {"objective":"reg:linear",'colsample_bytree': 0.4,
     'learning_rate': 0.02, 'n_estimators': 500, 'max_depth': 4,
     'alpha': 10, 'silent':1}

wine_xg = xgb.train(params=params, dtrain=data_matrix,
     num_boost_round=500)
xgb.plot_importance(wine_xg)
plt.rcParams['figure.figsize'] = [5, 5]
plt.savefig('wineGBM_variable_importance.png', dpi=500)
plt.show()


Printed Output:
['fixed acidity', 'volatile acidity', 'citric acid', 'residual sugar',
'chlorides', 'free sulfur dioxide', 'total sulfur dioxide', 'density',
'pH', 'sulphates', 'alcohol', 'quality']
Final training rmse [0.4301812 0.4299654 0.4296578 0.429428  0.4292482]
Final test rmse [0.5996246 0.5995986 0.599513  0.5995322 0.5994808]
```

The first section of code reads the data set, separates the attribute matrix from the targets, converts to numpy arrays, and then forms train and test subsets. The next step is to define a Python dictionary called params. This dictionary contains the values for parameters needed to define the GBM model. Some of these are more or less standard and some will vary considerably from one problem to the next. The first parameter is the objective function. Since this is a regression problem, reg:linear is the usual choice here. If you have a problem where the labels appear exponentially distributed (no negative values, positive values crowded near zero and spread more thinly for larger values), then you might try logistic regression.

Once the parameters are defined, the next step is to instantiate a model object. The training loop here is doing 5-fold cross-validation. The indices for train and test sets are defined in list comprehensions, which are used to define appropriate train and test sets for each fold. Then the model gets trained by invoking the fit function on the xgb.XGBRegressor object called reg_model. The parameter eval_set defined in the fit function is chosen to be a list of pairs. One pair is the training feature set and corresponding labels. The other pair is similar for the test data. eval_metric='rmse' tells the fit function to apply the model prediction to the features and then calculate root mean square error (RMSE) between the two. It follows the same process for the test data.

The XGBoost apparatus delivers a dictionary into reg_model.evals_result(). Each of these contains point-by-point train and test RMSE generated as trees are added to the ensembles in each of the cross-validation folds. That makes it easy to aggregate the results across the cross-validation folds with a list comprehension, convert the resulting list of arrays into a two-dimensional numpy array, and to then calculate average errors for train and test for each stage of the ensemble growth.

The last bit of code in the listing trains a new model on the full data set. The retraining is done using the XGBoost `"train"` function. This has a somewhat different character, although the underlying machinery is the same. Using the `train` function doesn't entail instantiating a class object. It's a function call. That function call requires that the input data (train and test sets) be in the XGBoost "DMatrix" data structure. You can see that this process only requires one line of code and accepts numpy arrays as input.

Assessing the Performance of a Gradient Boosting Model

Figure 7.1 and the printed output in Listing 7-1 show that gradient boosting gets slightly less than 0.6 RMS error. You'll see in the next section that random forest gets about the same. That's often the case, but problems exist where the difference is significant, so you might want to try them both to make sure. The plot in Figure 7.1 shows an oos error that flattens out midway along the x-axis. Sometimes you can squeeze out a little more performance by dropping the learning rate slightly and retraining. Give that a try and see what you can get.

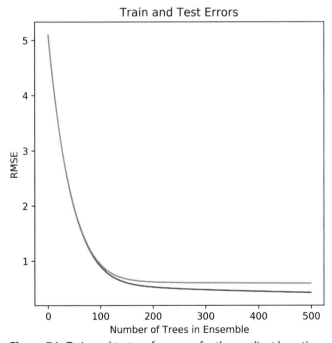

Figure 7.1: Train and test performance for the gradient boosting wine model

Figure 7.2 shows the variable importance determined as part of the gradient boosting implementation. Notice that alcohol is the second most important variable. It's switched places with volatile acidity from what you saw with penalized linear regression.

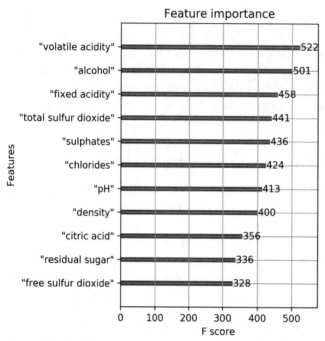

Figure 7.2: Variable importance as measured by gradient boosting

Building a Random Forest Model to Predict Wine Taste

Random forest is not available as part of XGBoost, but scikit-learn has a good random forest package. Evidence of competition performance and the relative intensity of development work in the last few years suggests that gradient boosting has a performance advantage over random forest. But random forest is unequivocally easier to use. If you follow Breiman's suggestion (the inventor) you grow trees to full depth and average. You can tweak the fraction of the data set that's sampled for training and you can tweak the number of features available at each split, but the performance is usually a fairly weak function of these two things. Gradient boosting, by contrast, has a learning rate, two regularization parameters, tree depth, and the list goes on. If you want a quick answer, random forest is a good bet.

The Python scikit-learn ensemble module houses a random forest algorithm for regression problems. That module also has a gradient boosting algorithm. First, this section explains the parameters required to instantiate a member of the RandomForestRegressor class. Then this section uses the `RandomForestRegressor` class to train a random forest model for the wine taste data and to explore the performance of the model.

Constructing a RandomForestRegressor Object

Here is the class constructor for `sklearn.ensemble.RandomForestRegressor`:

```
sklearn.ensemble.RandomForestRegressor(n_estimators=10, criterion=
'mse', max_depth=None, min_samples_split=2, min_samples_leaf=1,
max_features= 'auto', max_leaf_nodes=None, bootstrap=True,
oob_score=False, n_jobs=1, random_state=None, verbose=0,
min_density=None, compute_importances=
None)
```

The following description mirrors sklearn documentation but covers only the parameter values that you're most likely to want to alter. For those parameters, the list describes how to choose alternatives to the default values. To see descriptions of the parameters not covered here, see the sklearn package documentation. The following list describes the parameters:

■ **n_estimators**

integer, optional (default = 10)

This is the number of trees in the ensemble. The default is okay to use if you coded things correctly, but you'll generally want more than 10 trees to gain the best performance. You can experiment with the number and get a feel for how many are required. As emphasized throughout this book, the appropriate model complexity (tree depth and number of trees) depends on the complexity of the underlying problem and the amount of data that you have. A good starting point is 100–500.

■ **max_depth**

integer or None, optional (default=None)

If this parameter is set to None, the tree will be grown until all the leaf nodes are either pure or they hold fewer than `min_samples_split` examples. As an alternative to specifying the tree depth, you can use `max_leaf_nodes` to specify the number of leaf nodes in the tree. If you specify `max_leaf_nodes`, `max_depth` is ignored. There might be a performance advantage to leaving `max_depth` set to `auto` and growing full-depth trees. This is also a training time cost associated with full-depth trees. You may want to experiment with the depth if you need several training runs to complete your modeling process.

■ **min_samples_split**

integer, optional (default=2)

Nodes will not be split that have fewer than `min_samples_split` examples. Splitting nodes that are small is a source of overfitting.

■ **min_samples_leaf**

integer, optional (default=1)

A split is not taken if the split leads to nodes that have fewer than `min_sam-ples_leaf`. The default value for this parameter results in the parameter being ignored, which is often okay—particularly when you're making the first few training runs on your data set. You can think about selecting a meaningful value for this parameter in a couple of ways. One is that the value assigned to a leaf is the average of the examples in the leaf and that you'll get a lower variance average if there's more than one sample in the leaf node. Another way to think about this parameter is as an alternative way to control tree depth.

▪ **max_features**

integer, float or string, optional (default=None)

The number of features to consider when looking for the best split depends on the value set for `max_features` and on the number of features in the problem. Call the number of features in the problem `nFeatures`. Then:

▪ If the type of `max_features` is `int`, consider `max_features` features at each split. Note: `max_features` gt; `nFeatures` throws an error.

▪ If the type of `max_features` is `float`, `max_features` is the fraction of features to consider: `int(max_features * nFeatures)`.

▪ Possible string values include the following:

```
auto max_features=nFeatures
sqrt max_features=sqrt(nFeatures)
log2 max_features=log2(nFeatures)
If max_features=None, then max_features=nFeatures.
```

Breiman and Cutler recommend `sqrt(nFeatures)` for regression problems. The answers aren't generally terribly sensitive to `max_features`, but this parameter can have some effect, so you'll want to test a few alternative values.

▪ **random_state**

int, RandomState instance, or None (default=None)

▪ If the type is `integer`, the integer is used as the seed for the random number generator.

▪ If the `random_state` is an instance of `RandomState`, that instance is used as the random number generator.

▪ If `random_state` is `None`, the random number generator is the instance of `RandomState` used by `numpy.random`.

`RandomForestRegressor` has several attributes, including the trained trees that make up the ensemble. There's a predict method that will use the trained trees to make predictions, so you will not generally access those directly. You will want to access the variable `importances`. Here is a description:

- **feature_importances**

  This is an array whose length is equal to the number of features in the problem (called `nFeatures` earlier). The values in the array are positive floats indicating relative importance of the corresponding attribute. The `importances` are determined by a procedure Breiman invented in the original paper on random forests. The basic idea is that, one at a time, values of each attribute are randomly permuted, and the change in the model's prediction accuracy is determined. The more the prediction accuracy suffers, the more important the attribute.

Here are descriptions of the methods used:

- **fit(XTrain, yTrain, sample_weight=None)**

  `XTrain` is an array of attribute values. It has `nInstances` rows and `nFeature` columns. `yTrain` is an array of targets. `y` also has `nInstances` rows. In the examples you'll see in this chapter, `yTrain` will have a single column, but the method can fit several models having different targets. For that, `y` would have `nTargets` columns—one column for each set of outcomes. `sample_weight` makes it possible to assign different weights to each of the instances in the training data. It can take one of two forms. The default value of None results in equal weighting of all input instances. To apply different weights to each instance, `sample_weight` should be an array with `nInstances` rows and one column.

- **predict(XTest)**

  `XTest` is an array of attribute values for which predictions are produced. The array input to `predict()` has the same number of columns as the array used in the `fit()` method for training, but can have a different number of rows, including perhaps a single row. The rows in the output from `predict()` have the same form as rows in the target array `y` used in training.

Modeling Wine Taste with RandomForestRegressor

Listing 7-2 shows how to use the sklearn version of the random forest algorithm to build an ensemble model to predict wine taste.

The code reads the wine data set from UCI data repository; does some manipulation to get the attributes, labels, and attribute names into lists; and converts the lists to numpy arrays as required for input to `RandomForestRegressor`. A side benefit of having these input objects in the form of numpy arrays is that it enables the use of a sklearn utility, `train_test_split`, for building training and test versions of the inputs. The code sets `random_state` to a specified integer value instead of letting the random number generator pick an unrepeatable internal value. That's so that you'll get the same graphs and numeric values when you run the code as the results shown here. Setting `random_state` can also prove handy during development because randomness in the results can mask changes you're making. During real model training, you'll probably want to set `random_state` to its default value, None. Fixing `random_state` fixes the holdout set and, as a result, repeated parameter adjustments and retraining may start to overtrain on your holdout set.

The next step in the code is to define a list of ensemble sizes to produce performance graphs that show how the performance varies as the number of trees in the ensemble is changed. For producing detailed plots, the number chosen in Listing 7-2 trains 10 trees to start, then captures the results and trains more trees in batches. Training in increments enables you to see the shape of the curve of error versus number of trees. That way you can gauge how many trees you'll want in the final model. The code in Listing 7-2 shows how to use the `warm_start` parameter so as to accumulate training as new trees are added.

Listing 7-2: Build a Random Forest to Predict Wine Quality—wine_rf.py

```python
__author__ = 'mike_bowles'

import numpy as np
from sklearn.model_selection import train_test_split
from sklearn.ensemble import RandomForestRegressor
from sklearn.metrics import mean_squared_error
import matplotlib.pyplot as plt
from Read_Fcns import list_read_wine
from math import sqrt


# Read wine quality data from UCI website
names, xList, labels = list_read_wine()

nrows = len(xList)
ncols = len(xList[0])

X = np.array(xList)
y = np.array(labels)
wineNames = np.array(names)

#take fixed holdout set 30% of data rows
xTrain, xTest, yTrain, yTest = train_test_split(X, y, test_size=0.30,
        random_state=531)

#train random forest for various forest sizes - see how the mse changes
rmseOos = []
```

```python
depth = None  #None - gives max depth trees, try limiting
maxFeat  = 4 #try tweaking

num_iterations = 50 #train 10 additional trees 50 times
trees_per_iteration = 10

wineRFModel = RandomForestRegressor(n_estimators=trees_per_iteration,
                    max_depth=depth,
                    max_features=maxFeat,
                    oob_score=False,
                    random_state=531,
                    warm_start=True)

for iters in range(num_iterations):
    wineRFModel.fit(xTrain,yTrain)
    wineRFModel.n_estimators += trees_per_iteration

    #Accumulate mse on test set
    prediction = wineRFModel.predict(xTest)
    rmseOos.append(sqrt(mean_squared_error(yTest, prediction)))


print("RMSE" )
print(min(rmseOos))
print(rmseOos[-1])

#plot training and test errors vs number of trees in ensemble
num_trees = [i * trees_per_iteration for i in range(num_iterations)]
plt.plot(num_trees, rmseOos)
plt.xlabel('Number of Trees in Ensemble')
plt.ylabel('Root Mean Squared Error')
plt.title('RF Performance vs Number of Trees')
plt.savefig('wine_rf.png', dpi=500)
plt.show()

# Plot feature importance
featureImportance = wineRFModel.feature_importances_

# normalize by max importance
featureImportance = featureImportance / featureImportance.max()
sorted_idx = np.argsort(featureImportance)
barPos = np.arange(sorted_idx.shape[0]) + .5
plt.barh(barPos, featureImportance[sorted_idx], align='center')
plt.yticks(barPos, wineNames[sorted_idx])
plt.xlabel('Variable Importance')
plt.subplots_adjust(left=0.2, right=0.9, top=0.9, bottom=0.1)
plt.title('Relative Importance of Features')
plt.savefig('wine_rf_var_imp.png', dpi=500)
plt.show()
```

```
Printed Output
RMSE
0.5618291717498893
0.5644169041290903
```

Most of the parameters affecting training are set as part of the constructor that instantiates a `RandomForestRegressor` object. The call to the constructor is pretty simple in this case. The only parameter that is not left at default values is the `max_features` parameter. The default value (`None`) results in all the features being considered at each node of the tree, which means that it's actually implementing bagging because no random selection of attributes is involved.

After instantiating a `RandomForestRegressor` object, the next step is to invoke the `fit()` method the training sets as arguments. Once that is done, invoking the `predict()` method with the attributes from the test set generates predictions that can be compared to the test set labels. The code in the listing uses the sklearn.metrics function `mean_squared_error` to calculate the prediction error. The resulting mean squared error numbers are collected in a list and then plotted. Figure 7.3 shows the resulting plot.

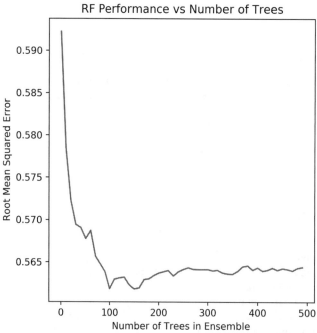

Figure 7.3: Train and test performance for the random forest wine quality model

The smallest value and the last value of mean squared error are also printed and copied at the bottom of Listing 7-2. Notice that the last value is somewhat higher than the minimum value. I would trust the last (higher) value over the minimum one. Random forest is minimizing variance by averaging over more and more somewhat independent high-variance trees. Conceptually the error should be declining monotonically. To the extent that it isn't, the variations are random fluctuations. By the end of the graph in Figure 7.3, the graph has become more or less flat. The minimum close to the beginning is likely random fluctuation, not achievable performance.

Visualizing the Performance of a Random Forest Regression Model

The curve in Figure 7.3 demonstrates the variance reduction properties of the random forest algorithm. The level of the error decreases as more trees are added, and the amount of statistical fluctuation in the curve also decreases.

> **NOTE**   To get a feel for the behavior of the algorithm, try changing some of the parameters used in Listing 7-1 and see how the plots change. Try running more trees to see whether you can reduce the error further. Try altering the tree-depth parameter to see how sensitive the answers are to tree depth. The wine quality data set has roughly 1,600 instances (rows), so a depth of 10 or 11 could result in almost every point having its own leaf node. A depth of 8 could ideally have 256 leaf nodes, so each one would have an average of about 6 instances. Try some depths in that range to determine whether it affects performance.

Random forest generates estimates of how important each variable is to the accuracy of predictions. Listing 7-2 extracts the data member `feature_importance_`, rescales importance values to between 0 and 1, orders the resulting importance values, and then plots them in a bar chart. Figure 7.4 shows that plot. The most important variable has scaled importance of 1.0 and is the top bar in the bar chart. The random forest model has ranked alcohol as the most important feature and volatile acidity as second most important. That reversed from gradient boosting, but the same as penalized linear regression as you saw in Chapter 5.

Incorporating Non-Numeric Attributes in Python Ensemble Models

Non-numeric attributes are ones that take several discrete non-numeric values. A census record has myriad non-numeric attributes—married, single, divorced, for example; state in which the household is located is another. Non-numeric attributes can improve prediction accuracy, but Python ensemble methods need numeric input. In Chapters 4, "Penalized Linear Regression," and 5, "Building Predictive Models Using Penalized Linear Methods," you saw how to code factor variables so that they could be incorporated in penalized linear regression. The same technique will work here. The problem of estimating the age of abalone will serve as an example to illustrate the technique.

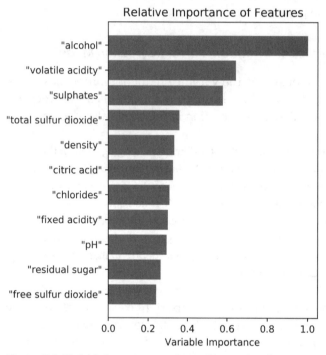

Figure 7.4: Variable importance estimated by random forest

Coding the Sex of Abalone for Gradient Boosting Regression in Python

Suppose that your problem has an attribute that takes n values. The attribute "States in the US" takes 50 values, and "Marital Status" takes 3. To code the n-valued factor variable, you create $n - 1$ new dummy attributes. If the variable takes its ith value, the ith dummy variable is 1 and all other dummies are 0. If the factor variable takes its nth value, all the dummy variables are 0. The abalone data will illustrate. Listing 7-3 contains the code to train a gradient boosting model.

Listing 7-3: Train a Gradient Boosting Model to Predict Abalone Age—abalone_gbm.py

```
__author__ = 'mike_bowles'

import matplotlib.pyplot as plt
import numpy as np
```

```python
from sklearn.metrics import mean_squared_error
from Read_Fcns import list_read_abalone
import xgboost as xgb


#read abalone data
xList, labels = list_read_abalone()

names = ['Sex', 'Length', 'Diameter', 'Height', 'Whole weight',
'Shucked weight', 'Viscera weight', 'Shell weight', 'Rings']

#code three-valued sex attribute as numeric
xCoded = []
for row in xList:
    #first code the three-valued sex variable
    codedSex = [0.0, 0.0]
    if row[0] == 'M': codedSex[0] = 1.0
    if row[0] == 'F': codedSex[1] = 1.0

    numRow = [float(row[i]) for i in range(1,len(row))]
    rowCoded = list(codedSex) + numRow
    xCoded.append(rowCoded)

namesCoded = np.array(['Sex1', 'Sex2', 'Length', 'Diameter', 'Height',
        'Whole weight', 'Shucked weight', 'Viscera weight',
        'Shell weight', 'Rings'])


nrows = len(xCoded)
ncols = len(xCoded[1])

#form x and y into numpy arrays and make up column names
X = np.array(xCoded)
y = np.array(labels)


data_dmatrix = xgb.DMatrix(data=X,label=y,
feature_names=namesCoded[0:(-1)])

# Train gradient boosting model to minimize mean squared error
params = {"objective":"reg:linear",
        'colsample_bytree': 0.6,
        'learning_rate': 0.02,
        'max_depth': 5,
        'alpha': 0,
        'silent':1}

cv_results = xgb.cv(dtrain=data_dmatrix,
                    params=params, nfold=5,
                    num_boost_round=500,
                    early_stopping_rounds=50,
                    metrics="rmse",
                    as_pandas=True, seed=123)
```

```
print(cv_results.head())
print(cv_results.tail())
plt1 = cv_results['train-rmse-mean']
plt2 = cv_results['test-rmse-mean']

plt.plot(plt1)
plt.plot(plt2)
plt.xlabel('Number of Trees in Ensemble')
plt.ylabel('RMSE')
plt.title('Train and Test Errors')
plt.savefig('abaloneXGB_train_test_rmse.png', dpi=500)
plt.show()

#retrain on full set for importance calc
abalone_xg = xgb.train(params=params,
                       dtrain=data_dmatrix,
                       num_boost_round=500)
xgb.plot_importance(abalone_xg)
plt.rcParams['figure.figsize'] = [5, 5]
plt.savefig('abaloneGBM_variable_importance.png', dpi=500)
plt.show()

Printed Output:
    train-rmse-mean  train-rmse-std  test-rmse-mean  test-rmse-std
0         9.783807        0.037574        9.783015       0.150659
1         9.600569        0.036505        9.599989       0.150391
2         9.421384        0.036425        9.421522       0.149063
3         9.246224        0.035644        9.247294       0.147877
4         9.074526        0.035122        9.076285       0.147339
      train-rmse-mean  train-rmse-std  test-rmse-mean  test-rmse-std
397        1.648841        0.022800        2.135843       0.061627
398        1.647947        0.022618        2.135824       0.061578
399        1.647266        0.022787        2.135831       0.061678
400        1.646389        0.022872        2.135730       0.061664
401        1.645507        0.023043        2.135672       0.061829
```

Assessing Performance and the Importance of Coded Variables with Gradient Boosting

The printed output in Listing 7-3 shows how gradient boosting performs on the abalone data. GBM gets down to errors on the test data of 2.13 without a great deal of tuning. The tuning that was done indicated that limiting the features used for tree training seemed helpful. See if you can improve on these results by doing some further tuning. You can find code in the online code repository for this book. You can either run it in a Python notebook or use the individual functions for each block. In the section "Classifying Glass Using Gradient Boosting" later in this chapter, you'll see how to implement grid search to automate the tuning process. Try implementing that in this problem to speed up your tuning process. Figure 7.5 shows how the training and test errors decay as more trees are added to the ensemble. This is another one that has leveled out. Decreasing the learning rate might help.

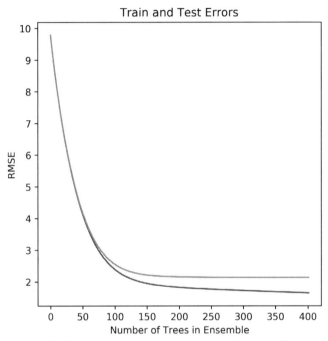

Figure 7.5: Train and test performance for gradient boosting abalone age model

Figure 7.6 shows the variable importance for gradient boosting. Notice that the sex variables that got coded numerically are at the bottom of the list. You'll see that they also occupy the bottom spot with random forest.

This section has gone through predicting abalone age—the number of rings found by slicing the shell and counting them under a microscope. The measurements available for making the prediction are other more easily measured quantities like the weight of the shell, the weight without the shell, and the sex of the animal. Since the sex is indeterminate at some stages of the abalone's life, the sex variable has three values. This section demonstrated how to handle coding the variable and demonstrated how that works with a gradient boosting model. You'll see this again in the section "Predicting Abalone Age with PySpark Ensemble Methods."

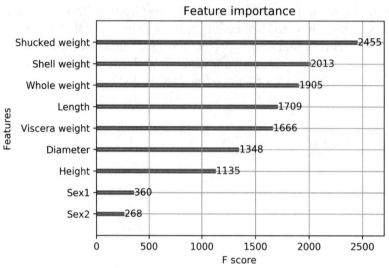

Figure 7.6: Gradient boosting estimates of variable importance in the abalone model

Coding the Sex of Abalone for Input to Random Forest Regression in Python

Listing 7-4 shows the steps for training a random forest model to predict abalone age from data on the abalone's weight, shell size, and so forth. The objective in this problem is to predict the age of the abalone from various physical measurements (weights of various parts of the abalone, dimensions, and so on). That makes this a regression problem amenable to the algorithms used for building models for predicting taste scores for wines in the previous two sections.

Listing 7-4: Train a Random Forest Model to Predict Abalone Age—abalone_rf.py

```
__author__ = 'mike_bowles'

import numpy as np
import matplotlib.pyplot as plot
from sklearn.model_selection import train_test_split
from sklearn.ensemble import RandomForestRegressor
from sklearn.metrics import mean_squared_error
from Read_Fcns import list_read_abalone


#read abalone data
xList, labels = list_read_abalone()

names = ['Sex', 'Length', 'Diameter', 'Height', 'Whole weight',
         'Shucked weight', 'Viscera weight', 'Shell weight',
         'Rings']
```

```
#code three-valued sex attribute as numeric
xCoded = []
for row in xList:
    #first code the three-valued sex variable
    codedSex = [0.0, 0.0]
    if row[0] == 'M': codedSex[0] = 1.0
    if row[0] == 'F': codedSex[1] = 1.0

    numRow = [float(row[i]) for i in range(1,len(row))]
    rowCoded = list(codedSex) + numRow
    xCoded.append(rowCoded)

namesCoded = np.array(['Sex1', 'Sex2', 'Length', 'Diameter', 'Height',
        'Whole weight', 'Shucked weight', 'Viscera weight', \
        'Shell weight', 'Rings'])

nrows = len(xCoded)
ncols = len(xCoded[1])

#form x and y into numpy arrays and make up column names
X = np.array(xCoded)
y = np.array(labels)

#break into training and test sets.
xTrain, xTest, yTrain, yTest = train_test_split(X, y,
                                test_size=0.30,
                                random_state=531)

#instantiate model
depth = None
maxFeat = 4
subsamp = 0.5

#train random forest over ensemble sizes to see how the mse changes

num_iterations = 50 #train 10 additional trees 50 times
trees_per_iteration = 10

abaloneRFModel = RandomForestRegressor(
                            n_estimators=trees_per_iteration,
                            max_depth=depth,
                            max_features=maxFeat,
                            oob_score=False,
                            random_state=531,
                            warm_start=True)

rmseOos = []
for iters in range(num_iterations):
    abaloneRFModel.fit(xTrain,yTrain)
    abaloneRFModel.n_estimators += 10
```

```
                #Accumulate mse on test set
                prediction = abaloneRFModel.predict(xTest)
                rmseOos.append(sqrt(mean_squared_error(yTest, prediction)))

        print("RMSE" )
        print(min(rmseOos))

        #plot training and test errors vs number of trees in ensemble
        num_trees = [i * trees_per_iteration for i in range(num_iterations)]
        plt.plot(num_trees, rmseOos)
        plt.xlabel('Number of Trees in Ensemble')
        plt.ylabel('Root Mean Squared Error')
        plt.title('Random Forest RMSE on Abalone Data')
        #plt.ylim([0.0, 1.1*max(mseOob)])
        plt.savefig('abalone_rf.png', dpi=500)
        plt.show()

        # Plot feature importance
        featureImportance = abaloneRFModel.feature_importances_

        # normalize by max importance
        featureImportance = featureImportance / featureImportance.max()
        sortedIdx = np.argsort(featureImportance)
        barPos = np.arange(sortedIdx.shape[0]) + .5
        plt.barh(barPos, featureImportance[sortedIdx], align='center')
        plt.yticks(barPos, namesCoded[sortedIdx])
        plt.xlabel('Variable Importance')
        plt.title('Relative Importance of Features')
        plt.subplots_adjust(left=0.2, right=0.9, top=0.9, bottom=0.1)
        plt.savefig('abalone_rf_var_imp.png', dpi=500)
        plt.show()

        Printed Output:
        RMSE
        2.0709035863949925
```

The printed output in Listing 7-4 gives the RMSE error for random forest to be 2.07. That's lower than what gradient boosting showed after a little tuning. It may well be that there's little performance difference between the two methods. It's already fairly low (0.06 ~ 3%). Those differences may be important to you. On the other hand, random forest didn't require a lot of tuning, so it got its answer in less developer time.

One of the attributes in the data set is the sex of the abalone. There are three possible values for an abalone's gender: male, female, and infant (although the gender of an abalone is indeterminate in infancy). So, the gender attribute is a three-valued factor variable. In the data set, the gender attribute is one of three character variables: M, F, or I. The section of the program that codes this attribute starts with a list filled with two float zeros. If the attribute value is M, the first list element is changed to a 1.0. If the attribute value is F, the second list element is changed to a 1.0. Otherwise, the list is left with two zeros (that is, if the attribute value is I). Then the new two-element list replaces the old character variable and the result is used to build a random forest model.

Assessing Performance and the Importance of Coded Variables

Figure 7.7 shows how the mean square prediction error decreases as the number of trees in the random forest ensemble is changed. The RMS error in predicting the age of abalone was 2.07, making the squared error 4.54. Compare that to the summary statistics that you saw in Chapter 2. The standard deviation of the age (shell rings) was 3.22, meaning that the mean squared variation in the age was 10.37. Therefore, random forest is able to predict about 56% of the squared variation in the age of the abalone in the population that was tested.

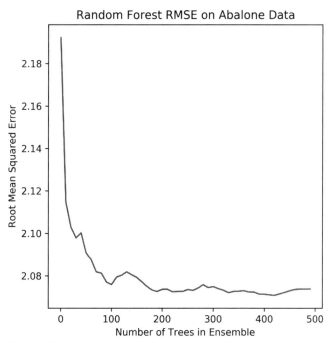

Figure 7.7: Train and test performance for random forest abalone age model

Figure 7.8 shows the relative variable importance for the random forest model. The gender-related variables that were created to deal with the non-numeric gender variable do not turn out to be very important in this model.

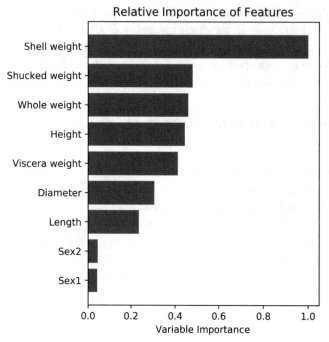

Figure 7.8: Random forest estimates of variable importance in the abalone model

Solving Binary Classification Problems with Python Ensemble Methods

This section covers two basic types of classification problems: binary classification and multiclass classification. Binary classification problems are ones with two possible outcomes. Those outcomes might be "clicked on the ad" or "didn't click on the ad," for example. The example used here to illustrate the use of ensemble methods is the rocks versus mines problem, where the task is to use sonar returns to determine whether the object being scanned by the sonar is a rock or a mine.

Multiclass problems are ones with more than two possible outcomes. Classifying glass samples according their chemical composition serves to illustrate the use of Python ensemble methods for this class of problem.

Detecting Unexploded Mines with Python Gradient Boosting

Listing 7-5 shows the code for building a binary classifier for detecting unexploded mines using XGBoost. This example is using the functional form of XGBoost in order to implement cross-validation as part of the training. You may be struck with how little difference there is in the arguments. The difference shows up in three places. One is that the objective needs to be changed from regression. The second is that the labels need to be 2-valued. The third is that the metric for performance needs to be changed.

Three objectives are available for binary classification. Those are `binary:logistic`, `binary:logitraw`, and `binary:hinge`. The code in Listing 7-5 uses `binary:logistic`. Try changing among these choices and see how it affects the performance you get. These have some important differences. One possibility is `error` or `error@t`. Gradient boosting will calculate estimates of class probabilities for each of the two classes. The `error` metric will compare predicted probabilities to a 0.5 threshold. Predictions above 0.5 will result in a prediction of 1 and those below in a prediction of 0. The metric `error` is then to add up the mistakes relative to true labels. It may be that your problem requires that you be more cautious with one type of error that with the other. Perhaps a classification of 1 results in a dangerous surgery, for example. Adjusting the threshold up will result in fewer predictions of 1. You can adjust the threshold upwards to 0.6 by using `error@0.6`.

Besides these classification error counting metrics, you can choose `auc` (area under the ROC curve) as a metric. Bigger is better with this metric and it has the benefit that doesn't require picking a threshold value. There is also `aucpr`, which is area under the precision recall curve. Listing 7-5 uses `auc`.

Listing 7-5: Build a Gradient Boosting Model to Distinguish Underwater Mines from Rocks—rocks_v_mines_gbm.py

```python
__author__ = 'mike_bowles'

from math import sqrt, fabs, exp
import matplotlib.pyplot as plt
from sklearn.metrics import roc_auc_score, roc_curve
import numpy as np
from Read_Fcns import list_read_rvm
import xgboost as xgb

#read data from uci data repository
xList, labels = list_read_rvm()


#number of rows and columns in x matrix
nrows = len(xList)
ncols = len(xList[1])

#form x and y into numpy arrays and make up column names
X = np.array(xList)
y = np.array(labels)
rocksVMinesNames = np.array(['V' + str(i) for i in range(ncols)])

data_dmatrix = xgb.DMatrix(data=X,label=y,
                     feature_names=rocksVMinesNames)

# Train gradient boosting model to minimize mean squared error
params = {"objective":"binary:logistic",
```

```
                'colsample_bytree': 0.3,
                'learning_rate': 0.5,
                'max_depth': 5,
                'lambda': 1.0,
                'alpha': 0,
                'silent':1}


cv_results = xgb.cv(dtrain=data_dmatrix,
                    params=params, nfold=5,
                    num_boost_round=200,
                    early_stopping_rounds=100,
                    metrics="auc",
                    as_pandas=True, seed=123)

print(cv_results.head())
print(cv_results.tail())
plt1 = cv_results['train-auc-mean']
plt2 = cv_results['test-auc-mean']

plt.plot(plt1)
plt.plot(plt2)
plt.xlabel('Number of Trees in Ensemble')
plt.ylabel('AUC')
plt.title('Train and Test Performance')
plt.savefig('rvmXGB_train_test_rmse.png', dpi=500)
plt.show()

Printed Output:
Best AUC
0.940052
```

	train-auc-mean	train-auc-std	test-auc-mean	test-auc-std
0	0.969936	0.009852	0.839870	0.080966
1	0.996107	0.001422	0.873191	0.061629
2	0.999883	0.000143	0.885021	0.053079
3	0.999971	0.000058	0.895060	0.042255
4	1.000000	0.000000	0.900222	0.049393
	train-auc-mean	train-auc-std	test-auc-mean	test-auc-std
95	1.0	0.0	0.938621	0.041431
96	1.0	0.0	0.938641	0.042119
97	1.0	0.0	0.939091	0.041444
98	1.0	0.0	0.939582	0.042113
99	1.0	0.0	0.940052	0.042141

The printed output from XGBoost classifier shows best AUC of 0.94. Given that perfect performance is 1.0, this is a pretty good number.

Determining the Performance of a Gradient Boosting Classifier

Figure 7.9 plots two curves. One is the AUC on the training set. The other is the AUC (on test data). These are both plotted against the number of trees in the ensemble to show how the performance is changing as the number of trees increases (or equivalently more gradient steps are taken; each step results in training an additional tree).

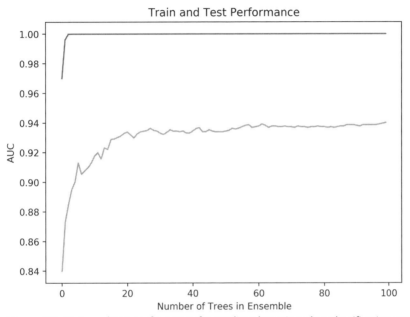

Figure 7.9: Train and test performance for gradient boosting glass classification model

Figure 7.10 plots the variable importance for the most important variables in the gradient boosting mine detector. The variable importances in Figure 7.10 are difficult to evaluate intuitively because they aren't as easily identified as shell weight or alcohol that occur in other data sets. In this case these correspond to different frequencies of sonar bouncing back from the targets. If we had the original data and the experimental conditions, we might be able to identify characteristic features on the rocks and mines that would correspond to the wavelengths of the most important features. If this were a problem you were working on, that might be a good direction to take.

In this section you have seen how ensemble methods can be used to solve binary classification problems. In most respects, using the application of ensemble methods to binary classification problems is the same as for regression problems.

You also understand that many of the differences between building ensemble models for classification and regression stem from differences in measuring errors and otherwise characterizing errors between the two classes of problems.

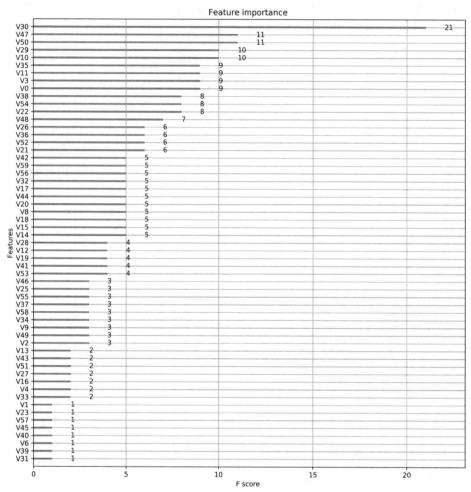

Figure 7-10: Gradient boosting estimates of variable importance in the rocks versus mines model

The next section shows how these methods can be used for multiclass problems.

Detecting Unexploded Mines with Python Random Forest

The lists that follow show the constructor and its arguments for RandomForestClassifier. Most of the arguments for the RandomForestClassifier are the same as for RandomForestRegressor. The arguments for RandomForestRegressor were outlined and discussed in the section on using

`RandomForestRegressor` for predicting wine quality. This section highlights only the elements of the `RandomForestClassifier` class that differ from their regression counterparts.

The first difference is the criterion used for judging the quality of splits. Recall from Chapter 6 that the process of training a tree involves trying all possible attributes and all possible split points for each attribute and then picking the attribute and split point that give the best split. For regression trees, the quality of the split was judged on the basis of sum squared error. Sum squared error does not work for classification problems. Something more like misclassification error is required.

Here is the class constructor for `sklearn.ensemble.RandomForestClassifier`:

```
sklearn.ensemble.RandomForestClassifier(n_estimators=10, criterion=
'gini', max_depth=None, min_samples_split=2, min_samples_leaf=1,
max_features='auto', max_leaf_nodes=None, bootstrap=True, oob_score=
False, n_jobs=1, random_state=None, verbose=0, min_density=None,
compute_importances=None)
```

The following describes the criterion parameter:

▪ **criterion**

  string, optional (default='gini')

  Possible values include the following:

  `gini`—Use gini impurity measure.

  `entropy`—Use entropy-based information gain.

For more information on these two measures of node impurity, see the Wikipedia page on binary decision trees at `http://en.wikipedia.org/wiki/Decision_tree_learning`. As a practical matter, the choice does not make a lot of difference for ensemble performance.

Classification trees naturally produce probabilities of class membership based on the percentages of different classes from the training data that wind up in each of the leaf nodes. Depending on the application you have, for the answers you might prefer to work directly with those probabilities, or you may want to have the value of the most numerous class returned as the prediction for those examples that wind up in the leaf node. If you're going to adjust thresholds used in conjunction with the prediction, you'll want to have the probabilities. For generating area under the curve (AUC), you'll get better fidelity on the receiver operating curve (ROC) with probabilities. If you want to calculate misclassification errors, you'll want the probabilities converted to a prediction of a specific class.

The following list describes the methods:

▪ **fit**(X, y, sample_weight=None)

  The description of the arguments for the classification version of random forest differs only in the nature of the labels y. For a classification problem, the labels are integers taking values from 0 to the number of different classes minus 1. For binary classification the labels are 0 or 1. For a multiclass problem with `nClass` different classes they are integers from 0 to `nClass - 1`.

▪ **predict**(X)

For an attribute matrix (two-dimensional numpy array) X, this function produces a specific class prediction. It yields a single column array with the same number of rows as X. Each entry is a predicted class, whether the problem is a binary classification problem or a multiclass problem.

▪ **predict_proba**(X)

This version of the prediction function produces a two-dimensional array. The number of rows matches the number of rows in X. The number of columns is equal to the number of classes being predicted (two columns for a binary classification problem, for example). The entry in each row is the probability of the associated class.

▪ **predict_log_proba**(X)

This version of the prediction function produces a two-dimensional array similar to the `predict_proba`. Instead of showing probabilities, this version shows log of probability.

Constructing a Random Forest Model to Detect Unexploded Mines

Listing 7-8 shows how to build a Random Forest Model for detecting unexploded mines using sonar. The overall structure of the data setup and training should be familiar from the other random forest examples earlier in this chapter and in Chapter 6. Differences stem from properties of classification problems. First, you'll notice that the labels are 0 and 1. That's an input requirement for `RandomForestClassifier`. The next differences show up after training when evaluating performance on the test set. For a binary classification problem, you have the choice of using area under the ROC curve (AUC) or misclassification error. I usually prefer AUC when it is available because it gives an overall measure of performance.

To calculate AUC, the `predict_proba` version of the `predict()` function is used. You cannot get a useful ROC curve with predictions that are already reduced to a specific class. (More correctly, the ROC curve you calculate only has three points on it: the two end points and one point in the middle.) The sklearn metric utilities make calculating the AUC simple, with just a couple lines of code. Those get accumulated into a list to plot AUC performance as a function of the number of trees in the ensemble. The code in Listing 7-6 then plots the AUC versus number of trees, the feature importance for the 30 most important features, and the ROC curve for the largest ensemble of the ones that are generated. The last section of the code picks three different threshold levels and prints out the confusion matrix for each of these threshold levels. The threshold levels are chosen at the three quartile boundaries, and the results show how false positives and false negatives change as the threshold moves to favor one versus the others.

Listing 7-6: Build a Random Forest Model to Distinguish Underwater Mines from Rocks—rocks_v_mines_rf.py

```
__author__ = 'mike_bowles'

from math import sqrt, fabs, exp
import matplotlib.pyplot as plt
from sklearn.model_selection import train_test_split
from sklearn.ensemble import RandomForestClassifier
from sklearn.metrics import roc_auc_score, roc_curve
import numpy as np

#read data from uci data repository
xList, labels = list_read_rvm()

#number of rows and columns in x matrix
nrows = len(xList)
ncols = len(xList[1])

#form x and y into numpy arrays and make up column names
X = np.array(xList)
y = np.array(labels)
rocksVMinesNames = np.array(['V' + str(i) for i in range(ncols)])

#number of rows and columns in x matrix
nrows = len(X)
ncols = len(X[1])

#break into training and test sets.
xTrain, xTest, yTrain, yTest = train_test_split(X, y, test_size=0.30,
random_state=531)

#define classifier
depth = None
maxFeat  = 8 #try tweaking

num_iterations = 50  #train 10 additional trees 50 times
trees_per_iteration
rocksVMinesRFModel = RandomForestClassifier(n_estimators=
trees_per_iteration,
```

```
                            max_depth=depth,
                            max_features=maxFeat,
                            oob_score=False,
                            random_state=531,
                            warm_start=True)

auc = []   #accumulate auc scores

for iters in range(num_iterations):

    rocksVMinesRFModel.fit(xTrain,yTrain)
    rocksVMinesRFModel.n_estimators += trees_per_iteration

    #Accumulate auc on test set
    prediction = rocksVMinesRFModel.predict_proba(xTest)
    aucCalc = roc_auc_score(yTest, prediction[:,1:2])
    auc.append(aucCalc)

print("AUC" )
print(auc[-1])


#plot training and test errors vs number of trees in ensemble
num_trees = [i * trees_per_iteration for i in range(num_iterations)]
plt.plot(num_trees, auc)
plt.xlabel('Number of Trees in Ensemble')
plt.ylabel('Area Under ROC Curve - AUC')
plt.title('AUC performance for Random Forest')
#plt.ylim([0.0, 1.1*max(mseOob)])
plt.savefig('rvm_rf_auc_performance_v_num_trees.png', dpi=500)
plt.show()

# Plot feature importance
featureImportance = rocksVMinesRFModel.feature_importances_

# normalize by max importance
featureImportance = featureImportance / featureImportance.max()

#plot importance of top 30
idxSorted = np.argsort(featureImportance)[30:60]
idxTemp = np.argsort(featureImportance)[::-1]
print(idxTemp)
barPos = np.arange(idxSorted.shape[0]) + .5
plt.barh(barPos, featureImportance[idxSorted], align='center')
plt.yticks(barPos, rocksVMinesNames[idxSorted])
plt.xlabel('Variable Importance')
plt.title('Variable importance for Random Forest')
plt.savefig('RVM_variable_importance_rf.png', dpi=500)
plt.show()
```

```
#plot best version of ROC curve
fpr, tpr, thresh = roc_curve(yTest, list(prediction[:,1:2]))
ctClass = [i*0.01 for i in range(101)]

plt.plot(fpr, tpr, linewidth=2)
plt.plot(ctClass, ctClass, linestyle=':')
plt.xlabel('False Positive Rate')
plt.ylabel('True Positive Rate')
plt.title('Rocks v Mines ROC curve with Random Forest')
plt.savefig('rocksVMines_roc_rf.png', dpi=500)
plt.show()

#pick some threshold values and calc confusion matrix for best
predictions
#notice that GBM predictions don't fall in range of (0, 1)
#pick threshold values at 25th, 50th and 75th percentiles
idx25 = int(len(thresh) * 0.25)
idx50 = int(len(thresh) * 0.50)
idx75 = int(len(thresh) * 0.75)

#calculate total points, total positives and total negatives
totalPts = len(yTest)
P = sum(yTest)
N = totalPts - P

print('')
print('Confusion Matrices for Different Threshold Values')

Printed Output:
AUC
0.9452332657200812


Confusion Matrices for Different Threshold Values

Threshold Value =    0.724
TP =   0.3492063492063492 FP =   0.015873015873015872
FN =   0.19047619047619047 TN =   0.4444444444444444

Threshold Value =    0.63
TP =   0.4603174603174603 FP =   0.031746031746031744
FN =   0.07936507936507936 TN =   0.42857142857142855

Threshold Value =    0.516
TP =   0.5079365079365079 FP =   0.15873015873015872
FN =   0.031746031746031744 TN =   0.30158730158730157
```

Determining the Performance of a Random Forest Classifier

Figure 7.11 shows a plot of AUC versus number of trees. The plot appears upside down from the plots you've seen involving mean squared error or misclassification error. For mean squared error and misclassification error, smaller is better. For AUC, 1.0 is perfect, and 0.5 is perfectly bad. So, with AUC, larger is better, and instead of looking for a valley in the plot, you're looking for a peak. Figure 7.11 shows a peak toward the left side of the plot. However, because random forest only reduces variance and does not overfit, the peak can be attributed to random fluctuation. As was the case with some of the regression problems earlier in the chapter, the best choice of model is the one including all the trees whose performance is the rightmost point on the curve.

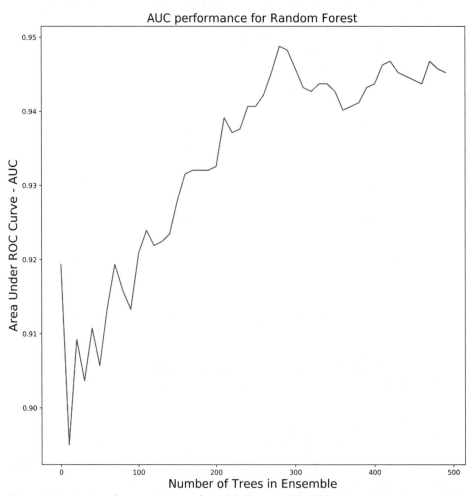

Figure 7.11: Random forest estimates of variable importance in the rocks versus mines model

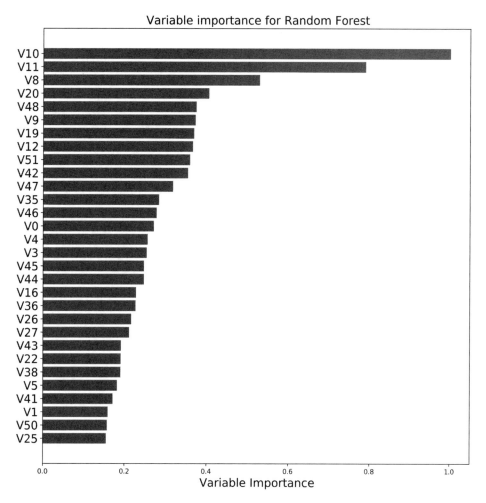

Figure 7.12: Random forest estimates of variable importance in the rocks versus mines model

Figure 7.12 plots the variable importance for the most important 30 variables in the random forest mine detector. The different attributes in the mine detection problem correspond to different frequencies of sonar signal and therefore different wavelengths. If you were given the problem of designing the machine learning for this problem, your next step might be to determine the wavelengths corresponding to these variables and compare those wavelengths to the characteristic dimensions of the rocks and mines in the test and training set. That could help you get some faith and understanding of the model.

Figure 7.13 shows the ROC curve that random forest achieves. The model is getting remarkably high AUC, and the ROC curve is correspondingly good. It doesn't quite square the corner in the upper left, but it comes pretty close.

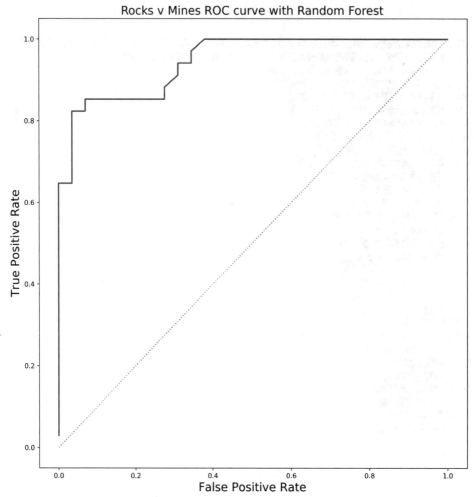

Figure 7.13: Receiver operating curve (ROC) for random forest rocks versus mines model

Solving Multiclass Classification Problems with Python Ensemble Methods

The gradient boosting and random forest packages in XGBoost and the Python sklearn library will build both binary and multiclass classification models. The two types of models have a few natural differences between them. One is that the labels (y) take more values. The discussion of the gradient boosting and random forest packages described the manner in which the labels are specified. For a classification problem having nClass different classes, the labels take integer values from 0 to nClass - 1. Another manifestation of the number of classes is the output of the various predict methods.

The predict methods that are predicting classes generate the same integer values that the labels take. The methods predicting probabilities yield probabilities for nClass possible classes.

The other area where there is a noticeable difference is in specifying performance. Misclassification error still makes sense, and you'll see that the example code uses that to measure oos performance. AUC is more complicated to use when you have more than two classes, and trading off different error types becomes more challenging.

Dealing with Class Imbalances

The code in this section will use the classifiers applied in the sections "Detecting Unexploded Mines with Python Gradient Boosting" and "Constructing a Random Forest Model to Detect Unexploded Mines," but accommodation will need to be made for the glass data. One important difference is that the glass data are unbalanced. "Unbalanced" means that some of the classes have significantly more examples than others. You'll see in the code listings how many examples there are of each type of glass. Some of the types have relatively many examples (in the 70s). Some types of glass are not as well represented. One in particular only has nine examples.

Imbalanced classes can sometimes cause problems because random sampling of the underrepresented classes may result in wildly different proportions in the sample than in the original data. For example, the glass data has only nine examples of one class. If you wanted to do 10-fold cross-validation, one of the test folds would have no examples from that class. To avoid these problems, the code goes through a process called *stratified sampling*. What that means in this case is that the data are segregated according to labels (stratified), and then each of those groups is sampled to obtain training and test sets within each class. Then the class-specific training sets are combined into a training set that has proportions of different classes that exactly match the original data. The gradient boosting code in the following section accomplishes this by using the sklearn StratifiedKFold package. The random forest code shows how to build the stratification yourself.

Classifying Glass Using Gradient Boosting

Listing 7-7 uses XGBoost to build models for classifying glass. This is a multiclass classification problem. The code in Listing 7-7 also shows how to build a grid search for the best parameter values from a number of different parameter combinations. The basic idea for a grid search is to choose some values for several of the parameters and then to run through all the possible combinations to find the best one. The code uses a dictionary called grid_dict to contain the parameters being tweaked. Each of the parameter names is used as a key and the dictionary holds a list of values for each key. Then a `for` loop runs through a list of all possible combinations of values. The code shows how you can use the Python itertools package to form the list of combinations from the dictionary of lists.

As the grid search iteration proceeds, the parameter values corresponding to best performance are updated as better performing parameter combinations are found. Then the best parameter set is used to retrain the model, and the train performance and test performance are printed. The process illustrated in Listing 7-7 will help you to automate the process of arriving at a best model for your problem.

Listing 7-7: Build a Gradient Boosting Model to Distinguish Different Types of Glass—glass_gbm.py

```python
__author__ = 'mike_bowles'

from math import sqrt, fabs, exp
import matplotlib.pyplot as plt
from sklearn.metrics import roc_auc_score, roc_curve, confusion_matrix
from sklearn.model_selection import StratifiedKFold
import numpy as np
from Read_Fcns import list_read_glass
import xgboost as xgb
from itertools import product

#read in glass data
names, xNum, labels, yOneVAll = list_read_glass()

glassNames = np.array(['RI', 'Na', 'Mg', 'Al', 'Si', 'K', 'Ca', 'Ba',
'Fe',
                      'Type'])

#number of rows and columns in x matrix
nrows = len(xNum)
ncols = len(xNum[1])

#Labels are integers from 1 to 7 with no examples of 4.
#gb requires consecutive integers starting at 0
newLabels = []
labelSet = set(labels)
labelList = list(labelSet)
labelList.sort()
nlabels = len(labelList)
for l in labels:
    index = labelList.index(l)
    newLabels.append(index)

X = np.array(xNum)
y = np.array(newLabels)
```

```
#Class populations:
#old label      new label      num of examples
#1               0                70
#2               1                76
#3               2                17
#5               3                13
#6               4                9
#7               5                29
#

n_fold = 5

#Since some of the classes are bit thin, use stratified sampling
#Stratified sampling yields test sets whose class probs match full data
skf = StratifiedKFold(n_splits=n_fold)
skf.get_n_splits(xNum, newLabels)


#set up params to search - two examples
grid_dict = {'colsammple_bytree': [0.5, 0.7, 1.0],
             'learning_rate':[0.1, 0.5, 1.0],
             'max_depth':[3,4],
             'alpha':[0]}
grid_dict = {'colsammple_bytree': [0.7],
             'learning_rate':[0.001],
             'max_depth':[3,4,5,6],
             'alpha':[0]}
#set to keep track of best values
best_test_err = 1.0

#use itertools product function to do simple grid search
for colsample_bytree, learning_rate, max_depth, alpha \
            in list(product(*grid_dict.values())):

    params = {'objective':'multi:softmax',
              'num_class': 6,
              'colsample_bytree': colsample_bytree,
              'subsample': 0.5,
              'learning_rate': learning_rate,
              'n_estimators': 300,
              'max_depth': max_depth,
              'alpha': alpha,
              'verbosity':1}

    clf_model = xgb.XGBClassifier(**params)
    results_list = []
    for idx_train, idx_test in skf.split(X, y):

        x_test = X[idx_test]
        y_test= y[idx_test]
```

```
        x_train = X[idx_train]
        y_train = y[idx_train]

        clf_model.fit(x_train, y_train,
                eval_set=[(x_train, y_train), (x_test, y_test)],
                eval_metric='merror',
                verbose=False)
        results_list.append(clf_model.evals_result())

    train_err = [eval['validation_0']['merror'] for \
                        eval in results_list]
    test_err = [eval['validation_1']['merror'] for \
                        eval in results_list]

    train_err_array = np.array(train_err)
    test_err_array = np.array(test_err)

    train_avg = np.mean(train_err_array, axis = 0)
    test_avg = np.mean(test_err_array, axis = 0)

    print('colsample_bytree=', colsample_bytree, 'learning_rate=',
            learning_rate, 'max_depth=',max_depth,
            'alpha=', alpha, 'avg error=', np.amin(test_avg))

    if np.amin(test_avg) < best_test_err:
        best_params = [colsample_bytree, learning_rate, max_depth,
alpha]

#retrain with best values
[colsample_bytree, learning_rate, max_depth, alpha] = best_params

params = {'objective':'multi:softmax',
        'num_class': 6,
        'subsample': 0.5,
        'colsample_bytree': colsample_bytree,
        'learning_rate': learning_rate,
        'n_estimators': 300,
        'max_depth': max_depth,
        'alpha': alpha,
        'verbosity':1}

clf_model = xgb.XGBClassifier(**params)
results_list = []
for idx_train, idx_test in skf.split(X, y):

    x_test = X[idx_test]
    y_test= y[idx_test]
    x_train = X[idx_train]
    y_train = y[idx_train]
```

```
        clf_model.fit(x_train, y_train,
                    eval_set=[(x_train, y_train), (x_test, y_test)],
                    eval_metric='merror', verbose=False)
        results_list.append(clf_model.evals_result())

    train_err = [eval['validation_0']['merror'] for eval in results_list]
    test_err = [eval['validation_1']['merror'] for eval in results_list]

    train_err_array = np.array(train_err)
    test_err_array = np.array(test_err)

    train_avg = np.mean(train_err_array, axis = 0)
    test_avg = np.mean(test_err_array, axis = 0)

    print('\nFinal training error', train_avg[-5:])
    print('Final test error', test_avg[-5:])

    plt.plot(train_avg)
    plt.plot(test_avg)
    plt.xlabel('Number of Trees in Ensemble')
    plt.ylabel('Multiclass Error')
    plt.title('Train and Test Errors')
    plt.savefig('glassXGB_train_test_merror.png', dpi=500)
    plt.show()

    Printed Output:
    colsample_bytree= 0.7 learning_rate= 0.001 max_depth= 3 alpha= 0 avg
        error= 0.3361334
    colsample_bytree= 0.7 learning_rate= 0.001 max_depth= 4 alpha= 0 avg
        error= 0.3211646
    colsample_bytree= 0.7 learning_rate= 0.001 max_depth= 5 alpha= 0 avg
        error= 0.3115134
    colsample_bytree= 0.7 learning_rate= 0.001 max_depth= 6 alpha= 0 avg
        error= 0.3115134

    Performance with best params:
    Final train error [0.1086792 0.1086792 0.1074956 0.1074956 0.1086652]
    Final test error [0.3115134 0.3115134 0.3115134 0.3115134 0.3115134]
```

It is worth noting that the best choice of parameters in the search process in Listing 7-7 included a search on the parameter `colsample_bytree`. This parameter was fixed at 0.7 in the optimization that's printed in the code listing, but you'll see that `grid_dict` has two different definitions in the listing. Only the second one counts for the execution of the program, but the first version was run as a prelude. That version of `grid_dict` included a range of possibilities for `colsample_bytree`. The parameter `colsample_bytree` controls random sampling of features to be used in growing each tree. If the parameter is set to 1.0, then all the features are used. If it's set to 0.7, then 70% of the parameters are chosen at random each time a new tree is built. This is edging toward the random forest base learners, where at each split point a random selection of features is chosen. It's usually worth doing some experimentation with these parameters at some point in the process of reaching the best-performing model.

Determining the Performance of the Gradient Boosting Model on Glass Classification

Figure 7.14 shows how the performance of the gradient boosting classifier improves as trees are added to the ensemble. The best performance comes at the far-right end of the graph. That suggests that more trees might be added or perhaps the learning rate increased a bit to improve performance.

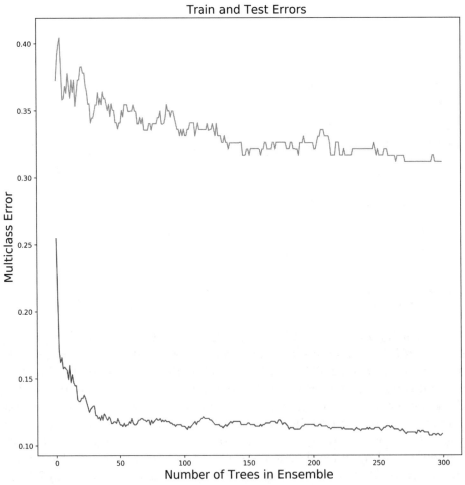

Figure 7.14: Train and test performance for gradient boosting glass classification model

Classifying Glass with Random Forests

Listing 7-8 follows a similar outline to the code used for detecting mines. In this example, a more manual method is used to deal with class imbalance so you can visualize how this might work. The input data are separated by class and then each class is separately split into 70:30 train test sets. Then class-by-class train sets are aggregated into an overall train set and similar for the test sets.

Listing 7-8: Build a Random Forest Model to Distinguish Different Glass Types—glass_rf.py

```python
__author__ = 'mike_bowles'

from math import sqrt, fabs, exp
import matplotlib.pyplot as plt
from sklearn.metrics import accuracy_score, confusion_matrix, roc_curve
from sklearn.model_selection import train_test_split
from sklearn import ensemble
import numpy as np
from Read_Fcns import list_read_glass

#read in glass data
names, xNum, labels, yOneVAll = list_read_glass()

glassNames = np.array(['RI', 'Na', 'Mg', 'Al', 'Si', 'K', 'Ca', 'Ba', 'Fe',
                        'Type'])

#number of rows and columns in x matrix
nrows = len(xNum)
ncols = len(xNum[1])

#Labels are integers from 1 to 7 with no examples of 4.
#gb requires consecutive integers starting at 0
newLabels = []
labelSet = set(labels)
labelList = list(labelSet)
labelList.sort()
nlabels = len(labelList)
for l in labels:
    index = labelList.index(l)
    newLabels.append(index)

#Class populations:
#old label      new label      num of examples
#1              0              70
#2              1              76
#3              2              17
#5              3              13
#6              4              9
#7              5              29
#
```

```
#Drawing 30% test sample may not preserve population proportions

#stratified sampling by labels.
xTemp = [xNum[i] for i in range(nrows) if newLabels[i] == 0]
yTemp = [newLabels[i] for i in range(nrows) if newLabels[i] == 0]
xTrain, xTest, yTrain, yTest = train_test_split(xTemp, yTemp,
test_size=0.30,
                                                 random_state=531)
for iLabel in range(1, len(labelList)):
    #segregate x and y according to labels
    xTemp = [xNum[i] for i in range(nrows) if newLabels[i] == iLabel]
    yTemp = [newLabels[i] for i in range(nrows) if newLabels[i] ==
                iLabel]

    #form train and test sets on segregated subset of examples
    xTrainTemp, xTestTemp, yTrainTemp, yTestTemp = train_test_
split(xTemp,
                             yTemp, test_size=0.30, random_state=531)

    #accumulate
    xTrain = np.append(xTrain, xTrainTemp, axis=0)
    xTest = np.append(xTest, xTestTemp, axis=0)
    yTrain = np.append(yTrain, yTrainTemp, axis=0)
    yTest = np.append(yTest, yTestTemp, axis=0)

num_iterations = 50
trees_per_iteration = 10
depth = None
maxFeat  = 4 #try tweaking

glassRFModel = ensemble.RandomForestClassifier(
                    n_estimators=trees_per_iteration,
                    max_depth=depth,
                    max_features=maxFeat,
                    oob_score=False,
                    random_state=531,
                    warm_start=True)

missCLassError = []

for iteration in range(num_iterations):

    glassRFModel.fit(xTrain,yTrain)
    glassRFModel.n_estimators += trees_per_iteration

    #Accumulate auc on test set
    prediction = glassRFModel.predict(xTest)
    correct = accuracy_score(yTest, prediction)
```

```
        missCLassError.append(1.0 - correct)

print("Misclassification Error" )
print(missCLassError[-1])

#generate confusion matrix
pList = prediction.tolist()
confusionMat = confusion_matrix(yTest, pList)
print('')
print("Confusion Matrix")
print(confusionMat)

#plot training and test errors vs number of trees in ensemble
num_trees = [i * trees_per_iteration for i in range(num_iterations)]
plt.plot(num_trees, missCLassError)
plt.xlabel('Number of Trees in Ensemble')
plt.ylabel('Misclassification Error Rate')
plt.title('Random Forest Classifier Perf on Glass Data')
plt.savefig('rf_glass_perf.png', dpi=500)
#plt.ylim([0.0, 1.1*max(mseOob)])
plt.show()

# Plot feature importance
featureImportance = glassRFModel.feature_importances_

# normalize by max importance
featureImportance = featureImportance / featureImportance.max()

#plot variable importance
idxSorted = np.argsort(featureImportance)
barPos = np.arange(idxSorted.shape[0]) + .5
plt.barh(barPos, featureImportance[idxSorted], align='center')
plt.title('RF Variable Importance on Glass Data')
plt.yticks(barPos, glassNames[idxSorted])
plt.xlabel('Relative Variable Importance')
plt.savefig('rf_glass_var_importance.png', dpi=500)
plt.show()


Printed Output:
Misclassification Error
0.2272727272727273

Confusion Matrix
[[17  2  1  0  0  1]
 [ 2 18  1  2  0  0]
 [ 2  0  4  0  0  0]
 [ 0  1  0  3  0  0]
 [ 0  1  0  0  2  0]
 [ 0  2  0  0  0  7]]
```

The code generates random forest models and plots the training progress and the variable importance. It also prints out a confusion matrix which shows how the prediction model treats each class in the data population. It show how many from each class the predictor maps to the correct class and how many it maps to the wrong classes. If the classifier is perfect, there should be no off-diagonal entries in the matrix.

Determining the Performance of the Random Forest Model on Glass Classification

Figure 7.15 shows how the performance of random forest improves as more trees are included in the ensemble. The curve generally drops as more trees are added. The rate of improvement decreases as more trees are added. It has slowed considerably at the point where the graph stops.

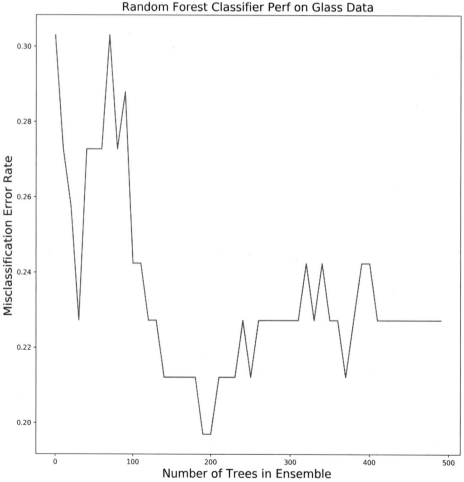

Figure 7.15: The overall performance of random forests

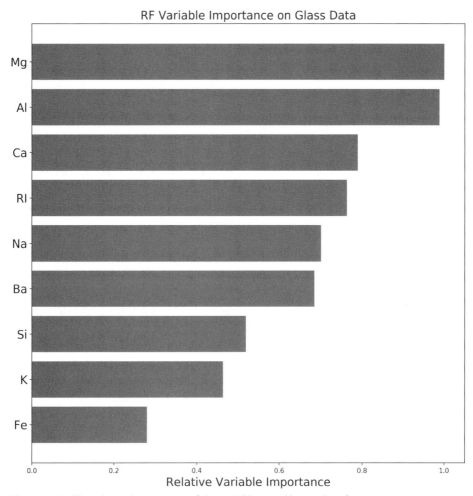

Figure 7.16: The relative importance of the variables used by random forest

Figure 7.16 is a bar chart showing the relative importance of the variables used by random forests. The chart shows that a number of the variables are roughly equal in performance. This is unusual behavior. In many cases the variable importance drops off quickly after the first few variables. This problem contains several equally important variables.

Solving Regression Problems with PySpark Ensemble Packages

This section will run through the examples you've seen throughout the book and demonstrate how to use ensemble methods available in PySpark to build a model for each example. This section combines what you learned about in

Chapter 5 and what you've just seen about using ensemble methods to build models. Using ensemble methods in PySpark involves the exact same data preparation steps that you saw in Chapter 5, and uses the same gradient boosting and random forest algorithms that you've learned so far in this chapter. The PySpark gradient boosting and random forest algorithms have the same parameters to twiddle as what you've seen earlier. Once the data is prepped as it was in Chapter 5, it's just a matter of learning some slight differences in notation and variable names.

Data preparation in PySpark only depends on the data set. The PySpark regression packages take the same input whether you choose to use penalized linear regression or gradient boosting. The next section, "Predicting Wine Taste with PySpark Ensemble Methods," will demonstrate that only a few lines of code need be changed to switch from using gradient boosting to using random forest. Subsequent sections covering the remaining problems (abalone, rocks versus mines, and glass classification) will include the data prep for the gradient boosting example and in a separate code listing the code for random forest.

You've seen from the PySpark examples covered in Chapter 5 that data preparation in PySpark is more complicated than with numpy or pandas in Python. The ensemble algorithms, on the other hand, are simpler from the user's standpoint. They don't have as many options as what you've seen in XGBoost or sklearn random forest. The user interface is simpler with PySpark because programming the algorithms is much harder in a distributed environment and it is therefore more difficult to offer as many features to tweak as with the packages you learned earlier in this chapter.

The features for gradient boosting and random forest are similar enough that they can be covered in a single description, with some notes in the few instances where differences exist.

First, the functions available for training and making predictions with your model once you've got it instantiated are `fit()` and `transform()`. The only argument to the `fit` function is the data frame that you use for training. As you saw in Chapter 5, the input PySpark data frame carries the feature set and the labels. The `transform` function also takes a single argument, usually the test version of the data frame that was used for training.

Predicting Wine Taste with PySpark Ensemble Methods

Listing 7-9 steps through the process of building the data frame that will be used for training and testing a PySpark gradient boosting model. You'll be familiar with the vector assembler that you saw in Chapter 5. What you see here is exactly the same code up to the point where the GBTRegressor model is instantiated. The instantiation identifies which columns from the data frame will be features and labels, and it defines the training parameters required for any gradient boosting model—number of trees in the ensemble, the depths of those trees, the size of the random subsample to be drawn from the training set for training each tree, and the learning rate. In the PySpark gradient boosting model, the number of trees is called `maxIter`, the depth of the trees is called `maxDepth`, the subsample size is called `subsamplingRation`, and the learning rate is called `stepSize`. The function of those is the same as their function in the XGBoost models you saw earlier in this chapter. Generating predictions takes just two steps. First, the `transform` function uses the trained model to transform the test data frame to predictions. The next step instantiates a `RegressionEvaluator`, which defines the prediction and truth columns from the transform output and selects a regression metric. You'll see two different evaluators—one to generate root mean squared error and another to generate explained variance (r squared). The performance shown here is 0.739. You know from previous studies that this can be improved. Try adjusting the parameters to get a better result.

Listing 7-9: Using PySpark GBM to Predict Wine Quality—wine_taste_pred_spark_gbm.py

```python
__author__ = 'mike_bowles'

#Import sparksession
from pyspark.sql import SparkSession
from pyspark.ml.feature import VectorAssembler
from pyspark.ml.regression import GBTRegressor
from pyspark.ml.evaluation import RegressionEvaluator
import matplotlib.pyplot as plt

spark = SparkSession.builder.appName("regress_wine_data").getOrCreate()

#read in abalone data as pandas data frame and create Spark data frame.
import pandas as pd
from pandas import DataFrame
from Read_Fcns import pd_read_wine

wine_df = pd_read_wine()

#Create spark dataframe for wine data
wine_sp_df = spark.createDataFrame(wine_df)
print('Column Names', wine_sp_df.columns, '\n\n')

vectorAssembler = VectorAssembler(inputCols = ['fixed acidity', \
    'volatile acidity', 'citric acid', 'residual sugar', 'chlorides', \
    'free sulfur dioxide', 'total sulfur dioxide', 'density', 'pH', \
                    'sulphates', 'alcohol'], outputCol = 'features')
v_wine_df = vectorAssembler.transform(wine_sp_df)
vwine_df = v_wine_df.select(['features', 'quality'])


splits = vwine_df.randomSplit([0.66, 0.34])
x_train_sp = splits[0]
x_test_sp = splits[1]
```

```
gbt = GBTRegressor(featuresCol = 'features',
                   labelCol = 'quality',
                   maxIter=100,
                   maxDepth=5,
                   subsamplingRate=0.5,
                   stepSize=0.1)

gbt_model = gbt.fit(x_train_sp)
gbt_predictions = gbt_model.transform(x_test_sp)
gbt_predictions.select('prediction', 'quality').show(5)



gbt_evaluator1 = RegressionEvaluator(
        labelCol="quality",
        predictionCol="prediction",
        metricName="rmse")
rmse = gbt_evaluator1.evaluate(gbt_predictions)
gbt_evaluator2 = RegressionEvaluator(
        labelCol="quality",
        predictionCol="prediction",
        metricName="r2")
r2 = gbt_evaluator2.evaluate(gbt_predictions)

print("Root Mean Squared Error (RMSE) on test data = %g" % rmse)
print('R-squared on test data =', r2)

Printed Output:
Column Names ['fixed acidity', 'volatile acidity', 'citric acid',
              'residual sugar', 'chlorides', 'free sulfur dioxide',
              'total sulfur dioxide', 'density', 'pH', 'sulphates',
              'alcohol', 'quality']



+-----------------+-------+
|       prediction|quality|
+-----------------+-------+
|5.888749136462941|      4|
|6.160043612129055|      6|
|4.770216506879649|      5|
|5.238104393216513|      5|
|3.957840392301747|      4|
+-----------------+-------+
only showing top 5 rows

Root Mean Squared Error (RMSE) on test data = 0.739396
R-squared on test data = 0.18213112569257273
```

Listing 7-10 shows how to use PySpark random forest to build a model for predicting wine taste. The data preparation is identical to that in Listing 7-9 using GBM. Random Forest is run with default parameters—namely `numTrees=20` and `maxDepth=5`. Try changing these to see what effect they have on performance and run time. The performance is evaluated using the same approach as gradient boosting in Listing 7-9. Random forest's ease of tuning (virtually none required) makes it an easy first choice. Gradient boosting gives better performance (sometimes), but takes more work and compute time.

Listing 7-10: Using PySpark RF to Predict Wine Quality—wine_taste_prediction_spark_rf.py

```
__author__ = 'mike_bowles'

#Import sparksession
from pyspark.sql import SparkSession
from pyspark.ml.feature import VectorAssembler
from pyspark.ml.regression import RandomForestRegressor
from pyspark.ml.evaluation import RegressionEvaluator
import matplotlib.pyplot as plt


spark = SparkSession.builder.appName("regress_wine_data").getOrCreate()


#read in abalone data as pandas data frame and create Spark data frame.
import pandas as pd
from pandas import DataFrame
from Read_Fcns import pd_read_wine


wine_df = pd_read_wine()


#Create spark dataframe for wine data
wine_sp_df = spark.createDataFrame(wine_df)
print('Column Names', wine_sp_df.columns, '\n\n')


vectorAssembler = VectorAssembler(inputCols = ['fixed acidity', \
    'volatile acidity', 'citric acid', 'residual sugar', 'chlorides', \
    'free sulfur dioxide', 'total sulfur dioxide', 'density', 'pH', \
                    'sulphates', 'alcohol'], outputCol = 'features')
v_wine_df = vectorAssembler.transform(wine_sp_df)
vwine_df = v_wine_df.select(['features', 'quality'])


splits = vwine_df.randomSplit([0.66, 0.34])
x_train_sp = splits[0]
x_test_sp = splits[1]
```

```
rf = RandomForestRegressor(featuresCol = 'features', labelCol =
'quality')
rfModel = rf.fit(x_train_sp)
rf_predictions = rfModel.transform(x_test_sp)

#use evaluator to assess performance
rf_predictions.select('prediction').show(10)
rf_evaluator1 = RegressionEvaluator(
                labelCol="quality",
                predictionCol="prediction",
                metricName="rmse")
rmse = rf_evaluator1.evaluate(rf_predictions)
rf_evaluator2 = RegressionEvaluator(
                labelCol="quality",
                predictionCol="prediction",
                metricName="r2")
r2 = rf_evaluator2.evaluate(rf_predictions)
print("Root Mean Squared Error (RMSE) on test data = %g" % rmse)
print('R-squared on test data =', r2)

Printed Output:
Column Names ['fixed acidity', 'volatile acidity', 'citric acid',
'residual sugar', 'chlorides', 'free sulfur dioxide', 'total sulfur
dioxide', 'density', 'pH', 'sulphates', 'alcohol', 'quality']


+------------------+
|        prediction|
+------------------+
|   5.69127321080815|
|  4.674311642629709|
|    7.0567290737358|
|5.4275048042025125|
|  5.745206950323335|
|  5.298549695208836|
|  5.892330445514402|
|   5.36424137629707|
|  5.246211813151428|
|5.4748655383336695|
+------------------+
only showing top 10 rows

Root Mean Squared Error (RMSE) on test data = 0.62608
R-squared on test data = 0.3916738063214933
```

This section has demonstrated data preparation and model building for predicting wine taste—a regression problem with real-number inputs and outputs. You've seen that the two models share exactly the same data preparation. Subsequent sections will omit the second repetition of the data preparation. If you're running these examples in a Jupyter Notebook, you can paste the gradient boosting code (Listing 7-11 into a cell, execute it, and then paste the random forest listing into a subsequent cell and execute it.

Predicting Abalone Age with PySpark Ensemble Methods

This section employs the same GBTRegressor and RandomForestRegressor that you saw in the last section. The main difference is in the data preparation. The sex attribute is a three-valued categorical variable and needs to be one-hot encoded for use in these packages. Listing 7-11 walks through that process and then instantiates a GBTRegressor model. The results are printed at the end of the code. The printed output shows the schema before and after the vector assembler output is incorporated. Notice in particular that the feature vector shows up as an added column in the second schema.

Listing 7-11: Using PySpark Gradient Boosting to Predict Abalone Age—abalone_gbm_spark.py

```python
__author__ = 'mike_bowles'

#Import sparksession
from pyspark.sql import SparkSession
from pyspark.ml.feature import VectorAssembler
from pyspark.ml.evaluation import RegressionEvaluator
from pyspark.ml.regression import GBTRegressor
import matplotlib.pyplot as plt
from pyspark.ml.feature import StandardScaler

spark = SparkSession.builder.appName("abalone_regression").getOrCreate()

#read in abalone data as pandas data frame and create Spark data frame.
import pandas as pd
from pandas import DataFrame
from Read_Fcns import pd_read_abalone

abalone_df = pd_read_abalone()

#Create spark dataframe for abalone data
abalone_sp_df = spark.createDataFrame(abalone_df)
print('Column Names', abalone_df.columns, '\n\n')

cols = abalone_sp_df.columns
abalone_sp_df.printSchema()
```

```
numeric_cols = ['Length', 'Diameter', 'Height', 'Whole weight',
                'Shucked weight', 'Viscera weight', 'Shell weight']

from pyspark.ml.feature import OneHotEncoderEstimator, StringIndexer,
                                        VectorAssembler
from pyspark.ml import Pipeline

stages = []
stringIndexer = StringIndexer(inputCol = "Sex", outputCol = "SexIndex")
encoder = OneHotEncoderEstimator(inputCols=[
                        stringIndexer.getOutputCol()],
                        outputCols=["SexClassVec"])
stages +=[stringIndexer, encoder]

assembler_inputs = ["SexClassVec"] + numeric_cols

assembler = VectorAssembler(
            inputCols=assembler_inputs,
            outputCol="features")
stages += [assembler]

pipeline = Pipeline(stages = stages)
pipelineModel = pipeline.fit(abalone_sp_df)
df = pipelineModel.transform(abalone_sp_df)
selectedCols = ['features'] + cols
df = df.select(selectedCols)
df.printSchema()

pd.DataFrame(df.take(4), columns=df.columns).transpose()

train, test = df.randomSplit([0.7, 0.3], seed = 2018)
print("Training Dataset Count: ", train.count())
print("Test Dataset Count: ", test.count())

gbt = GBTRegressor(featuresCol = 'features',
                labelCol = 'Rings',
                maxIter=100)
gbt_model = gbt.fit(train)
gbt_predictions = gbt_model.transform(test)
gbt_predictions.select('prediction', 'Rings').show(5)


Column Names Index(['Sex', 'Length', 'Diameter', 'Height', 'Whole
weight',
                'Shucked weight', 'Viscera weight', 'Shell weight',
                'Rings'], dtype='object')


root
 |-- Sex: string (nullable = true)
 |-- Length: double (nullable = true)
```

```
 |-- Diameter: double (nullable = true)
 |-- Height: double (nullable = true)
 |-- Whole weight: double (nullable = true)
 |-- Shucked weight: double (nullable = true)
 |-- Viscera weight: double (nullable = true)
 |-- Shell weight: double (nullable = true)
 |-- Rings: long (nullable = true)


root
 |-- features: vector (nullable = true)
 |-- Sex: string (nullable = true)
 |-- Length: double (nullable = true)
 |-- Diameter: double (nullable = true)
 |-- Height: double (nullable = true)
 |-- Whole weight: double (nullable = true)
 |-- Shucked weight: double (nullable = true)
 |-- Viscera weight: double (nullable = true)
 |-- Shell weight: double (nullable = true)
 |-- Rings: long (nullable = true)


Training Dataset Count:  2924
Test Dataset Count:  1253
+-----------------+-----+
|       prediction|Rings|
+-----------------+-----+
| 8.509670984422382|    6|
| 8.706689087368456|    5|
| 8.845143090365704|   12|
|10.344913796129237|    9|
| 9.292785676640456|    9|
+-----------------+-----+
only showing top 5 rows


gbt_predictions = gbt_model.transform(test)
gbt_predictions.select('prediction', 'Rings').show(5)
gbt_evaluator1 = RegressionEvaluator(
                labelCol="Rings",
                predictionCol="prediction",
                metricName="rmse")
rmse = gbt_evaluator1.evaluate(gbt_predictions)
gbt_evaluator2 = RegressionEvaluator(
                labelCol="Rings",
                predictionCol="prediction",
                metricName="r2")
r2 = gbt_evaluator2.evaluate(gbt_predictions)


print("Root Mean Squared Error (RMSE) on test data = %g" % rmse)
print('R-squared on test data =', r2)
```

```
+------------------+-----+
|        prediction|Rings|
+------------------+-----+
| 8.509670984422382|    6|
| 8.706689087368456|    5|
| 8.845143090365704|   12|
|10.344913796129237|    9|
| 9.292785676640456|    9|
+------------------+-----+
only showing top 5 rows


Root Mean Squared Error (RMSE) on test data = 2.43757
R-squared on test data = 0.4803196949324039
```

Listing 7-12 shows the code you'll need to add to build a random forest model in addition to the gradient boosting model in Listing 7-11. The modeling process and performance evaluation for the random forest model is the same.

Listing 7-12: Using PySpark Random Forest to Predict Abalone Age—abalone_rf_spark.py

```python
__author__ = 'mike_bowles'
#Use the same data pipeline as for gbt.

from pyspark.ml.regression import GBTRegressor
rf_abalone = RandomForestRegressor(featuresCol = 'features',
                                   labelCol = 'Rings')
rf_model = rf_abalone.fit(train)
rf_predictions = rf_model.transform(test)
rf_predictions.select('prediction', 'Rings').show(5)

#use evaluator to assess performance
rf_evaluator1 = RegressionEvaluator(
        labelCol="Rings",
        predictionCol="prediction",
        metricName="rmse")
rmse = rf_evaluator1.evaluate(rf_predictions)
rf_evaluator2 = RegressionEvaluator(
        labelCol="Rings",
        predictionCol="prediction",
        metricName="r2")
r2 = rf_evaluator2.evaluate(rf_predictions)

print("Root Mean Squared Error (RMSE) on test data = %g" % rmse)
print('R-squared on test data =', r2)


+------------------+-----+
|        prediction|Rings|
+------------------+-----+
|7.948640573830748|     6|
```

```
|7.992553171937639|     5|
| 9.17707071700458|    12|
|9.766365653629238|     9|
| 9.37061976521712|     9|
+-----------------+-----+
only showing top 5 rows

Root Mean Squared Error (RMSE) on test data = 2.46559
R-squared on test data = 0.46830523987797523


rf_evaluator1 = RegressionEvaluator(
        labelCol="Rings",
        predictionCol="prediction",
        metricName="rmse")
rmse = rf_evaluator1.evaluate(rf_predictions)
rf_evaluator2 = RegressionEvaluator(
        labelCol="Rings",
        predictionCol="prediction",
        metricName="r2")
r2 = rf_evaluator2.evaluate(rf_predictions)

print("Root Mean Squared Error (RMSE) on test data = %g" % rmse)
print('R-squared on test data =', r2)


Root Mean Squared Error (RMSE) on test data = 2.46559
R-squared on test data = 0.46830523987797523
```

This section has gone through the process of data preparation and model building using the two most used ensemble methods—gradient boosting and random forest. The next two sections, "Distinguishing Mines from Rocks with PySpark Ensemble Methods" and "Identifying Glass Types with PySpark Ensemble Methods," will show you how to build PySpark models for regression problems.

Distinguishing Mines from Rocks with PySpark Ensemble Methods

This section shows how to use PySpark's gradient boosting package to build models for the rocks versus mines problem that you've seen throughout the book. In most regards the data preparation code mirrors the data preparation code in the regression examples in the previous section. The major difference is that you need to use the StringAssembler to code the 0, 1 label into the correct form for PySpark classifiers. The code in this example uses the pipeline structure that's available in PySpark. The various stages in the processing of the input data are captured in a single "pipeline" that can be reused. Use of the pipeline makes subsequent code neater.

Listing 7-13: Using PySpark to Distinguish Mines from Rocks—rocks_v_mines_gbt_spark.py

```python
__author__ = 'mike_bowles'

#Import sparksession
from pyspark.sql import SparkSession
from pyspark.ml.feature import VectorAssembler
from pyspark.ml.classification import GBTClassifier
from pyspark.ml.classification import RandomForestClassifier
from pyspark.ml.evaluation import BinaryClassificationEvaluator
import matplotlib.pyplot as plt
from pyspark.ml.feature import StandardScaler


spark = SparkSession.builder.appName("log_regress_rvm").getOrCreate()


#read in abalone data as pandas data frame and create Spark data frame.
import pandas as pd
from pandas import DataFrame
from Read_Fcns import pd_read_rvm


rvm_df = pd_read_rvm()


#Create spark dataframe for wine data
rvm_sp_df = spark.createDataFrame(rvm_df)
print('Column Names', rvm_sp_df.columns, '\n\n')


cols = rvm_sp_df.columns


assembler_inputs =
        ['V0', 'V1', 'V2', 'V3', 'V4', 'V5', 'V6', 'V7', 'V8', 'V9',
         'V10', 'V11', 'V12', 'V13', 'V14', 'V15', 'V16', 'V17', 'V18',
         'V19', 'V20', 'V21', 'V22', 'V23', 'V24', 'V25', 'V26', 'V27',
         'V28', 'V29', 'V30', 'V31', 'V32', 'V33', 'V34', 'V35', 'V36',
         'V37', 'V38', 'V39', 'V40', 'V41', 'V42', 'V43', 'V44', 'V45',
         'V46', 'V47', 'V48', 'V49', 'V50', 'V51', 'V52', 'V53', 'V54',
          'V55', 'V56', 'V57', 'V58', 'V59']
from pyspark.ml.feature import OneHotEncoderEstimator, StringIndexer,
VectorAssembler
stages = []
label_string_idx = StringIndexer(inputCol = 'V60', outputCol = 'label')
stages += [label_string_idx]


assembler = VectorAssembler(inputCols=assembler_inputs, outputCol=
"features")
stages += [assembler]
from pyspark.ml import Pipeline
pipeline = Pipeline(stages = stages)
pipelineModel = pipeline.fit(rvm_sp_df)
df = pipelineModel.transform(rvm_sp_df)
selectedCols = ['label', 'features'] + cols
```

```
df = df.select(selectedCols)
df.printSchema()

train, test = df.randomSplit([0.7, 0.3], seed = 2018)
print("Training Dataset Count: " + str(train.count()))
print("Test Dataset Count: " + str(test.count()))

gbt = GBTClassifier(featuresCol = 'features', labelCol = 'label',
maxIter=100) gbt_model = gbt.fit(train)


predictions = gbt_model.transform(test)
predictions.select('rawPrediction', 'prediction', 'probability').
show(10)

evaluator = BinaryClassificationEvaluator()
print("Test Area Under ROC: " + str(evaluator.evaluate(predictions,
{evaluator.metricName: "areaUnderROC"})))

Column Names ['V0', 'V1', 'V2', 'V3', 'V4', 'V5', 'V6', 'V7', 'V8',
'V9', 'V10', 'V11', 'V12', 'V13', 'V14', 'V15', 'V16', 'V17', 'V18',
'V19', 'V20', 'V21', 'V22', 'V23', 'V24', 'V25', 'V26', 'V27', 'V28',
'V29', 'V30', 'V31', 'V32', 'V33', 'V34', 'V35', 'V36', 'V37', 'V38',
'V39', 'V40', 'V41', 'V42', 'V43', 'V44', 'V45', 'V46', 'V47', 'V48',
'V49', 'V50', 'V51', 'V52', 'V53', 'V54', 'V55', 'V56', 'V57', 'V58',
'V59', 'V60']


root
 |-- label: double (nullable = false)
 |-- features: vector (nullable = true)
 |-- V0: double (nullable = true)
 |-- V1: double (nullable = true)
 |-- V2: double (nullable = true)
 ............
 |-- V58: double (nullable = true)
 |-- V59: double (nullable = true)
 |-- V60: string (nullable = true)

Training Dataset Count: 146
Test Dataset Count: 62
+--------------------+----------+--------------------+
|       rawPrediction|prediction|         probability|
+--------------------+----------+--------------------+
|[-1.7597810427667...|       1.0|[0.02876072590667...|
|[1.82542450921326...|       0.0|[0.97468825140490...|
|[-2.2263645624067...|       1.0|[0.01151265329721...|
|[-0.1228667018215...|       1.0|[0.43887393096213...|
|[-0.2634614568499...|       1.0|[0.37123485505299...|
|[-2.2152521276024...|       1.0|[0.01176834016224...|
```

```
|[-2.2091975339739...|        1.0|[0.01191000394705...|
|[-2.2291594195578...|        1.0|[0.01144921510524...|
|[0.00969027556420...|        0.0|[0.50484498613265...|
|[-0.310090868679...|         1.0|[0.34974011922974...|
+--------------------+----------+--------------------+
only showing top 10 rows


Test Area Under ROC: 0.8885416666666667
```

Listing 7-14 shows code that runs on the same `'label'` and `'features'` columns that were generated by the pipeline in Listing 7-13.

Listing 7-14: Using PySpark Random Forest to Distinguish Mines from Rocks—rocks_v_mines_rf_spark.py

```python
from pyspark.ml.classification import RandomForestClassifier
rf = RandomForestClassifier(featuresCol = 'features',
                           labelCol = 'label')
rf_model = rf.fit(train)


predictions = rf_model.transform(test)
predictions.select('rawPrediction', 'prediction', 'probability').
show(10)


evaluator = BinaryClassificationEvaluator()
print("Test Area Under ROC: " +
      str(evaluator.evaluate(predictions,
      {evaluator.metricName: "areaUnderROC"})))
```

```
+--------------------+----------+--------------------+
|       rawPrediction|prediction|         probability|
+--------------------+----------+--------------------+
|[9.93333333333333...|       1.0|[0.49666666666666...|
|        [10.0,10.0]|       0.0|         [0.5,0.5]|
|[2.69292929292929...|       1.0|[0.13464646464646...|
|[12.8213463947460...|       0.0|[0.64106731973730...|
|[9.77578633164038...|       1.0|[0.48878931658201...|
|[4.03959627329192...|       1.0|[0.20197981366459...|
|[1.37476943346508...|       1.0|[0.06873847167325...|
|[6.90565178640626...|       1.0|[0.34528258932031...|
|[11.1235640964849...|       0.0|[0.55617820482424...|
|        [8.05,11.95]|       1.0|[0.4025,0.5974999...|
+--------------------+----------+--------------------+
only showing top 10 rows


Test Area Under ROC: 0.9104166666666667
```

This section introduced the pipeline process for encapsulating the data preparation steps leading up to fitting a predictive model. It showed how you can use PySpark ensemble methods for binary regression problems.

Identifying Glass Types with PySpark Ensemble Methods

Listing 7-15 shows how to build a multiclass classifier using random forest in PySpark. The `StringIndexer` gets used to encode the categorical multiclass labels similar to the way it was used in the two previous examples. This example uses the pipeline framework. The performance of the model is shown at the end of the code.

Listing 7-15: Using PySpark Random Forest to Identify Glass Types—glass_multiclass_rf_ spark.py)

```
__author__ = 'mike_bowles'

#Import sparksession
from pyspark.sql import SparkSession
from pyspark.ml.feature import VectorAssembler
from pyspark.ml.classification import RandomForestClassifier
import matplotlib.pyplot as plt
from pyspark.ml import Pipeline
from pyspark.ml.feature import OneHotEncoder, StringIndexer,
VectorAssembler
import pandas as pd
from pandas import DataFrame
from Read_Fcns import pd_read_glass
from pyspark.ml.tuning import ParamGridBuilder, CrossValidator

spark = SparkSession.builder.appName("glass_mc_log_regress").
getOrCreate()

# read glass data into pandas data frame and create spark df
glass_df = pd_read_glass()

#Create spark dataframe for glass data
glass_sp_df = spark.createDataFrame(glass_df)

cols = glass_sp_df.columns
print('Column Names', cols, '\n\n')

glass_sp_df.printSchema()

pd.DataFrame(glass_sp_df.take(5), columns=glass_sp_df.columns).
transpose()

feature_cols = ['RI', 'Na', 'Mg', 'Al', 'Si', 'K', 'Ca', 'Ba', 'Fe']

label_stringIdx = StringIndexer(inputCol = "Type", outputCol = "label")
assembler = VectorAssembler(inputCols=feature_cols,
                            outputCol='features')
pipeline = Pipeline(stages=[assembler, label_stringIdx])

pipelineFit = pipeline.fit(glass_sp_df)
dataset = pipelineFit.transform(glass_sp_df)
```

```
#have a look at the dataset
dataset.show(5)

#train test split
trainingData, testData = dataset.randomSplit([0.7, 0.3], seed = 1011)

#select model p
lr = RandomForestClassifier(featuresCol = 'features',
                            labelCol = 'label')
lrModel = lr.fit(trainingData)

predictions = lrModel.transform(testData)

from pyspark.ml.evaluation import MulticlassClassificationEvaluator
evaluator = MulticlassClassificationEvaluator(predictionCol="predict
ion")
print(evaluator.evaluate(predictions))

Column Names ['Id', 'RI', 'Na', 'Mg', 'Al', 'Si', 'K', 'Ca', 'Ba', 'Fe',
'Type']

root
 |-- Id: long (nullable = true)
 |-- RI: double (nullable = true)
 |-- Na: double (nullable = true)
 |-- Mg: double (nullable = true)
 |-- Al: double (nullable = true)
 |-- Si: double (nullable = true)
 |-- K: double (nullable = true)
 |-- Ca: double (nullable = true)
 |-- Ba: double (nullable = true)
 |-- Fe: double (nullable = true)
 |-- Type: long (nullable = true)

+---+------------------+-----+----+----+-----+----+----+---+---+----+---
----------------+-----+
| Id|                RI|   Na|  Mg|  Al|   Si|   K|  Ca| Ba| Fe|Type|
          features|label|
+---+------------------+-----+----+----+-----+----+----+---+---+----+---
----------------+-----+
|  1|           1.52101|13.64|4.49| 1.1|71.78|0.06|8.75|0.0|0.0|
  1|[1.52101,13.64,4....|  1.0|
|  2|1.5176100000000001|13.89| 3.6|1.36|72.73|0.48|7.83|0.0|0.0|
  1|[1.51761000000000...|  1.0|
|  3|1.5161799999999999|13.53|3.55|1.54|72.99|0.39|7.78|0.0|0.0|
  1|[1.51617999999999...|  1.0|
|  4|           1.51766|13.21|3.69|1.29|72.61|0.57|8.22|0.0|0.0|
  1|[1.51766,13.21,3....|  1.0|
|  5|           1.51742|13.27|3.62|1.24|73.08|0.55|8.07|0.0|0.0|
  1|[1.51742,13.27,3....|  1.0|
```

```
+---+------------------+-----+----+----+-----+----+----+---+---+----+---
---------------+-----+
only showing top 5 rows

0.8098768104960057
```

In this section you've seen how to build a random forest model for a multiclass prediction problem. There's no gradient boosting model, because the PySpark version of GBTClassifier doesn't support multiclass problems as of the time of this writing.

Summary

This chapter demonstrated ensemble methods available as XGBoost, Python sklearn, and PySpark packages. The examples show these methods at work building models on a variety of different types of problems. The chapter also covered regression, binary classification, and multiclass classification problems, and discussed variations on these themes such as the workings of coding categorical variables for input to XGBoost, Python, and PySpark ensemble methods and stratified sampling. These examples cover many of the problem types that you're likely to encounter in practice.

The examples also demonstrate some of the important features of ensemble algorithms—the reasons why they are a first choice among data scientists. Ensemble methods are relatively easy to use—they do not have many parameters to tune, they give variable importance data to help in the early stages of model development, and they very often give the best performance achievable.

The chapter demonstrated the use of available XGBoost, Python sklearn, and PySpark packages. The background given in Chapter 6 helps you to understand the parameters and adjustments that you see in the Python packages. Seeing them exercised in the example code can help you get started using these packages.

References

1. J. H. Friedman. "Greedy Function Approximation: A Gradient Boosting Machine," `https://statweb.stanford.edu/~jhf/ftp/trebst.pdf`

2. J. H. Friedman. "Stochastic Gradient Boosting," `https://statweb.stanford.edu/~jhf/ftp/stobst.pdf`

3. sklearn documentation for GradientBoostingRegressor, `http://scikit-learn.org/stable/modules/generated/sklearn.ensemble.GradientBoostingRegressor.html`

4. sklearn documentation for RandomForestRegressor, `http://scikit-learn.org/stable/modules/generated/sklearn.ensemble.RandomForestRegressor.html`

5. Leo Breiman. (2001). "Random Forests." *Machine Learning*, 45(1): 5–32. doi:10.1023/A:1010933404324

6. J. H. Friedman. "Greedy Function Approximation: A Gradient Boosting Machine," `https://statweb.stanford.edu/~jhf/ftp/trebst.pdf`

7. sklearn documentation for RandomForestClassifier, `http://scikit-learn.org/stable/modules/generated/sklearn.ensemble.RandomForestClassifier.html`

8. sklearn documentation for RandomForestRegressor, `http://scikit-learn.org/stable/modules/generated/sklearn.ensemble.RandomForestRegressor.html`

9. L. Breiman, "Bagging predictors," `http://statistics.berkeley.edu/sites/default/files/tech-reports/421.pdf`

10. Tin Ho. (1998). "The Random Subspace Method for Constructing Decision Forests." *IEEE Transactions on Pattern Analysis and Machine Intelligence*, 20(8): 832–844. doi:10.1109/34.709601

11. J. H. Friedman. "Greedy Function Approximation: A Gradient Boosting Machine," `https://statweb.stanford.edu/~jhf/ftp/trebst.pdf`

12. J. H. Friedman. "Stochastic Gradient Boosting," `https://statweb.stanford.edu/~jhf/ftp/stobst.pdf`

13. J. H. Friedman. "Stochastic Gradient Boosting," `https://statweb.stanford.edu/~jhf/ftp/stobst.pdf`

14. sklearn documentation for GradientBoostingClassifier, `http://scikit-learn.org/stable/modules/generated/sklearn.ensemble.GradientBoostingClassifier.html`

Index